PSYCHIATRIC DIAGNOSIS: A BIOPSYCHOSOCIAL APPROACH USING DSM-III-R

Jess Amchin, M.D.

Assistant Professor of Psychiatry
University of Pittsburgh School of Medicine
Western Psychiatric Institute and Clinic
Pittsburgh, Pennsylvania

American Psychiatric Press, Inc.

Washington, DC
London, England

Diagnostic criteria and other material in this book are reprinted with permission from the *Diagnostic and Statistical Manual of Mental Disorders, Third Edition, Revised.* Copyright © 1987 American Psychiatric Association.

93 92 91   4 3 2

American Psychiatric Press, Inc.
1400 K Street, N.W., Washington, DC 20005

The paper used in this publication meets the minimum requirements of the American National Standard for Information Sciences—Permanence of Paper for Printed Library Materials ANSI Z39.48-1984.   ∞

Library of Congress Cataloging-in-Publication Data
Amchin, Jess, 1955–
    Psychiatric diagnosis : a biopsychosocial approach using DSM-III-R / Jess Amchin.—1st ed.
        p.   cm.
    Includes bibliographical references.
    Includes index.
    ISBN 0-88048-166-8 (alk. paper)
    1. Mental illness—Diagnosis. 2. Mental illness—Classification. I. Title. II. Title: DSM-III-R.
    [DNLM: 1. Mental Disorders—classification. 2. Mental Disorders—diagnosis.
    3. Psychiatry—nomenclature. WM 141 A496p]
    RC469.A47   1991
    616.89'075—dc20
    DNLM/DLC
    for Library of Congress   90-874
                                                                                         CIP

British Cataloguing in Publication Data
A CIP record is available from the British Library

For my parents, Abe and Rita, who taught me throughout my life to examine, respect, and appreciate the workings of the human mind, and for my wife, Lori, and daughter, Arielle, who so enrich my life.

Contents

List of Tables and Figures

Preface

Psychiatric diagnosis occupies a central role in the clinical practice of modern psychiatry. In this book I seek to achieve two primary aims, both of which are necessary for the clinician to master psychiatric diagnosis. The book is also organized so that the reader may choose to focus on both or solely on either of these aims, as described below.

First, I describe a biopsychosocial approach to psychiatric assessment, articulating five elements that result in an integrated assessment process. This is crucial to the ability to achieve psychiatric diagnoses, since the diagnostic process is inexorably linked to the ability to pursue an expert psychiatric assessment. The five elements that the clinician must master to achieve this required assessment include the abilities to gather an empirical data base, to develop a descriptive differential diagnosis correctly applying DSM-III-R (American Psychiatric Association 1987), to apply psychiatric theory, to develop a diagnostic case formulation, and to synthesize additional clinical information as it becomes available. This book is structured to parallel the mastery of each of these elements: one chapter is devoted to each of these five elements, yet each presents only a concise review, always with an eye toward integrating each element into an overall assessment process. The common theme throughout the book, unifying the separate elements under one overarching theory, is the application of the comprehensive yet flexible biopsychosocial model described in Chapter 1.

Second, I aim to provide a review of DSM-III-R, found in Chapter 3, as part of the third element of the psychiatric assessment, labelled the descriptive diagnosis. *Diagnostic and Statistical Manual of*

Mental Disorders, Third Edition, Revised (DSM-III-R) and its pre-decessor (DSM-III) have contributed to the acceptance of standard clinical and research criteria defining psychiatric disorders. In order to apply DSM-III-R, which is required as one of the five elements in the psychiatric assessment, one must master these rigorous de-scriptive criteria. The "walk-through" of DSM-III-R in Chapter 3 pro-vides a narrative description of these diagnoses, closely repeating or following the definitional language of DSM-III-R, and occasionally including additional clinical or conceptual points—all of which will enable the clinician to review and apply these carefully designed criteria accurately, while also appreciating the limitations and proper place of DSM-III-R as only one element of the overall psychiatric assessment.

By structuring the book in this way, I have given the reader the option of focusing on either of the book's two primary goals, attain-ing knowledge concisely, but without necessarily reading the book from cover to cover. One may selectively review one element or each element that makes up the entire assessment process but skip the review of DSM-III-R diagnosis in Chapter 3. Alternatively, one may achieve a relatively quick and concise review of DSM-III-R in its en-tirety, or select specific areas of DSM-III-R for focused and relatively rapid review or reference by reading only the appropriate passages in Chapter 3.

Overall, this is very much a "how-to" book. It provides a descrip-tion of how to go about making an accurate, comprehensive, yet appropriately focused psychiatric diagnosis, while also providing a succinct and critical review of DSM-III-R. The book is written for students and clinicians in medicine, psychiatry, psychology, social work, nursing, and other fields in which professional skills are re-quired to develop psychiatric diagnoses. In a practical sense, I hope that this book will be valuable for clinical training, actual clinical practice, and for review, including preparation for examinations.

While there are advantages in providing an integrated and fo-cused description of the process of modern psychiatric diagnosis, this book has certain limitations. An academic understanding of the process of psychiatric diagnosis must be complemented by actual clinical experience and expert supervision. No book can provide this experience. Further, in emphasizing the diagnostic process, this book de-emphasizes informational content. This permits a clear and thorough description of the framework for understanding the di-agnostic process, unencumbered by the overloading of factual ma-terial. A more detailed working knowledge of psychiatric skills, disorders, and theories is also vital to the clinician. After mastering the framework provided by this book, the student or clinician will be able to build on this foundation by adding information provided by textbooks, journals, lectures, and supervisors. For example, while Chapter 3 summarizes the psychiatric disorders as described in DSM-III-R for basic training and review purposes, the reader should consult DSM-III-R itself and other sources to gain a more thorough knowledge of these disorders. Similarly, Chapter 4 describes the role of psychiatric theory in the diagnostic process, but it does not describe the theories themselves except for a few illustrative examples.

Based on my own experience in initially learning the material found in this book and later preparing for Board Examinations, I decided not to include lengthy, detailed case material. Such case material would detract from the relatively rapid acquisition or review of the basic framework of knowledge that this book is intended to convey. Further, there are a number of excellent books and chapters that provide detailed case review, if desired. Rather, I sought to write a book that provided what I myself sought as a trainee and in preparation for exams: a concise framework of the salient points and integrated approach to diagnosis, with a relatively rapid, concise, and critical review of DSM-III-R. Once having mastered the framework and review presented in this book, the clinician may learn to apply this framework through his or her work with real cases and supervisors, or by reference to the many excellent books, chapters, and papers that apply assessment techniques and diagnostic criteria (several of which are listed under Further Reading).

Finally, I thank those who helped in the development and preparation of this book. Iris Lowe and Joanne Cobb provided much-appreciated help in preparing the manuscript. Lori Amchin provided emotional support as well as a thorough review of the draft. I thank the American Psychiatric Press, especially Robert Hales and Carol Nadelson, who helped nurture the concept for this book, and Tim Clancy, who provided understanding editorial assistance throughout the process. My colleagues at Western Psychiatric Institute and Clinic, especially Loren Roth, have provided invaluable ideas, inspiration, and support. David Kupfer and Thomas Detre deserve special recognition for creating and maintaining a department of psychiatry that permits faculty, such as myself, to pursue their academic interests and achieve their maximum professional potential. I wish to extend additional thanks to those who read segments or various drafts, including Carlos Placci and the anonymous reviewers for American Psychiatric Press who provided helpful comments on earlier drafts of this book. Finally, I would like to thank the many teachers, students, residents, and patients with whom I have worked during my training and professional career at Columbia University College of Physicians and Surgeons, Payne-Whitney Psychiatric Clinic, and Western Psychiatric Institute and Clinic—collectively they have provided the clinical experience and teaching upon which much of this book is based.

CHAPTER 1

Psychiatric Diagnosis in Perspective

The Goal of Psychiatric Diagnosis

The goal of psychiatric diagnosis is to achieve a meaningful understanding of another human being's mental functioning and behavior, incorporating biological, psychological, and social perspectives.

This defined goal for psychiatric diagnosis underscores several concepts. First, the diagnosis should be *meaningful* to the clinical or research task at hand. To say that a patient "meets DSM-III-R criteria" for a particular psychiatric disorder—as is sometimes heard in a modern psychiatric setting—may be entirely accurate and sufficient in some clinical or research situations, but may be inadequate for understanding of a patient whose problems significantly reflect interpersonal or psychodynamic conflict, for example. The diagnostic process should integrate the correct application of the descriptive criteria of DSM-III-R (American Psychiatric Association 1987), which the clinician must master, with the application of theoretical constructs in order to achieve a more meaningful diagnostic case formulation and treatment plan. Further, generalized descriptions or theories of psychiatric disorders must be as reliable (i.e., reproducible by different clinicians) and valid (i.e., actually true) as our scientific knowledge permits, and must be individualized to be meaningful for the particular patient, whether in the clinical or research setting.

Second, psychiatric diagnosis seeks *understanding.* Understanding implies a professional yet empathic appreciation of the patient's problems, both intellectually and emotionally. Thus, the diagnostic process is really part of the therapeutic process, building

1

the understanding that is at the core of the therapeutic alliance. Admittedly, psychiatric diagnoses are "labels." Labels may be misapplied or misused. But properly applied, these labels should serve only as a kind of shorthand summary—frequently inadequate—to communicate both a description and an appreciation of the problem. Additional facets to a patient's mental functioning and behavior, such as etiology or cultural implications, may not be communicated by such labels. A comprehensive diagnostic case formulation should convey these aspects of the patient's functioning. As the diagnostic process proceeds, the patient should be increasingly "understood" by the mental health professional.

Third, psychiatric diagnosis seeks to understand *mental functioning and behavior*. Thus, the clinician must consider both cognitive processes and conduct. Although a person's conduct usually reflects cognitive processes, they may be discordant. Conduct may appear unremarkable, for example, while internal mental processes may reflect a psychiatric problem such as a mood disturbance or psychotic thinking. Conversely, thinking may appear unremarkable even though behavior appears to be disturbed, implying an underlying mental disturbance that is not yet apparent. In either case, the mental health professional should scrutinize both mental functioning and behavior in an attempt to reach a diagnostically accurate and comprehensive understanding of the patient.

Finally, psychiatric diagnosis should incorporate three perspectives: *biological, psychological, and social*. By considering each of these three spheres of human functioning, the clinician will have a more complete understanding of the patient's psychiatric problems. This approach reflects the "biopsychosocial" model.

The Biopsychosocial Perspective

Psychiatric diagnosis reflects a philosophical model of the human mind and disease.

In the traditional "medical model," disease is defined by physical parameters and implies a physical etiology for biological dysfunction. In the most extreme application of the medical model, psychological, social, and behavioral dimensions are considered unrelated to the concept of illness. The medical model thus reflects a philosophy of reductionism, in that disease phenomena are thought to be ultimately derived from a single principle (i.e., the biological cause), and the doctrine of mind-body dualism, which separates mental from somatic functions.

Despite the success of the medical model, it is increasingly apparent that psychological and social influences affect physical processes, and that all three dimensions interact, particularly in psychiatric disorders. Schizophrenia, for example, seems to reflect not only genetic or other biological vulnerabilities, but also experiential and cultural factors. While the effectiveness of antidepressant medication in many depressed patients suggests a biological aspect to depression, psychological and social treatments are also effective, and understanding the psychological impact of a social loss may be crucial to understanding depression in a patient. Our expanding knowledge of neuroendocrinology, immunology, and the effects of stress on biological systems further supports the importance of considering the interaction of biological, psychological, and social factors as causes of psychiatric disorders.

The "biopsychosocial model" provides a more comprehensive conceptual framework than the medical model.[1] According to the biopsychosocial model, the clinician's approach to any patient incorporates three interacting dimensions of the patient's functioning: biological (physical or organic processes), psychological (aspects of mental functioning, including thought, behavior, and emotion), and social (interactions with others, including family, friends, colleagues at work, professionals, and others important to the patient). These three variables interact in complex and interdependent ways to affect the patient's experience of illness as well as the development of the psychiatric disorder or syndrome. By considering each of these factors, the clinician is more likely to achieve "meaningful understanding" of the patient. Reflecting this philosophy, psychiatric abnormalities are sometimes designated as "disorders" or "conditions" rather than as "diseases" implying a sole physiological cause. In short, the biopsychosocial model permits a more comprehensive and humanistic approach to diagnostic assessment and treatment.

It may not always be necessary or practical to pursue all three aspects of the biopsychosocial model fully in every patient. Although the clinician should retain the biopsychosocial perspective, he or she must also be flexible and individualize the diagnostic assessment and treatment. For example, if a patient's problems clearly reflect a primary biological process, then the clinician should focus on the biological dimension of the biopsychosocial assessment. In other patients, psychological or social factors may predominate, and the

---

[1]The biopsychosocial model and its application to psychiatry were perhaps most articulately described by George Engel (see Further Reading).

clinician should then emphasize these areas of functioning. In most circumstances, however, all three factors—biological, psychological, and social—must be considered in order to understand the patient.

There is also a practical reason to maintain a biopsychosocial perspective: even without a clear etiological explanation for a psychiatric disorder, successful interventions typically involve biological, psychological, and social strategies. In order to achieve maximally effective treatment, therefore, the clinician should consider each of these three factors.

In summary, psychiatric diagnosis requires a biopsychosocial perspective, which should be applied to each of the five components of the diagnostic process. The basic biopsychosocial approach and five components of the diagnostic process apply equally well to the nonpsychiatric medical setting, but this book describes only their application to psychiatry.

The Five Components of the Diagnostic Process

There are five components to the process of developing a psychiatric diagnosis:

1. The empirical data base
2. The descriptive diagnosis
3. The application of psychiatric theory
4. The psychiatric diagnostic case formulation
5. The ongoing diagnostic synthesis

From the moment the clinician first meets the patient—or even begins learning about the patient before this first meeting—until their final interaction, the clinician is pursuing each of these five tasks: gathering data, considering descriptive diagnoses, applying theory, developing a case formulation, and synthesizing new information. Each of these components develops simultaneously with every other component throughout the assessment and treatment of the patient. However, each component typically predominates in a certain phase of the diagnostic process. Thus, in this book, these components of the diagnostic process are considered in a sequence analogous to their usual chronological importance.

Chapter 2 examines the gathering of the empirical data base, focusing on the historical, physical, and laboratory data, the diagnostic psychiatric interview, and a consideration of settings and symptoms. Gathering the empirical data base is usually thought of as a first step in patient assessment. However, more detailed historical information and its important emotional context may be developed only after some time and the building of the therapeutic alliance. Basic clinical information is crucial to each of the other components in the diagnostic process.

As pieces of clinical information are gathered, the descriptive differential diagnosis becomes more focused. Chapter 3 reviews these descriptive psychiatric diagnoses, including an overview of DSM-III-R and a review of each of the major DSM-III-R diagnostic categories. This review provides the basic language for modern psychiatric diagnoses and is designed as a training guide, clinical review, and reference to be used in conjunction with DSM-III-R and other psychiatric texts.

Theoretical hypotheses are usually more meaningful after the descriptive diagnosis becomes clearer. Chapter 4 describes the role and application of diagnostic theory in the development of a more meaningful diagnostic understanding of the patient.

Armed with empirical data, a descriptive differential diagnosis, and theoretical hypotheses, the clinician may develop a more formal, comprehensive, yet properly focused psychiatric diagnostic case formulation, as described in Chapter 5.

Finally, Chapter 6 discusses the ongoing diagnostic synthesis. This component requires that the psychiatric diagnosis be continually reviewed and revised based on additional information obtained as the psychiatric assessment and treatment proceeds. Thus, the skilled clinician realizes that his or her diagnostic thinking underlies the course of treatment and is always subject to review and modification. The diagnostic process and each of its five components continue until the patient's treatment is concluded.

Throughout the process of diagnostic assessment, it is wise to apply a seeming contradiction: rigorous clinical and scientific standards must be applied, but only in a flexible context. The mental health profession strives to be scientifically sound; the profession has made great progress in improving the reliability and validity of diagnoses. Yet, because mental functioning and behavior are both complex and often poorly understood, virtually any psychiatric diagnosis may be wrong or incomplete in at least two crucial ways: the clinician may be mistaken in evaluating an individual patient, and the mental health profession as a whole may be mistaken in describing and understanding a particular psychiatric problem. Many current psychiatric disorders may eventually be more clearly understood as neurological or medical disorders, as in the case of the old psychiatric disorder "paresis," now known to be due to the infectious agent causing syphilis. On a more fundamental level, even if we understand the biological intricacies of the brain such as neurotransmitter communications and brain biochemistry, an element of abstraction will probably always be required to understand the functioning of the mind.

The clinician faces the more practical reality, however, of trying to understand his or her patient in order to provide treatment and relieve suffering. Psychiatric diagnosis is the cornerstone to achieving effective psychiatric treatment. The challenge of modern psychiatric diagnosis, then, is to apply professional skills and the best currently available scientific knowledge to understand and ultimately help patients.

CHAPTER 2

The Empirical Data Base

The empirical data base is analogous to a funnel. One starts with a wide range of potential information about a patient, with many possible diagnoses to be considered. Gradually, information is presented to support or rule out certain diagnoses. The funnel narrows. The clinician, while maintaining objectivity, is actually building a case for a diagnostic conclusion. Finally, one reaches the tip of the funnel: the formulation. At this point, sufficient clinical information has been presented for the mental health professional to develop the working differential diagnosis. The recommendations then flow logically from the formulation.

While there are advantages to being comprehensive, the empirical data base must also be tailored to the clinical context. The clinician cannot—and frequently should not—try to obtain every piece of information available about the patient, as will become clearer in the discussion to follow. The clinician should, however, recognize the full range of information that could be appropriately pursued, screen certain areas to avoid clinical gaps, and then focus on the clinically important issues for the patient. The empirical data base, like all components of the diagnostic process, should be individualized.

Further, evaluating a patient and building the biopsychosocial empirical data base takes time. Several patient visits and the evolution of a clinician-patient relationship may be required. This process should be allowed to evolve.

The empirical data base is divided into the categories of the history, physical examination, and laboratory data. Among the many sources of information for developing the empirical data base, particularly important psychiatric information is obtained through the skillful diagnostic psychiatric interview and a consideration of the importance of the clinical setting and symptoms.

The History, Physical Examination, and Laboratory Data

Obtaining a thorough history and physical examination is the primary approach taught to medical students for pursuing a comprehensive evaluation of a new patient, and it should be applied to the evaluation of psychiatric disorders. A comprehensive history and physical systematically incorporates all biological, psychological, and social information.

The history and physical also organizes all historical and objective information logically. History begins with the most basic and currently important information: identifying facts, the reason for the patient's seeking help, sources of information, and the history of the current problem. Medical and psychiatric history is then reviewed. The data base next reviews family history, followed by other personal and social information. A review of systems completes a comprehensive picture of the patient's life and functioning. The objective data of the physical examination and laboratory findings complete the data base. The history, physical, and laboratory findings lead to clinical hypotheses, differential diagnoses, and other clinical conclusions, described under the heading "formulation." Finally, strategies for clinical management and treatment are summarized under the heading of "plan" or "recommendations."

The clinician should recall and apply the structured outline of the history and physical in order to gather, organize, record, and present clinical information (see Table 2-1).

A comprehensive biopsychosocial assessment requires evaluating each section of the history, physical, and laboratory data base. To neglect a category is to risk creating a gap in information. However, it is not always practical, possible, or even wise to be comprehensive in obtaining the empirical data base. It may be necessary to emphasize certain sections, de-emphasize others, and tailor information gathering to the clinical situation. Attempting to obtain every possible piece of information on a patient is not only inefficient, but also probably inhibits the task of focusing on the problem and developing a meaningful formulation and plan. Clinical judgment is required to individualize the empirical data base properly.

The mental health professional may need to emphasize those elements of the history and physical examination that are within

Table 2-1. Outline of the history and physical examination

1. Identifying information
2. Chief complaint
3. Sources of information
4. History of present illness
5. Past medical history (including past psychiatric history)
6. Family history
7. Personal history
8. Social history
9. Review of medical systems
10. Physical examination, including the mental status examination
11. Laboratory results
12. Formulation (including differential diagnoses)
13. Plan or recommendations

his or her expertise and are relevant to the psychiatric presentation. Multidisciplinary consultation may be needed to develop sufficient information for some sections of this data base. For example, medical and physical examination, when indicated, may require the expertise of a physician; psychological testing may require the expertise of a psychologist; and detailed social and family history may require the expertise of a social worker. When information is lacking in an area important to the case, the clinician should explicitly state that such information is unavailable, including any reasons why the information could not be obtained and whether such information will be evaluated later or by another member of an interdisciplinary team. All mental health professionals, no matter what their particular discipline, should be knowledgeable about each component of the empirical data base and be trained to develop most areas of the psychiatric history.

Mental health professionals must not overlook the importance of medical aspects of the empirical data base, especially when physical disease processes may explain a psychiatric presentation. For example, a mood disturbance may be related to thyroid dysfunction, and confusion may be due to substance abuse, central nervous system infection, metabolic disturbances, or other medical problems. A neurological assessment may be important, particularly in assessing certain organic deficits on the mental status examination. A review of current medications is also extremely important. For geriatric patients in particular, both prescribed and over-the-counter medications should be reviewed for their possible contributions to psychiatric disturbances.

In addition to the patient, certain other sources deserve special mention for their value in pursuing a biopsychosocial assessment.

The written medical and psychiatric record is a key source of information. The written record will often correct distortions and fill in otherwise missing or forgotten information.

The family may corroborate or provide key information; but in addition, an assessment of family dynamics, conflicts, stresses, and interpersonal relationships may lead to an understanding of the patient's psychological and social state. Similarly, assessment of significant nonfamily relationships may be extremely helpful.

Another source of crucial information, too often overlooked, is other therapists or physicians. They may help in clarifying history, diagnostic thinking, and the details of current treatments and responses, including medication trials. Less obvious but equally important, therapists may provide insight into significant transference issues, sometimes related to the ongoing therapy itself. For example, an outpatient therapist's vacation may be the crucial precipitant for a depression or an exacerbation of psychotic symptoms. Countertransference issues from another ongoing therapy situation may be vital to understanding a patient's current presentation.

The outline of the history and physical examination provides a structure for recalling, adding, organizing, and communicating information. It should be applied while collecting initial or new information, when organizing the data in one's own mind, and in written documentation and oral presentation.

Parts of the History and Physical

Identifying information. Basic identifying information may include the patient's full name, age, birth date, marital status, race, ethnic origin, religion, sex, occupation, number of children, and living situation. The clinician may note the number of past hospitalizations when this is a salient factor in the history, although past hospitalizations are typically described elsewhere.

Identifying information should describe how the patient arrived at the point of requesting or requiring a psychiatric assessment. Some patients are self-referred. Other patients are transferred from inpatient facilities or are referred from such sources as physicians, other mental health providers, or employers. When the referral is made for consultation, the clinician should note the source and reason for consultation.

Thus, in merely a sentence or two, the identifying information rapidly captures fundamental patient information, providing the context for understanding the patient's psychiatric problem.

Chief complaint. The chief complaint is the patient's reason for seeking help. In eliciting the chief complaint, the clinician may ask several questions, such as, Why are you here, why are you here with me, and why are you here now? The clinician should record the patient's exact words in quotes. Sometimes, the patient's words themselves will suggest psychiatric symptoms, diagnoses, or the need for urgency. For example, the chief complaint may reflect a psychotic process ("I'm hearing voices again and I want them to stop"), a specific diagnosis such as a mood disorder ("I'm depressed"), or a psychiatric emergency ("I'm going to kill myself with the gun I just bought"). In some situations, when the patient cannot articulate a chief complaint, the clinician should note the patient's exact answer, if any, to an inquiry designed to elicit the chief complaint. A common way to elicit the chief complaint is to ask, "What is the main problem that leads you to seek help?" Some patients, reflecting psychological denial, a lack of insight, a lie, or an inappropriate referral, will deny any chief complaint; this response should also be noted.

The patient's description of a chief complaint may differ from both the referral source's description of the main problem and the clinician's perception of the main problem—all should be recorded. While the referral source's reason for requesting an evaluation should already be recorded as part of "identifying information," the chief complaint is the place to record the patient's words and the mental health professional's conception of the main problem for which the patient seeks evaluation or treatment. Differences here may be clinically instructive in elucidating distortions, transference or countertransference issues, errors in judgment, or differing expectation of treatment on the part of the patient, the referral source, or the mental health professional. For example, a hospital consultation from a nonpsychiatric physician may be requested to evaluate depression, yet the patient may appear to be more confused than depressed, and the patient may provide the chief complaint, "My doctor thinks I'm crazy." These discrepancies suggest a need for further evaluation of the clinical presentation (i.e., confusion, depression, or a changing mental status observed by different professionals), denial or a distrust of the consultant or primary physician as suggested by the patient's chief complaint, and possible misdiagnosis by either the primary physician or the consultant.

The chief complaint provides a focused description of the primary problem for which the patient seeks professional help and is logically followed by immediate history that led up to this primary problem.

Sources of information.   Just prior to describing the patient's history, it is important to note the sources of information and their level of reliability. When possible, information should be obtained from the patient, family, friends, significant others, the medical record, and other professional staff, especially prior or current therapists and other health care providers. Knowing the sources and reliability of historical and objective information is key in deciding whether historical information is inaccurate, biased, or incomplete. The availability of important sources helps establish the credibility of the information to follow, while the lack of important sources— such as the medical record, a current or recent therapist, or a key family member—suggests gaps in the history that will follow. The patient is one source of information, of course, but it should be noted when the patient is uncooperative or unconscious and does not provide historical data. Even in these unusual situations, however, mental status and other information are still obtained by evaluating and perhaps interacting with the patient in some way.

When recording sources of information, the clinician should also describe the relationship of the source to the patient and may need to record phone numbers and addresses of important sources for future reference and contact.

History of present illness.   The history of present illness should provide a chronological description of psychiatric symptoms and clinically significant events and factors, beginning with the onset of the current psychiatric problem, continuing with the clinical course, and concluding with the current primary psychiatric presentation that results in the chief complaint. This chronology should include possible precipitating factors as well as a description of the impact of the psychiatric problem on the patient's life. Biological, psychological, and social aspects should be considered. Current psychiatric medications and psychotherapy should be described.

The onset of the present illness may or may not be clear. In circumscribed psychiatric problems of limited duration, the present illness may begin with the onset of symptoms and associated possible stressors or precipitants. In more chronic problems, it is sometimes difficult to determine when the present illness began. In such cases, the clinician may provide a brief sentence or two summarizing the chronic illness, which will be detailed later as part of the past psychiatric history, and then describe the present exacerbation of the chronic illness. For example, the clinician could report, "In the

ever committed suicide, attempted suicide, or seriously talked about suicide?" Other questions could specifically ask about family hospitalizations or diagnoses, such as, "Has anyone in your family ever been admitted to a psychiatric hospital?" and "Has anyone in your family ever been diagnosed as suffering from an emotional (or psychiatric) problem such as depression, schizophrenia, or other disorders the clinician could name?" Even with these questions, one cannot assume that the patient understands. The clinician should follow up with questions designed to clarify and expand the historical information elicited.

Personal history. The personal history provides a chronological description of important events and relationships in the patient's biological, psychological, and social development. A comprehensive personal history would review every stage of development: prenatal, infancy and early childhood, middle childhood, late childhood and adolescence, and adulthood. Early developmental history is particularly important in the assessment of children, but it may also be invaluable in reaching a deeper understanding of an adult psychiatric patient.

Social history. The social history provides a description of the patient's social development and functioning. Conceptually, the social history is sometimes combined with the personal history.

Social history should include a review of several areas of patient functioning: education, past and current employment, nature and quality of social and work relationships, significant aspects of religious or cultural upbringing, military history, sexual history, marital history, current social situation, and any aspects of the patient's family relationships not described under family history. In addition, detailed information should be obtained concerning alcohol and drug use.

Certain areas of the social history are frequently pursued too superficially, with the risk of missing information important for understanding the psychiatric presentation. For example, many clinicians are either too uncomfortable or poorly trained to obtain a good sexual history. Patients are often also uncomfortable discussing sex. An accurate history of drug and alcohol use is frequently difficult to obtain. Other important areas of social history that seem to be frequently overlooked include religion and military experiences.

Review of medical systems. In the medical setting, questions about each organ system provide a screen for all major physical illnesses. In a psychiatric setting, this review may also be valuable in order to ensure that no aspects of medical history or current medical symptoms are overlooked. A review of systems is particularly helpful in considering somatic manifestations of psychiatric disorders or, conversely, when patients present with psychiatric symptoms reflecting underlying physical disorders.

Physical examination including the mental status examination. A physical examination provides objective information about body functioning. A complete or partial physical examination may be appropriate in some psychiatric patients, particularly when physical signs may be related to psychiatric problems. Many psychiatric disorders involve certain physical symptoms or require ruling out physical conditions. A complete screening physical examination would include the following: general survey, vital signs, and examination of skin, head, eyes, ears, nose, throat, neck, nodes, back, lungs, breast, heart, abdomen, inguinal area, genitalia, rectum, extremities, peripheral vascular system, musculoskeletal function, and neurological examination. The neurological examination is further divided as follows: mental status, cranial nerves, motor function, sensory function, and reflexes.

Note the location of the mental status examination in the list of items covered in the physical examination. The mental status exam is technically part of the neurological examination, which in turn is part of the overall physical examination. Thus, the mental status examination is part of the *objective* information assessed as part of the physical examination. Psychiatrists and other mental health professionals are experts, along with neurologists, in assessing the mental status component of the physical examination. The mental status examination will be described later in this chapter.

Laboratory results. This section of the history and physical systematically reviews and organizes relevant laboratory results. Although there are as yet no pathognomonic tests for any psychiatric disorder, laboratory testing is increasingly important in psychiatry.

Typical medical screening tests (e.g., complete blood counts, blood electrolytes, liver function tests, urinalysis, VDRL, electrocardiograms, and chest X-rays) and other tests used in the medical settings (e.g., lumbar puncture) may help in evaluating psychiatric conditions and in selecting somatic treatments. Other tests helpful in evaluating biological aspects of psychiatric disorders include neuroendocrine tests (e.g., thyroid function tests to rule out thyroid abnormalities causing depression, and the dexamethasone suppression test for following certain depressed patients), toxicology screens (e.g., for illicit drugs in blood or urine), B_{12} and folate blood levels, medication blood levels, electroencephalograms to evaluate for seizures or delirium, sleep studies (e.g., polysomnography), computerized tomography scans, magnetic resonance imaging scans, tests for sexual dysfunctions (e.g., nocturnal penile tumescence, vascular flow studies, and endocrine tests), and standardized neuropsychiatric and psychological testing. Certain procedures, such as an Amytal interview, hypnosis, or the pentobarbital challenge test, may also provide objective diagnostic information. Advances in psychiatry promise new possibilities for objective laboratory testing, perhaps including positron emission tomography scans, testing for endorphins, provocative tests for panic disorder (e.g., intravenous lactate infusion), and genetic markers for psychiatric disorder.

Formulation (including differential diagnoses). The formulation describes the clinical hypotheses, differential diagnoses, and clinical conclusions that follow logically from the preceding history, physical, and laboratory data base. The psychiatric diagnostic case formulation will be described in Chapter 5.

Plan or recommendations. The plan or recommendation summarizes the treatment and management strategies that follow logically from the empirical data base and the preceding diagnostic case formulation.

Mental health consultants should consider that the referring clinician will probably focus on this section. In such cases, the plan should be clearly and sufficiently described to communicate information and educate the nonpsychiatric audience.

The Mental Status Examination

The mental status examination provides an objective description of all areas of the patient's current mental functioning. Although all physicians and mental health professionals should be qualified to perform a mental status examination, this is an area of special expertise for the mental health professional. Each category of the mental status examination provides potentially crucial information in evaluating the differential psychiatric diagnosis.

The mental status examination provides a logical structure for organizing clinical information. This structure is somewhat analogous to the chronological order in which information becomes available to the interviewer; the structure also roughly follows a progression from easily observed data to areas requiring deeper and more probing assessment. Even before talking with the patient, the clinician notes the patient's appearance and describes observed motor behavior. When verbal interactions begin, the clinician may describe

Table 2-2.   Outline of the mental status examination

1. Appearance
2. Behavior
3. Speech
4. Attitude toward interviewer
5. Mood and affect
6. Thought
   a. Thought process
   b. Thought content
   c. Perceptual disturbances
7. Formal cognitive function (or higher integrative function)
   a. Orientation
   b. Memory (immediate, recent, and remote)
   c. Attention and concentration
   d. Calculations
8. Abstractions
9. Intelligence
10. Insight
11. Judgment

contours and abnormalities in the patient's speech. The attitude of the patient toward the interviewer may then be ascertained, providing an important context for understanding the data to follow. Next, the clinician evaluates the information communicated by the patient, beginning with emotion (mood and affect) and followed by thought. Thought processes, which may color the reliability of later information, are observed first, followed by the actual content of thought and any perceptual disturbances. Formal cognitive functions are then described, often requiring structured questioning by the interviewer. Finally, the mental status examination concludes with the most advanced areas of mental functioning: ability to abstract, intelligence, insight, and judgment.

As with the history and physical, the clinician should recall and apply the structured outline of the mental status examination to avoid overlooking important information and in order to gather, organize, record, and orally present mental status information properly (see Table 2-2).

Certain aspects of the mental status examination deserve special emphasis.

First, the mental status examination is part of the physical examination, providing *objective* information for the overall empirical data base. Trainees often confuse this point. Historical information is not part of the mental status examination. Recent past suicidal ideation related to the psychiatric presentation, for example, is appropriately included in the history of present illness. This should be distinguished from a finding or patient report of current suicidal ideation, which is appropriately included in the description of mental status. Subjective impressions and hypotheses also do not belong in the objective description of the mental status, but they may be incorporated into the case formulation. The patient's statements and responses to questions should be recorded in quotes; they are empirical data. All other recorded information should indicate the interviewer's observations and findings. The mental status report should always reflect current, objective information.

Second, the clinician should consciously consider the categories of the mental status outline as the interview progresses but should not let the structure of the outline significantly interfere with the flow of the interview or the development of a rapport with the patient. This is a difficult task. Information will not usually be gathered in the order of the mental status outline. The most skilled interviewers will be able to engage the patient in a smoothly flowing interview while still extracting all the necessary mental status information by the end of the interaction.

Third, the mental status examination should be applied as a screening test. When an abnormality is suggested in any one component of the mental status functioning, the clinician should note the finding and pursue that area in more depth. It may or may not turn out to be meaningful; its significance may become clear only with further probing. Inaccurate recall of the date, for example, should prompt a deeper assessment of cognitive functioning to determine whether the patient simply did not know or forgot the date, or whether the patient is truly disoriented or confused or suffers from another mental status deficit. As another example, reported perceptual disturbances may be normal in certain situations, such as when falling asleep, in response to severe sensory deprivation, or in normal grieving. But perceptual disturbances may also suggest psychopathology. Depending on the nature of the disturbance, the clinician may gain a clue as to whether the disturbance relates to a psychotic process (more likely with auditory hallucinations) or an organic process (more likely with visual or gustatory hallucinations) or suggests another psychiatric disorder. More detailed information about a mental status disturbance may also help in assessing potential risk; for example, command hallucinations are thought to increase the risk of dangerous behaviors, although this assumption is controversial.

Fourth, the clinician must balance the advantages of comprehensiveness with the advantages and necessity of selectivity. A rigorous examination of each area of mental functioning would ensure a complete assessment but can be taken to excess, distracting the clinician from properly focusing the assessment. The clinical situation may help define the proper balance. For example, an emergency psychiatric assessment following a suicide attempt should include a detailed assessment of suicidal ideation and risk factors for suicide. But an outpatient office visit by a patient seeking psychotherapy for a focused interpersonal problem may not require in-depth suicide assessment. The psychoanalytically oriented clinician may be reluctant to ask mental status questions that might interfere with the developing transference. The clinician should constantly consider how any given information helps clarify a meaningful diagnostic understanding of the patient. The application of the mental status examination, like other aspects of the assessment process, must be tailored to the needs of the individual patient; but the clinician should have a good clinical rationale for not pursuing a potentially important area of the mental status examination.

Certain components of the mental status examination deserve special emphasis because they screen for the more significant psychiatric disturbances and risk. These include evidence for suicidal ideation, psychotic symptoms, mood disturbance, and formal cognitive function deficits.

The psychiatric assessment of suicide potential should include any evidence for suicidal ideation, the extent of any such thoughts, suicidal plans, and any suicidal behaviors. Inexperienced clinicians are often reluctant to ask about suicidal thoughts, but specific questioning may be the only way to obtain such information. The patient will usually be relieved. One approach is to ask a series of questions that are increasingly specific, and to continue in more depth if there is any suggestion of suicidal ideation. For example, if a patient reports feeling depressed, the clinician may ask a general question, "Have you been so depressed that you thought life was not worth living anymore?" followed by, "Have you had any thoughts about hurting yourself, or of suicide?" Often, the clinician should ask at least one question using the word "suicide," to be sure the patient knows what is being asked and to break any possible taboo in using the term. Depending on the patient's response, the clinician will decide whether to press further. The goal is to have as clear an understanding as possible of the patient's self-destructive risk in order to reach a proper assessment and disposition.

Psychotic symptoms are symptoms suggesting grossly impaired "reality testing," and they may reflect a significant psychiatric disorder or a risk for destructive behavior. Psychotic thinking may be obvious, as demonstrated by a blatant hallucination or delusion, but symptoms of psychosis may also be hidden or subtle—an unusual appearance, abnormalities in behavior or thought processes, or an unexpectedly guarded response to a question. Sometimes the psychotic symptoms will be undetected unless elicited by specific questions (e.g., "Do you think people are trying to hurt you?") or an unstructured projective inquiry (e.g., proverb interpretation).

Mood disturbances, particularly depression, may reflect a serious psychiatric or physical disorder as well as a risk factor for destructive behavior. Even when mood disturbance is not the focus of the initial contact, the clinician may wish to pursue an assessment of mood.

Finally, the clinician may need to introduce specific structured questions in order to assess formal cognitive function, including orientation, memory, attention and concentration, and calculations (see the section on formal cognitive function later in this chapter). Trainees are sometimes reluctant to introduce the structured questions during the interview, fearing the questions will be seen as condescending or demeaning. However, without formal cognitive screening questions, the clinician risks missing a significant cognitive deficit. Some patients with cognitive deficits are skilled at appearing oriented and otherwise cognitively intact during a casual social conversation, yet they may be concocting convincing stories to cover cognitive deficits ("confabulation"). Alcoholics in particular are notorious for confabulation. Where there is a suspicion of deficits in formal cognitive functions, it is important to pose the appropriate structured questions. The interviewer need not apologize for introducing formal cognitive questions into the interview if they are an important part of the assessment. In general, patients will understand that these formal questions are necessary for the professional evaluation. If a patient raises objections, the clinician should consider that the patient is either attempting to mask cognitive or other deficits, or that the patient's response reflects some aspect of the patient's personality. These possibilities should be explored, if possible, as part of the diagnostic assessment.

Parts of the Mental Status Examination

Appearance. The clinician should begin with a description of the patient's appearance, noting prominent and unique features. Here clinicians may use literary skills in painting an individualized portrait, but they should not get carried away. The focus should be on aspects of appearance that have diagnostic significance. For example, misaligned buttoning of the shirt may suggest confusion or difficulty in concentrating, and unusual jewelry or skin markings may suggest unusual beliefs or cultural practices. Other notable facets of appearance may include apparent age, facial expression, eye contact, clothing, hygiene, neatness, posture, or other features.

Behavior. This description should include any aspects of the patient's observed behavior that are distinctive, unusual, or diagnostically significant. The clinician should observe behavior throughout the interview. Sometimes an unusual behavior occurs at a particular point during the interview; these events should be noted for their possible significance in diagnostic and dynamic assessment. A stressful or threatening topic, for example, may prompt the patient to look away, tap one foot repeatedly, stand up, or pace. Abnormal tongue or other movements may suggest tardive dyskinesia; restlessness may suggest akathisia. Descriptions of behavior may include overall activity level ("psychomotor state," which may be characterized in a variety of ways, such as "agitated," "excited," or "retarded," meaning slowed), coordination, stiffness, rigidity, posturing, tremors, tics, mannerisms, gestures, grimaces, tongue movements, restlessness, bizarre stereotype behaviors, and compulsive rituals. This is only a partial list; the experienced clinician will selectively describe those behaviors that contribute most to the diagnostic understanding of the patient.

Speech. Many contours and qualities of speech may be described, including rate, volume, pitch, range, spontaneity, clarity, and response time. Speech may be described as rapid or slow, pressured, hesitant, monotonous, loud, whispered, slurred, mumbled, or in many other ways. Defects in spoken language are sometimes included here, such as stuttering, echolalia, evidence of aphasia, and unusual use of vocabulary. Once again, the clinician should selectively describe aspects of speech that may have diagnostic significance. It is sometimes difficult to separate a description of speech from a description of thought.

Attitude toward interviewer. The clinician should describe the degree to which the patient became engaged in the interview, and the manner in which the patient related to the interviewer throughout the clinical examination. Patients may be described as cooperative or friendly or otherwise. Other descriptions of patient attitude include mature, childlike, argumentative, passive, aggressive or hostile, evasive, defensive or resistant, guarded, paranoid, controlling, dramatic, or seductive. Shifts in attitude at certain points in the interview, like shifts in behavior, may identify topics that are diagnostically important or emotionally charged, or have unconscious significance, suggesting transference issues and areas of resistance. Overall, a description of attitude provides a context for appreciating the interview, clinician-patient interaction, and quality of the information in the history and mental status examination.

The clinician's reaction to the patient may also be diagnostically useful. Countertransference responses may signal certain patient characteristics. For example, anger toward a patient may be a clue that the patient is controlling or manipulative; overconcern for a patient may suggest that the patient is insecure or psychologically fragile.

Mood and affect. Mood refers to the patient's primary sustained level of emotion, often described with reference to a spectrum of possible moods. At least several distinct mood levels may be described, ranging from the "lowest" to the "highest": depression (or "dysphoria," meaning unpleasant mood), euthymia (mood within a "normal" range), elevated mood (happier than usual, but not abnormal), euphoria (more elevated than normal), and mania. "Hypomania," a frequently used term, means "less than mania," implies a mood abnormality, and probably fits somewhere between elevated mood and mania on the mood continuum. "Expansive" mood refers to somewhat unrestrained feelings or mood. "Irritable" mood applies to a patient who appears tense and whose anger is easily provoked. Other common terms are available to describe mood.

Mood should be described from two perspectives. The clinician should record, in quotes, the patient's own description of mood. Although some patients will spontaneously describe their mood, others will do so only after a specific inquiry from the interviewer. Second, the clinician should record his or her impression of the patient's mood, with a clear designation that this is the clinician's impression. Discrepancies between the patient and clinician in describing mood may indicate that the patient is not consciously aware of mood, which is nevertheless communicated in other ways. When faced with such discrepancies, the clinician will usually need to evaluate the patient's mood further as well as why the patient might be denying an emotional experience.

Affect refers to the quality, range, and appropriateness of emotional expression. The clinician may consider facial expression as well as other behaviors in assessing affect. The quality of affect may include pure description or expression, such as "tearful" or "smiling," and may also include evidence for mood or other emotions, as when a patient appears "sad" or "happy." Affect that is devoid of expression or feelings is described as "flat affect," typically associated with schizophrenia. A "full range of affect" means that the patient demonstrates a natural and wide variety of emotions or feelings. Such patients may smile, laugh, and also appear sad at various times during the interview. "Blunted" or "constricted" affect reflects a narrower range of emotional expressiveness. Affect is described as "labile" when it jumps around, often without warning and between emotional extremes. Appropriateness of affect refers to the relationship between emotional expression and content. Appropriate affect is illustrated by smiling when discussing a pleasant topic, or appearing sad when discussing a recent family death. When a patient's emotional expression is inconsistent with the expected response to a given topic, such as smiling when discussing a sad topic, affect is described as "inappropriate."

Thought. The mental status examination of thought is divided into three categories: thought process, thought content, and perceptual disturbances.

Thought process refers to the logical connection and quality of thought, but not to actual content or substance. The apparent productivity of thought may be described according to the amount of thought (paucity or overabundance) and rate of thinking (rapid or slow). Normal thought processes may further be described as "logical," "goal-directed," and "relevant."

Certain abnormal thought processes are well recognized. These are sometimes labelled "formal thought disorders" because they indicate abnormalities in the form rather than the content of thought (but see the discussion of formal cognitive function later in this chapter for another use of the term "formal"). "Loose associations" refers to a thought pattern that lacks logical connections—thoughts jump from idea to idea without logical basis, or based only on some obscure or idiosyncratic logic. Loose associations may be subtle; the clinician should avoid the natural inclination to assume logical connections that are not actually present. "Tangential" thought refers to a thought pattern in which the stream of ideas departs from its starting point, never to return. "Circumstantial" thought also departs from its starting point but does eventually return to that original topic. Tangentiality and circumstantiality may involve long, detailed monologues unless interrupted by the interviewer; however, they are unlike loose associations in that they remain logical. "Perseveration" indicates the continual repetition of words or ideas (excluding the normal use of favorite expressions). "Blocking" refers to an interruption in the stream of thought marked by a moment or two of silence, in which the patient reports an inability to recall what was being said or what the patient intended to say. "Flight of ideas" describes rapid jumping from subject to subject based on some type of association or play on words. Other descriptions of abnormal thought process include "illogical," "distractable," "irrelevant," and "evasive."

Thought content refers to the main themes and actual substance of the patient's thoughts. The clinician should specifically note any evidence for suicidal ideation or thoughts suggesting danger to others. Thought content may include a description of relevant unconscious material (e.g., dreams, so-called Freudian slips of the tongue), preoccupations, obsessions (thoughts that are persistent, recurrent, intrusive, and seemingly not under voluntary control), fears or phobias, paranoid ideation, ideas of influence (e.g., fears of being controlled), ideas of reference (the belief that objects, events, and people's actions have special significance and meaning for the patient), and delusions.

Delusions are firmly held, fixed personal beliefs based on incorrect reasoning and inferences, which are not consistent with widely held religious or cultural beliefs. Delusions belong at one extreme of a spectrum extending from less to more strongly held beliefs: strong opinion, "overvalued ideas," "ideas of reference," and frank delusions, which may also vary in degree and intensity. In a delusion, even in the face of contrary evidence or reasoning, the patient will not consider the possibility that the belief may be untrue or an opinion. The hallmark of a delusion is that it is unshakable, not that it is untrue in reality.[1] A patient's belief that people are conspiring against him may be delusional if based on erroneous inferences from other people's comments and stares, even if it turns out that people truly are plotting against him. Delusions should be described in quality (e.g., whether they are systematized, or mood congruent) and content (e.g., persecutory, somatic, grandiose, nihilistic, self-referential, jealous, guilty, involving thought broadcast-

---

[1]Note that some authors and texts, including DSM-III-R, disagree and take the position that a delusion must be false in fact. Such a definition is problematic, however; a patient may have the same unshakable belief at two different times, yet the belief may be factually false at one time and factually true the other time (e.g., believing a war had begun the day before and the day after the war *had* actually begun)—it would not be particularly clinically useful to consider such a patient to be delusional one day and nondelusional the next day, given that the clinical status and appropriate interventions for that patient were unchanged.

ing or thought insertion, or of being controlled). Delusions should be distinguished from perceptual disturbances.

Perceptual disturbances require an abnormality in a sensory experience. These may involve hearing, sight, smell, taste, and touch. "Illusions" should be distinguished from "hallucinations." An illusion is a misperception of a real external stimulus. For example, a gust of wind in some nearby trees may be misperceived as a whispering voice. A "hallucination," however, is a sensory experience with no basis in any external stimuli. For example, hearing a voice that is not really there and is not the misperception of another sound is an example of an auditory hallucination. It is sometimes difficult to distinguish a hallucination from a delusion, and both may occur together. A patient may recognize an auditory hallucination as purely a sensory phenomenon, but may still hold the delusional belief that the voice is of a real person talking to the patient.

The circumstances in which the illusion or hallucination occurred may be important. An unusual sensory experience occurring only while going to sleep ("hypnagogic hallucination") or while waking up ("hypnopompic hallucination"), for example, is not usually clinically significant.

The sensory modality affected by a hallucination may have diagnostic and etiologic significance. Auditory hallucinations more likely suggest a psychiatric diagnosis with elements of psychosis, such as schizophrenia, but visual hallucinations more likely suggest an organic etiology for the psychiatric problem, such as drug use or a brain lesion. Olfactory and gustatory hallucinations also suggest an organic process. "Formication" is a specific type of tactile hallucination characterized by the sensation of something crawling on or under the skin, usually accompanied by the delusion that insects are causing the sensation; formication is seen in the delirium that follows alcohol withdrawal and withdrawal from cocaine intoxication.

The content of the hallucination may be diagnostically useful, especially when suggesting themes of depression, grandiosity, guilt, and other mood or thought processes. Some clinicians believe that the auditory hallucination of a voice telling a patient to act in a self-destructive manner (an example of a "command" hallucination) increases the risk for a self-destructive act, although this belief is controversial. Less controversial is the notion that the presence of psychosis, as would be indicated by hallucinations, should raise at least some concern that the patient may act impulsively.

Other possible perceptual disturbances include "depersonalization" and "derealization." Depersonalization is the sense of having lost one's reality or sense of self; body parts may seem distorted or unfamiliar, and the person may experience viewing himself or herself from a distance. Derealization is the sense that the external environment is strange or unfamiliar.

Formal cognitive function (or higher integrative function). As previously noted, certain areas of mental functioning are labeled "formal" because they define aspects of the form rather than the content of thought. When used in this part of the mental status examination, "formal cognitive functions" is a term referring to a specific set of cognitive abilities assessed through the use of formal questions. Because of a lack of agreement on the use of the term "formal," it is perhaps preferable to label these as "higher integrative functions," suggesting mental functions mediated by the cortex. Abnormalities in these functions are frequently associated with organic, physiological abnormalities and are therefore sometimes called "organic" findings. They do not, however, invariably indicate an organic problem. Deficits in higher integrative function may occur without a psychiatric disorder or may suggest a nonorganic disorder such as depression. Some clinicians attribute the cognitive deficits found in depression to problems with attention and concentration. Standardized sets of clinical questions, such as the 30-point scale Mini-Mental State Exam (Folstein et al. 1975) or the 6-Item Orientation-Memory-Concentration Test (Katzman et al. 1983) may be used to assess and follow the patient's cognitive status. More detailed neuropsychological and psychological testing may also be pursued.

"Pseudodementia" is an imprecise and, in this author's view, an unfairly pejorative term sometimes used to indicate deficits in formal cognitive function resulting from depression. "Pseudodementia" implies a "false" cause of dementia, suggesting that the dementia is illegitimate. But dementia is a descriptive term for a syndrome, and its cause requires further assessment. In fact, depression is statistically the second most common explanation of dementia or a dementialike presentation, second only to dementia of the Alzheimer's type. The conventional belief is that "organic" nonpsychiatric causes of delirium have direct brain effects, but "functional" psychiatric disorders such as depression merely indirectly result in cognitive deficits due to inattention or lack of concentration. But no one knows the precise mechanism that explains the cognitive deficits found in delirium, no matter what the cause. Perhaps depression has direct biological effects, and perhaps other medical causes of cognitive deficits are mediated through attention and concentration brain functions. The term "pseudodementia" implies an antipsychological bias and is inconsistent with a biopsychosocial philosophy that acknowledges the complex interaction between biological and psychological processes. "Pseudodementia" should be dropped from the clinician's vocabulary.

Specific formal questions are quite important in assessing higher integrative functions. Abnormalities in these cognitive functions may be evident during the interview; specific questioning would then help pinpoint the areas of deficit. Further, even though these functions may appear normal in a casual conversation, the clinician may be fooled. In such cases, the clinician must ask specific structured questions to be sure that a deficit in formal cognitive functioning is not overlooked. As noted earlier, patients, especially alcoholics, who concoct convincing stories to cover cognitive deficits ("confabulation"), are notorious for fooling clinicians into missing organic deficits. Finally, more detailed questioning should follow any significant errors detected with the routine screening questions typically used in assessing higher integrative functions.

There are three spheres of *orientation*: time, place, and person. To assess orientation to time, the clinician may ask the patient to state the date, day of the week, time of day, season, the year, how long the patient has been in a particular place such as the hospital, or other facts regarding time. To assess orientation to place, the clinician may ask where the patient currently is located, including the building, city, state, or other facts regarding location. To assess orientation to person, the clinician may ask for the patient's name, and the names and roles of others.

Three aspects of *memory* may be assessed: immediate, recent, and remote. Tests of memory frequently require other cognitive functions, such as attention and concentration, so that it may be difficult to determine whether an error exclusively reflects deficits in memory.

One commonly used screening test of immediate memory is digit span recall. In this test, the clinician asks the patient to repeat a random sequence of numbers, beginning with three or four digits and gradually increasing the digit span length one digit at a time. By starting with a shorter digit span, the clinician helps ensure that the patient understands and is confident in the task, and can also more precisely define the point at which errors begin. Each digit span test should involve a newly generated random sequence, and the patient should be given more than one chance at a given digit span length. Mnemonic strategies, such as associations or groupings of numbers, may create larger apparent memory capacity. In order to avoid inadvertent suggestion of such mnemonic advantages, the clinician should present the digit span at a slow, steady pace and in a monotonous voice. A useful device to help generate digit spans is for the clinician to use sequences he or she already knows, such as a telephone number, provided the patient will not recognize the sequence or groupings within the sequence. The clinician should be sure to provide clear instructions, including an illustration of the task with a three- or four-digit sequence. Most people will recall between five and nine digits, reflecting the common number of "slots" for immediate memory recall, referred to as "seven, plus or minus two."

The clinician may also ask the patient to repeat a random number sequence backwards, a more difficult task that requires even more concentration. A common variant is to ask a patient to spell a five-letter word, such as "world," backwards. Normal performance in recalling digits backwards would be less than expected for forward digit span recall. Five-digit recall backwards is a good result. Again, the clinician should begin with a short digit span and gradually increase the length, one digit at a time, until the patient cannot perform this task. The clinician then records the length of digit span recalled both forwards and backwards.

Recent memory refers to the ability to recall events over the past few minutes to days. The clinician may inquire whether the patient recalls recent events, such as what the patient ate for breakfast or watched on television the night before. However, it must be possible to confirm the validity of the patient's response. Otherwise, confabulation may fool the clinician.

One commonly used screening test of recent memory is to ask the patient to recall three objects after approximately 5 minutes. In this test, after providing instructions about what will occur, the clinician lists three objects in a steady, monotonous voice in order to avoid inadvertent grouping of the objects. Such groupings may create inaccuracies in conclusions from the test, suggesting a better memory capacity than the patient actually has. The objects are also usually unrelated in order to avoid inadvertent groupings. The clinician then asks the patient to repeat the objects to establish immediate recall. This test is not primarily a test of immediate recall. The clinician may remind the patient that he or she will be asked to recall these objects a little later in the interview. The clinician then continues with the interview, and approximately 5 minutes later asks the patient to recall the three objects. If the patient has difficulty, the clinician may give a multiple choice of possible objects, including one from the original three. However, doing so transforms the test to an assessment of the easier task of recognition recall; such a patient should be noted to have demonstrated deficits in the initial recall test. It is often reassuring to tell the patient that he or she will not be asked to recall these objects again. In a subsequent interview, a new set of three objects should be used; otherwise recall from the earlier interview may interfere with the test. However, the clinician may find it useful to test for the same three objects in every initial interview of a new patient; in this way the clinician need not struggle to think up three new objects for each evaluation and remember them during the interview.

Remote memory refers to the ability to recall events from the more distant past, months or years earlier. Questions about the patient's early life may help establish remote memory, but one must then confirm the accuracy of the memory. A common test of remote memory is to ask a patient to recall widely known events. A typical approach is to ask the a patient to name the presidents in reverse chronological order, or to recall well-known historical events. Education and culture may bias such tests, however, since some people may simply be unaware of or inattentive to certain events.

Attention and concentration refers to the ability to maintain a focus on a specific activity. Problems in attention and concentration often overlap with deficits in other areas of mental functioning, such as mood, thought, memory, and ability to perform calculations. The interview process itself may reveal problems in attention and concentration; patients with such problems are easily distracted and have difficulty recalling or paying attention to questions.

Formal tests of attention and concentration are available, although results may overlap with other mental functions. One common test, known as "serial 7s," involves asking the patient to subtract 7 from 100 and to continue subtracting 7 from each result. To clarify the instructions, the interviewer may need to illustrate the first subtraction or so. Patients may become unusually proficient at this task if they have performed this test frequently before, reflecting their learning and memory capacity rather than concentration. Other patients are more mathematically skilled. In such cases, the clinician may vary the test or make it more difficult, for example asking the patient to subtract 13 or 19 from some large number. Conversely, patients who have difficulty with serial 7s may be asked an easier version of the test, such as subtracting serial 3s or simply counting backwards from 100.

Asking patients to solve problems, such as providing directions to a given location or performing a mathematical calculation, is another method of testing attention and concentration. A particularly sensitive test of cognitive function, including attention and concentration as well as memory, is to ask a patient to state the months of the year in reverse order.

Calculation skills are the ability to perform mathematical tasks and manipulate numbers. Several tests of attention and concentration, such as serial subtractions, also reflect calculation ability. Additional calculation tests include asking the patient to solve a specific mathematical problem, or to determine the proper amount of change from a hypothetical purchase.

Abstractions. Abstractions refers to the ability to understand concepts and formulate generalizations. The absence of ability to abstract is called "concrete thinking." Tests for abstraction may also function as projective tests, revealing idiosyncratic or bizarre thoughts.

Abstraction can be observed during the interview process. Abstract thinking may also be formally assessed by testing for similarities, differences, or proverbs. When testing for similarities, the clinician asks how two objects, such as a plane and a train, are similar. A common response indicating good abstract thinking would be that both are forms of transportation. Concrete thinking would be illustrated by the response that they both have doors. As another example, good abstract thinking is indicated by responding that an apple and an orange are both fruit. When testing for differences, the clinician asks how two objects are different. Finally, the clinician may ask the patient to interpret a proverb, such as, "People who live in glass houses shouldn't throw stones." A concrete response to this proverb would be, "You shouldn't tempt someone to throw a stone into your glass window because you could get hurt." The proverb need not be familiar to the patient. The clinician must take into account the patient's education, intelligence, culture, and values in order to understand proverb interpretations. It is useful for the clinician to be prepared in advance with set questions involving similarities, differences, and proverb interpretation to use as needed when evaluating patients.

Intelligence. Intelligence may be inferred from the patient's use of vocabulary, abstraction, problem-solving ability, use of insight, capacity to adapt to novel situations, and ability to learn from experience. Intelligence must always be considered in the context of the patient's education and culture. A more detailed assessment of intelligence requires specialized and standardized tests. The clinician may also comment on the patient's fund of information.

Insight. For the mental status examination, insight has two meanings. First, insight refers to the patient's awareness and understanding of his or her problem. The clinician should describe whether the patient knows he or she suffers from a problem, what the patient believes is causing the disorder, and what should be done about it. Second, insight refers to the patient's awareness and understanding of deeper emotions, motivations, and conflicts that may underlie behavior patterns or the psychiatric disorder. This deeper understanding, which requires more than merely self-observation, may be an important ingredient for the success of certain types of psychotherapy.

Judgment. Judgment refers to the ability to act or solve problems appropriately within the social context. A patient's judgment ability usually emerges from the details of the history and the process of the interview. However, the clinician could present the patient with a difficult hypothetical situation and assess the patient's judgment in solving the problem. A classic example is to inquire what a patient would do on discovering a fire in a crowded theater.

The Diagnostic Psychiatric Interview

The diagnostic psychiatric interview is the primary means employed by mental health professionals to develop a diagnostic formulation. No two psychiatric interviews follow the same script. But all psychiatric diagnostic interviews aim to develop a diagnostic case formulation by pursuing two main tasks: 1) extracting "content," and 2) working with "process." The line between content and process, however, is sometimes blurred. Following a review of these two concepts, some general principles of interview technique will be summarized.

Extracting Content

Content refers to factual information, which may be communicated verbally or nonverbally. The clinician should gather the information needed to develop the empirical data base. As previously described, the interviewer must apply the structured outlines of the history and physical and mental status examination in order to gather, organize, record, and orally present information. Yet the clinician must individually tailor the acquisition of facts to focus on the information useful to developing the differential diagnosis.

In gathering information, the mental health professional should particularly focus on psychiatric history and the mental status examination. The clinician should pursue information concerning the relevant clinical features for any psychiatric disorder under consideration, referring to the descriptive DSM-III-R diagnoses as discussed in Chapter 3. The clinician should also consider other biological, psychological, or social dimensions to the patient's presentation. These biopsychosocial factors will help lead to a fuller understanding of the patient, hypotheses for the causes of the disorder, and treatment strategies.

Working With Process

Process refers to the development of the interview and the underlying psychodynamic interactions. By recognizing aspects of the interview process, the clinician will achieve two separate goals: 1) obtaining significant diagnostic and dynamic information that may not be available solely from the superficial content of history and other factual data, and 2) beginning the treatment process by developing a therapeutic alliance and applying psychotherapeutic technique.

The clinician should observe and work with four main concepts regarding dynamic interactions during the interview: transference, resistance, countertransference, and the therapeutic alliance. A full discussion of these concepts is beyond the scope of this book, but brief working definitions and illustrations will provide a sufficient framework for considering the importance of these concepts in the interview process.

Transference is the unconscious projection of feelings, thoughts, wishes, or desires related to significant people in the patient's past onto persons in the patient's present. While transference may involve the patient's current interactions with any persons, interactions with the interviewer may be of particular importance in the diagnostic interview. Trainees sometimes believe that transference involves only the patient's developmental history. While understanding feelings about past figures may help the clinician or patient to understand transference, it should also be emphasized that the manifestations of these feelings are played out in the present. The emotional power behind the transference feelings will more likely be elicited by addressing the here-and-now manifestations of transference rather than retreating into the intellectualized past.

Observing and understanding transference may help in the diagnostic assessment, especially with regard to understanding personality characteristics and a patient's vulnerability to other disorders, such as depression or anxiety. Transference may also be important to understanding obstacles to the smooth flow of information gathering during the interview. A patient's unrealistic anger at a male therapist when asked a question, for example, may reflect the patient's transference. Understanding the meaning of this reaction may help the therapist to understand this patient's difficulty with other male authority figures, possibly a reason for seeking professional help. Ultimately the reaction may be related to issues of control or competition among males, and refer back to figures in the patient's past, such as a father. During the course of the interview, the clinician may suggest an interpretation of a transference issue, such as by pointing out the relationship between the patient's anger toward the interviewer and other competitive feelings with men, both to examine the transference issue further and to begin to assess whether the patient is prepared to work on this issue from an analytically oriented psychotherapeutic perspective.

Resistance refers to feelings, thoughts, attitudes and behaviors that oppose therapeutic goals, including the goal of obtaining important information in the initial diagnostic interviews. Resistance may reflect conscious or unconscious processes. Resistance is closely related to transference; the patient may be particularly resistant to change that requires confronting transference feelings which, despite appearing maladaptive, are vehemently retained for irrational or unconscious reasons. As with transference, an examination of resistance may suggest certain diagnoses as well as whether the patient is amenable to certain modes of psychotherapy. For example, a patient who does not directly answer questions about close relationships may have sexual fears, reflecting either long-standing personality issues, unconscious conflict, or perhaps a sexual disorder as defined in DSM-III-R. A patient who refuses to comply with formal cognitive testing may be trying to avoid the embarrassment of revealing an underlying cognitive deficit. The clinician has a choice of ignoring or in some way addressing the resistance. Confronting the resistance creates the risk of threatening or alienating the patient, but it could help elucidate the reasons for the resistance and whether the patient can work with the resistance psychotherapeutically. The clinician may succeed by addressing the resistance without being threatening—for example, by pointing out an inconsistency that the patient and clinician can examine together or by an empathic comment acknowledging a patient's urge to cry that may help the patient reveal his or her true emotional state.

Countertransference refers to the clinician's emotional reactions and unconscious projections regarding the patient, usually based on a combination of the patient's transference and the clinician's own personal transference issues. Examples of countertransference are a clinician's anger toward a manipulative antisocial patient, or overconcern for an insecure and dependent patient. The clinician's countertransference feelings may serve as a flag for identifying certain diagnoses, or simply alerting the clinician to whether he or she likes or dislikes the patient. Despite the pejorative connotation heard in some settings, countertransference does not reflect a value judgment about the clinician. Rather, countertransference provides a way to acknowledge that clinicians have feelings about patients, which in turn may help further understanding of the patient and maintenance of the professional role.

The *therapeutic alliance* is the rationally based, trusting rapport and understanding between the clinician and the patient. Even though the focus of the diagnostic psychiatric interview is on developing a diagnostic formulation, a therapeutic process is also at work. In order to provide meaningful and personal information, the patient must trust the clinician and believe the clinician can help. The clinician, in turn, must communicate interest, respect, and empathic understanding in order to facilitate the patient's trust. The development of a therapeutic alliance permits the interview to progress smoothly and establishes the basis for further psychotherapy.

These four concepts—transference, resistance, countertransference, and the therapeutic alliance—interact throughout the psychiatric interview. They provide a key for identifying and understanding diagnoses, personality, unconscious conflict, the use of defense mechanisms, the patient's ability to cope and adapt, and the potential efficacy of various treatments. The clinician must not only be astute in recognizing these dynamic factors but must also develop strategies to work with them during the interview. Transference issues, even though not initially on the interviewer's agenda, may point the way to the most diagnostically important information. Countertransference may identify important diagnostic areas as well, but it may also alert the clinician to potential pitfalls or blind spots in the assessment process. Although the interviewer's aim is to develop the therapeutic alliance through empathic understanding, resistance from the patient may emerge, threatening to undercut the therapeutic alliance. The clinician must then decide whether and how to avoid or address the resistance. Attention to these dynamic factors will enable the clinician to achieve a meaningful understanding of the patient, for both diagnostic and treatment purposes.

Principles of Interview Technique

There is no formula for conducting a diagnostic interview. Expertise in interviewing requires experience and training. Yet certain general principles may be articulated.

Perhaps most important, the clinician should embrace an attitude that facilitates the development of the therapeutic alliance. The clinician should be professional, empathic, nonjudgmental, and respectful. The mental health professional should respect confidentiality, provided there is no acceptable overriding reason to breach confidentiality. The clinician should appreciate possible unconscious or psychodynamic factors when working with the patient in order to allow the therapeutic alliance to develop. In short, the interview should be part of the attempt to develop a meaningful clinician-patient relationship.

When considering the flow of the interview as a whole, it is often useful to consider the interview as consisting of several phases: pre-interview, opening, middle, and closing. Each phase raises different priorities and uses different techniques. Prior to actually meeting the patient, preliminary contact such as a telephone conversation may help allay initial fears, answer early questions, focus the problem, and set realistic expectations about the assessment process. The opening phase of the interview is geared toward introductions, allaying fears, initially assessing the patient's attitude toward the interview process, and beginning to develop a trusting rapport. The content of the opening phase usually focuses on the primary problem motivating the patient to seek help. The middle phase usually involves a more detailed examination of the present illness and a review of other salient aspects of the empirical data base or interview process. In the closing phase, lasting at least several minutes, the patient should usually have the opportunity to raise any remaining topics or questions. Depending on the situation, this might be a good time to discuss reactions and impressions so far, or to arrange a future session.

The interview should feel natural, not stilted or contrived. Two factors need to be balanced: the interviewer's agenda and the patient's agenda. Although it is not always apparent, the interviewer and patient are actually working toward the same goal—achieving proper diagnosis and treatment. But psychodynamic factors or inexperience may get in the way of this goal. On the one hand, the interviewer should pursue the structured outline of the empirical data base and mental status examination, extracting content and working with process. On the other hand, the interviewer may often follow the patient's lead, permitting a more natural interchange and fostering the therapeutic alliance. The patient is thus assured of some control and knows there will be an opportunity to communicate what the patient believes is important. Information will not necessarily emerge in the order of the clinician's outline. However, at various points, the clinician may take control and direct the interview in order to fill in important information gaps or to address dynamic aspects of the interview process.

Thus, if the patient wishes to begin an interview with family psychiatric history, it would be appropriate for the interviewer to ask specific questions about that topic and wait for the patient to come to a discussion of the history of the present illness, which the interviewer would then pursue. By allowing the patient to have some control of the flow of the interview, the interviewer lets the patient feel that an alliance is developing and that the interviewer is working with and following the lead of the patient. However, at some point the interviewer may have to direct the patient in order to obtain important information in a given area. The interviewer should then interrupt the flow of the interview, interjecting a question or shifting topics in an appropriate and polite manner. If the patient is spending an inordinate amount of time on family history rather than present illness, for example, the clinician might say, "I think I have a good sense of the psychiatric problems that your family has encountered over the years. Perhaps now we could turn to the specific problem that brings you to my office at this time."

All the while, as the interview proceeds, the clinician notes information pertinent to the mental status exam. At some point, specific areas of mental status may need to be directly assessed, perhaps changing the natural flow of the interview. An experienced interviewer, however, can often cleverly intertwine mental status questions with the natural flow of the interview. For example, if some information or event during the interview suggests a mental status abnormality, the interviewer can follow up with questions about that area. A patient may state that he or she is sad; the clinician may then more directly inquire about depression and suicidal ideation. A patient who suddenly glances around the room may be responding to perceptual disturbances or paranoid thoughts; the clinician may then ask questions to establish whether there are any present hallucinations or delusions. Formal mental status questions may fit into the flow of the interview as well: for example, after eliciting the patient's age, the clinician may ask the patient to calculate his or her date of birth. The clinician should avoid being so clever that the patient feels manipulated. Sometimes it is best simply to state what you will be testing, and then ask the formal questions.

The clinician should employ a variety of questioning and other interactive techniques, such as open-ended and closed-ended questions, reflection, facilitating comments, transitions, reinforcement, manipulation, suggestion, clarification, confrontation, interpretation, and silence. Each approach may be effective in the proper interview situation. Although it is beyond the scope of this book to examine each of these techniques, the importance of using both open-ended and closed-ended questions will be briefly illustrated.

Open-ended or unstructured questions permit patients to peruse their own response to a general question, deciding for themselves what is important. For example, the clinician may ask, "What is the main problem that brings you here today?" or, "Tell me what you mean by anxiety." These types of questions give the patient control over the response, thereby facilitating the therapeutic alliance, and may provide an opportunity to assess the emotional significance of certain areas and identify areas for more detailed inquiry. These questions further allow the clinician to observe the patient's thought processes without any externally imposed structure, yielding information important to the mental status examination. For all these reasons, open-ended questions are useful in the early phases of an interview. Too many open-ended questions, however, may leave gaps in the empirical data base and may allow the patient too much control, thereby permitting the patient to avoid important areas.

Closed-ended or structured questions are questions which, if properly answered, require a specific answer. For example, closed-ended questions may inquire about specific facts in the history such as, "When did these symptoms begin?" or "Have you had any thoughts about hurting yourself?" Areas of the mental status examination, such as formal cognitive function, may require a series of closed-ended questions. Such questions provide information that may not otherwise be obtained. The patient may be resistant to discussing a certain topic without a pointed question from the interviewer. Further, the clinician may be more confident in the mental status assessment, including such areas as suicidal ideation or formal cognitive function, if specific closed-ended questions are asked. Too many structured questions, however, may stifle the patient. The proper balance must be struck.

Certain interview techniques or strategies tend to apply to certain patients. The clinician should therefore be flexible, adapting to the patient. A few examples will illustrate this point.

If an organic deficit may explain a patient's difficulty during the initial phases of the interview, the clinician should move to an assessment of formal cognitive functions. Otherwise, the clinician may waste time obtaining history that may turn out to be inaccurate. A withdrawn and depressed patient may provide virtually no response to open-ended questions; the clinician may need to address this withdrawal directly, or shift to structured questions. The discomfort of an anxious patient may be heightened by one interview approach and diminished by another. The clinician should use the approach that works, but also scrutinize why the earlier approach was unsuccessful. Obsessive patients tend to be either compliant or defiant; they may weave overdetailed answers to unstructured questions, requiring interruption by the interviewer, or overspecific short answers to closed-ended questions. Either possibility suggests obsessive traits and areas of resistance. Overdramatic patients may provide sensational stories in response to open-ended questions, which should usually be followed by clarifying, structured questions. Paranoid and psychotic patients, although needing reassurance to trust the clinician, may be threatened when questioned too directly; the resistance of such patients may need to be handled gingerly unless addressing resistance is otherwise clinically useful. It may be clinically appropriate, however, to aggressively confront manipulation by a patient whose personality traits are directly undercutting the clinician's ability to conduct the assessment or to pursue treatment.

When an interview grinds to a halt, the clinician should consider the extent to which psychopathology, such as psychotic paranoia, or psychodynamic factors, such as resistance, are affecting the interview process.

The clinician should also anticipate several practical considerations when conducting diagnostic interviews. Time limitations may dictate the extent of the material that can be covered. A well-staffed hospital may offer the luxury of more control over the time available for interviewing a patient, but the outpatient setting may offer precisely defined time limitations, often 50 minutes or less for a session. The clinician requires skill not only to use time well, but also to assess the meaning of the patient's use of time. For example, a patient who withholds important information until the end of the session may be resisting the evaluation or trying to extend the session for some reason. Fees may have both practical economic implications and symbolic meaning regarding control and the value of the interaction. Privacy should be ensured. Seating arrangements may have significance to both the clinician and the patient. Some clinicians prefer to face the patient directly; others sit behind a desk. The oppositional patient may sit farther from the interviewer, whereas the paranoid patient may be more comfortable sitting next to an office door.

Another practical consideration is that an assessment may require several interviews. In fact, a second interview provides a new opportunity for deeper understanding of the patient. The patient may have more security and trust in the interviewer and a clearer understanding of the interview process. The clinician, too, has had time to consider the diagnoses and which areas require further examination. The clinician and patient may examine the impact of the earlier interview and the patient's ability to work psychotherapeutically with the clinician from session to session. Personality disorders or other characterological difficulties, in particular, are exceedingly difficult to assess adequately in a limited number of interviews, although the diagnostician may generate hypotheses as to a patient's characterological functioning. Sometimes the first diagnostic interview itself can be quite therapeutic, and the presenting problem will look quite different by the second or subsequent sessions.

Potentially violent patients raise a practical concern. The clinician must feel physically secure in order to perform the assessment interview. A clinician cannot realistically evaluate a potentially violent patient while feeling physically threatened. In such situations, adequate security must be provided first. This is often reassuring to the patient as well, providing the security of external controls over acts that the patient fears cannot be otherwise held in check.

In summary, when conducting the diagnostic psychiatric interview, the clinician should maintain a comprehensive biopsychosocial viewpoint while also being flexible and selective and individually tailoring the interview to the clinically important needs of the patient. This is more easily said than done.

Setting-Based Priorities

The clinical context may suggest certain areas for information gathering and diagnostic emphasis. The clinician thus applies the knowledge that certain diagnoses or phenomena are more prevalent depending on the nature of the population, clinical setting, context of the referral, or timing. Several examples will illustrate this concept.

From a developmental perspective, the patient's age alone may suggest an emphasis. Certain diagnoses are associated with young children. Other disorders, such as eating disorders, may have their onset in adolescence. Traits that may be considered pathological in adults, such as age-appropriate impulsivity, may be considered normal in adolescence. Other disorders, such as schizophrenia, may first clearly begin in young adulthood. Assessment of college students, for example, should take this fact into account, as well as the stress faced by this group caused by separation from home, a new environment, and academic pressure. Mood disorders typically begin in early adulthood, and depression is more common in women than in men.

In the geriatric population, the clinician should be particularly concerned about psychiatric diagnoses more common in the elderly, such as dementia and depression. The biological and social aspects of the biopsychosocial assessment deserve special emphasis in this age group. Significant medical illnesses, lack of social support, and the death or illness of others are often important contributions to psychiatric problems in the elderly. A review of systems will help the clinician avoid overlooking the contribution of medical illnesses. The elderly frequently suffer from the psychiatric effects of both prescribed and over-the-counter medications, yet a superficial history may miss this area, especially because many patients do not consider nonprescribed substances as "medication." To remedy this potential oversight, the interviewer of a geriatric patient should review all medications, may inquire about medications purchased at a drugstore, and may ask a patient to describe or bring in the contents of the bathroom medicine cabinet.

In the medically ill population, including patients in a general medical hospital who may be seen by a consultation-liaison specialist, the clinician should be particularly concerned about psychiatric disorders that relate to medical illnesses, such as delirium. Prescribed medication is also a common cause of psychiatric disorders in the physically ill. A frequently encountered issue in this setting is the problem of distinguishing between depression and the demoralization or normal grieving reaction that may accompany medical illness.

In the acute assessment settings of the emergency room or acute care psychiatric ward, one should screen for the most significant psychiatric disorders and risks. In these settings, the mental status examination should usually note evidence for suicidal ideation, psychotic symptoms, mood disturbance, and formal cognitive function deficits.

When evaluating patients for substance abuse, it is sometimes difficult to distinguish between symptoms directly due to the drug and symptoms due to a psychiatric disorder that the patient is attempting to self-medicate with the drug. Antisocial personality disorders or traits are also common in this population. Such patients often seem convincing but are notoriously unreliable. The clinician should seek out other sources and try to corroborate any important information.

The nature of the referral may determine expectations and the agenda for the ensuing assessment and treatment. A referral for analysis or for a problem that requires analytically oriented psychotherapy, such as a characterological problem, implies an expectation that the assessment and treatment will proceed from an analytic framework. In contrast, a referral for psychotropic medication adjustments implies an entirely different expectation, with a focus on medication effects and perhaps limited psychotherapeutic support. Problems may emerge when the referral source, patient, and mental health professional have differing or uncertain expectations. Further, as the interview proceeds, the clinician may need to shift focus. For example, the analyst who discovers serious suicidal ideation may need to step out of the analytic framework to assess suicidal ideation. (Of course, this ideation could be a ploy by the patient for gratification.) Conversely, the clinician primarily addressing medication issues may need to explore the psychodynamic reasons for a patient's noncompliance, such as anger at being dependent on pills. At some point, the referral source, patient, or clinician may need to clarify the goals of the assessment or treatment. A clinician should try to clarify the initial reason for a consultation in order to develop a proper focus and anticipate both the patient's and referring clinician's expectations.

Other parameters, such as date or time of year, may turn out to be important to the assessment. The anniversary of a significant past event, such as the death of a loved one, may help explain the onset of psychiatric symptoms years later. Season and holidays may also be important. They may be reminders of significant past events or hold symbolic meaning for the patient. Rebirth and love are associated with spring, for example, and may evoke depression in some lonely patients. Disorders such as the recently described seasonal affective disorder may be specifically associated with time of year. It may be important to discover that the patient's therapist is on vacation, an event that may be associated with a regular time of year—traditionally August—and that may represent a significant "loss" for the patient. The patient's psychiatric symptoms may reflect an unwitting reaction to the temporary loss of the therapist. Current events may also be important to the evaluation; a recent tragic news or television story, or local school or peer events such as an adolescent suicide, may provide clues for areas of inquiry and possible diagnoses.

The setting, then, is important to the clinician in suggesting areas for emphasis in developing the empirical data base.

Symptom-Based Differential Diagnoses

In order to pursue information needed to evaluate a differential diagnosis, the clinician should understand the diagnostic significance of any specific empirical finding. Students sometimes believe that a particular psychiatric finding necessarily implies one specific diagnosis. This is an error. As in other medical illnesses, a psychiatric symptom may generate a broad differential diagnosis. Therefore, any finding should prompt the clinician to pursue further evidence to support or rule out these differential diagnoses. The most important illustrations of this point involve history and mental status abnormalities that may suggest severe psychiatric disorders—suicidal ideation or behavior, psychotic symptoms, mood disturbance, and deficits in formal cognitive function.

Suicidal ideation or behavior alone may suggest a wide range of differential diagnoses. The nonprofessional typically associates suicide with depression. But in addition to a single or recurrent episode of major depression, a wide range of disorders described in DSM-III-R may be associated with depression accompanied by suicidal ideation or behavior. These include organic mood syndrome, multi-infarct dementia, primary degenerative dementia of the Alzheimer's type, hallucinogen or phencyclidine mood disorder, bipolar disorder, and schizoaffective disorder. In addition to depression, suicidal ideation may suggest other feelings, such as impulsivity, anger, fear, or frustration. Suicidal ideation or behavior is included in possible criteria for the DSM-III-R diagnosis of borderline personality disorder and, although not part of formal criteria, may suggest a variety of other personality disorders, personality traits, or areas of unconscious conflict. A psychotic patient may become suicidal in response to auditory hallucinations, delusions, or other symptoms; this may suggest a number of diagnoses associated with psychosis, such as schizophrenia. A delirious patient may be suicidal because of cognitive confusion. Some chronic psychiatric patients experience and cope with frequent or constant suicidal ideation. Thoughts of suicide do not necessarily even imply a psychiatric disorder; they may be a normal response to stress, severe disappointment or frustration, loss, or demoralization. Finally, according to some ethical arguments that are not widely accepted in our society, suicide may be a rational alternative to other forms of death; a suffering, medically ill person who desires to die is not necessarily mentally disordered.

Psychotic symptoms, such as hallucinations and delusions, usually bring to mind such diagnoses as schizophrenia, delusional disorder, brief reactive psychosis, schizophreniform disorder, and schizoaffective disorder. But other DSM-III-R diagnoses may be associated with psychosis as well, including organic mental syndromes and disorders such as delirium and dementia, particular psychoactive substance-induced organic mental disorders, and mood disorders. Patients with certain personality disorders or traits may, when under stress, be vulnerable to developing psychotic symptoms. The original concept of borderline personality disorder was derived when some seemingly "neurotic" patients undergoing the frustration of psychoanalysis experienced brief psychotic episodes. Significant stress such as severe sensory deprivation may also trigger psychotic symptoms in otherwise healthy people.

After characterizing the nature of a mood disturbance, the clinician may need to consider a wide spectrum of differential diagnoses. Depression, for example, may be associated with normal grief and bereavement or with reactions to stress perhaps meeting criteria for an adjustment disorder, or it may extend to more serious psychiatric diagnoses such as major depression. Many other disorders in DSM-III-R may be associated with depression, however, including organic mental syndromes and disorders such as dementia or organic mood syndromes; psychoactive substance-induced organic mental disorders; other mood disorders such as bipolar disorder, dysthymia, or cyclothymia; and schizoaffective disorder. Finally, the clinician should consider that virtually any underlying psychiatric illnesses may be quite upsetting and evoke feelings of depression. For example, a patient with schizophrenia may become depressed when facing an exacerbation of this chronic mental illness. Euphoria or other mood disturbances may also suggest a range of possible diagnoses.

Deficits in formal cognitive functions, such as orientation and memory, are usually thought to be related to so-called organic disorders. Such disorders, however, include a wide range of possibilities, including delirium, dementia, and psychoactive substance-induced organic mental disorders. An entire section of DSM-III-R is devoted to the many possible diagnoses related to organic mental syndromes and disorders. Clinically, these diagnoses require further investigation into many possible medical etiologies. Deficits in formal cognitive function may also be associated with many other so-called nonorganic or functional diagnoses, especially when attention and concentration appear to be compromised. This association frequently occurs in major depression but may apply to other disorders as well.

When developing the empirical data base, therefore, the clinician should note the possible diagnostic implications of any psychiatrically important information and pursue those areas that will help rule in or rule out possible diagnoses. Doing so results in a more meaningful and accurate descriptive psychiatric differential diagnosis.

References

Folstein MF, Folstein SE, McHugh PR: "Mini-Mental State": a practical method for grading the cognitive state of patients for the clinician. J Psychiatr Res 12:189–198, 1975

Katzman R, Brown T, Fuld P, et al: Validation of a short orientation-memory-concentration test of cognitive impairment. Am J Psychiatry 140:734–739, 1983

CHAPTER 3

The Descriptive Diagnosis

The term *descriptive diagnosis* refers to a diagnosis based purely on the empirical data base, including clinical history, signs, and symptoms. It largely excludes psychiatric theory or etiology, although etiologic inferences are included in some descriptive diagnoses such as organic mental disorders, for which organic causes are known or presumed. The descriptive diagnosis is sometimes said to be "atheoretical" or "phenomenological." It is a kind of shorthand summary of clinically important findings from the empirical data base. In medicine, it would be comparable to making the diagnosis of pneumonia after a history and physical, without yet considering the many possible causes of the pneumonia. Descriptive diagnoses serve as the narrow neck in the funnel of information, concentrating the stream of clinical data for the forthcoming psychiatric diagnostic case formulation.

The most recent and widely accepted system of descriptive diagnoses in American psychiatry is *Diagnostic and Statistical Manual of Mental Disorders, 3rd Edition, Revised*, known as DSM-III-R, developed by the American Psychiatric Association and published in 1987.

Modern descriptive diagnosis represents a major advance for the mental health profession. Diagnostic terms are now more clinically useful because of increased reliability (i.e., different clinicians will arrive at the same diagnosis), improved validity (i.e., diagnoses describe actual clinical entities), wider acceptance of standardized terms, and increased compatibility between diagnostic systems (such as between DSM-III-R and the International Classification of Diseases [ICD]). Clinicians with differing theoretical orientations may now

47

agree on these more purely descriptive categories. Communication among professionals has improved. Finally, reliable diagnostic categories permit more meaningful psychiatric research and field trials.

The revisions and ongoing scientific debate on descriptive diagnoses in modern psychiatry signify two fundamental deficits in psychiatric knowledge. First, thoughts and behavior, unlike many medical diseases, cannot easily be classified into clinically meaningful diagnostic descriptions. Second, we know very little about the etiology of psychiatric problems. Psychiatric theory is important, as we shall see in later chapters, but is not included in this component of the diagnostic process.

An overheavy reliance on descriptive diagnoses entails several pitfalls. The clinician may be mistaken in the diagnosis applied to a case, or the diagnostic system itself may require further revision. DSM-III-R diagnoses are not necessarily the last word in describing and categorizing thought and behavior. There will be a DSM-IV. The clinician should consider a diagnosis even though the case may not precisely meet specific diagnostic criteria. Further, the clinician should initially consider a broad differential diagnosis, rather than a narrowly focused, seemingly definitive, but perhaps wrong single diagnosis. As will be reviewed in Chapter 5, the descriptive differential diagnosis should be included in the psychiatric diagnostic case formulation, prioritized both according to likelihood and clinical importance. The DSM-III-R descriptive diagnosis is a vital component of psychiatric diagnoses, but it does not represent the conclusion of the diagnostic process.

A thorough working knowledge of DSM-III-R is crucial for modern psychiatric diagnoses. The next section will provide a conceptual overview of DSM-III-R, followed by a capsule summary of the major diagnostic categories in DSM-III-R itself.

Understanding and Applying DSM-III-R

DSM-III-R has been criticized for being too much like a cookbook. In fact, it *is* very much like a cookbook; every diagnosis in DSM-III-R has specific and mostly descriptive criteria. But this is not necessarily a disadvantage, since the diagnostic criteria are quite useful. Problems occur when DSM-III-R is applied too rigidly or overemphasized in the diagnostic process. When applied properly, it offers a wide range of available dishes (i.e., diagnoses) and an opportunity to adapt recipes (i.e., diagnostic criteria) to meet the clinical situation.

Table 3-1.   Historical context of DSM-III-R

Year	Diagnostic categories or system	Basis
1952	DSM-I	Alternative to ICD-6
1968	DSM-II	ICD-8
1980	DSM-III	ICD-9-CM
1987	DSM-III-R	DSM-III
1993 (projected)	DSM-IV	DSM-III-R and ICD-10

Note.   CM = clinical modification, DSM = Diagnostic and Statistical Manual of Mental Disorders, ICD = International Classification of Disease, R = revision.

DSM-III-R in Historical Perspective

A historical perspective helps clarify the advances and limitations of DSM-III-R in the continuing evolution of psychiatric diagnoses in the United States (see Table 3-1).

The first edition of the *Diagnostic and Statistical Manual of Mental Disorders* (now called DSM-I in retrospect), published in 1952, introduced descriptions for diagnostic categories but primarily reflected Adolf Meyer's theories about mental disorders.

DSM-II, published in 1968, incorporated both description and psychiatric theory prominent at the time, such as the distinction between psychosis and neurosis. Beginning with DSM-II, American psychiatric diagnostic systems have been coordinated with the development of international systems (ICD).

Among all the diagnostic systems, DSM-III, published in 1974, represents the most revolutionary change. DSM-III sought to be more exclusively descriptive and atheoretical. DSM-III dropped terms suggesting psychodynamic theory, such as "neuroses," although remnants of the old "neurotic" diagnoses still appear in the current manual, usually redefined as descriptions of behavior patterns rather than unconscious conflict. These changes have been largely successful in improving reliability, validity, and the wide acceptance of the diagnostic system.

Whereas DSM-III represented a major shift in the official diagnostic manual, DSM-III-R represents merely a fine-tuning of DSM-III. Revisions reflect minor improvements in DSM-III and advances in the field but do not introduce any major conceptual changes in the diagnostic manual. Most of the ensuing discussion of DSM-III-R really focuses on the primary changes made earlier in DSM-III.

A historical perspective also points to humbling limitations in our diagnostic system. In many respects, diagnostic concepts have changed little over the centuries. For example, the older terms "mania" and "melancholia" (from the Greek "black bile" theory) are comparable to modern mood disorders; "monomania" resembles modern schizophrenia and other functional psychoses; the old term "dementia" relates to modern dementia classifications; and "dipsomania" relates to modern alcoholism. Further, an understanding of the etiology and pathophysiology of mental disorders often results in the reclassification of such disorders into fields other than psychiatry. For example, epilepsy, once considered a psychiatric disorder, is now considered a neurological disorder, and paresis is now known to be an infectious disease (syphilis). The lack of such reclassification for many of the early diagnoses suggests the limited progress psychiatry has made in understanding the causes of disorders.

In summary, the modern clinician working with DSM-III-R diagnoses inherits the benefit of significant progress as well as the reality of continuing limitations. It is both exciting and frustrating to realize that this process is ongoing, and the clinician will continually need to master new knowledge and revisions in psychiatric diagnosis.

DSM-III-R: Science and Politics

DSM-III-R reflects a scientific project undertaken by the American Psychiatric Association, but admittedly involved a political process as well. It reflects both research field trials and committee votes. Two factors explain the intrusion of politics into the creation of the manual. First, diagnoses have important political implications. Labeling certain behaviors as "disorders" presumes abnormality, evokes stigma and possible discrimination, and may have other legal or financial ramifications. Second, some diagnoses reflect subjective judgments of scientific information or simply lack of scientific rigor and are therefore open to debate.

The majority of diagnoses in DSM-III-R, however, were either unchanged from DSM-III or represent clarifications that evoked minimal debate. There are notable exceptions. For example, three controversial diagnoses (late luteal phase dysphoric disorder, sadistic personality disorder, and self-defeating personality disorder) were relegated to an appendix of nonofficial diagnoses entitled "Proposed Diagnostic Categories Needing Further Study." I believe that the names of certain disorders were also designed partly to minimize their emotional or political impact as well as for other reasons (i.e., "late luteal phase dysphoric disorder" instead of "premenstrual syndrome," or "sexual paraphilias" instead of "sexual deviations").

Further, I feel that in order to apply DSM-III-R properly, the clinician should understand that DSM-III and DSM-III-R were developed by a mixture of scientific and political processes, a situation that has both advantages and disadvantages. The primary advantage is that a wide range of views and data could be considered, including the best available research and advice from the nation's leading mental health experts. Unintended political ramifications could also be anticipated and avoided. The process may be criticized, however, for reflecting political pressure that may have influenced the objectivity of committee deliberations. The wide acceptance of the diagnostic manual and the clarity of descriptions of most of the diagnoses suggests that the resulting manual was quite successful. But DSM-III-R has its critics. Thus, the clinician should use DSM-III-R but retain a bit of skepticism.

The Role of Etiology in Using DSM-III-R

Although DSM-III-R aims to rely primarily on phenomenological descriptions, etiology must also be considered in two important respects.

First, many DSM-III-R diagnoses do, in fact, require the identification or presumption of a cause for the psychiatric diagnosis. For example, organic mental disorders require an identified or presumed organic cause. Adjustment disorder requires reaction to a stress. Other diagnoses infer psychiatric theory. Conversion disorder, for example, requires the determination that psychological factors are causally related to loss of or alteration in physical functioning, based on a temporal relationship between a stressor related to a psychological conflict and the onset or worsening of the physical symptom.

Second, as DSM-III-R itself points out, the descriptive approach to diagnosis should not diminish the importance of theories about the cause of mental disorders. Psychiatric theory is a crucial additional component of the clinical diagnostic process, as will become clear in later chapters.

The Role of Flexibility

The application of DSM-III-R should emphasize flexibility. DSM-III-R itself provides a "cautionary statement" explicitly stating that the specific DSM-III-R diagnostic criteria are offered as *guidelines*. Further, the cautionary statement notes that other conditions not included in the manual may be legitimate for treatment or research. A psychiatric diagnosis may not apply in other contexts. For example, the diagnosis of a mental disorder does not necessarily relieve the person diagnosed of legal responsibility for his or her actions, and the increasingly important role of DSM-III-R for insurance purposes is controversial. Elsewhere, the DSM-III-R cautions that application of the diagnoses may need to take into account cultural differences.

In addition to these explicit cautions, the DSM-III-R diagnostic categories themselves include flexible options. Patients who do not precisely meet criteria for a specific subcategory of a broader diagnostic group may nevertheless be diagnosed under the broader diagnosis with the additional label "not otherwise specified." Some diagnoses incorporate criteria for severity. In others, the clinician may specify a range of severity by using the following terms in parentheses after the diagnosis: mild, moderate, severe, in partial remission (or residual state), or in full remission.

The range of diagnostic categories itself offers much flexibility. Some diagnoses form a spectrum, and the boundaries between these diagnoses may not be distinct. For example, a patient's depression may not qualify as a full-blown major depression, but may more closely meet criteria for dysthymia or an adjustment disorder with depressed mood. The so-called V Codes (so named to be consistent with ICD-9), although not true diagnoses, are nevertheless available in the DSM-III-R system to identify conditions that are not attributable to a mental disorder. Multiple diagnoses may be listed. When there is insufficient information to make a firm diagnosis, the clinician may follow the working diagnosis with the parenthetical term "(provisional)" to indicate significant uncertainty, and may then include other diagnoses to be ruled out. Finally, DSM-III-R provides additional codes for varying levels of diagnostic uncertainty: "unspecified mental disorder" (enough information to determine the presence of a mental disorder but not enough for further specification), "diagnosis or condition deferred" (inadequate information to make a diagnostic determination), and "no diagnosis or condition" (i.e., there is a code for no diagnosis).

In short, DSM-III-R should be used as a flexible guide to descriptive diagnoses, and only as one part of the larger diagnostic process.

Defining "Mental Disorder"

A key paragraph in DSM-III-R is the definition of a mental disorder.

In DSM-III-R each of the mental disorders is conceptualized as a clinically significant behavioral or psychological syndrome or pattern that occurs in a person and that is associated with present distress (a painful symptom) or disability (impairment in one or more important areas of functioning) or with a significantly increased risk of suffering death, pain, disability, or an important loss of freedom. In addition, this syndrome or pattern must not be merely an expectable response to a particular event, e.g., the death of a loved one. Whatever its original cause, it must currently be considered a manifestation of a behavioral, psychological, or biological dysfunction in the person. Neither deviant behavior, e.g., political, religious, or sexual, nor conflicts that are primarily between the individual and society are mental disorders unless the deviance or conflict is a symptom of a dysfunction in the person, as described above. (DSM-III-R, p. xxii)

According to this definition, a psychiatric diagnosis should be made only when the syndrome is *clinically significant*, as manifested by distress, disability, or certain increased risks. The definition attempts to distinguish psychiatric disorders from psychological experiences and behaviors within the realm of normal experience, such as bereavement. Behavior that is considered abnormal in a social context may not necessarily meet the requirements of a mental disorder. But the boundary distinguishing mental disorders from the range of normal mental functioning may not be clear. V Codes may apply to some conditions that do not meet the definition of a mental disorder. Other situations may simply not imply a true psychiatric diagnosis.

Hierarchies

DSM-III-R employs the concept of diagnostic hierarchies, but to a much more limited extent than its predecessor, DSM-III. The presumption behind using hierarchies is that diagnoses higher in the hierarchy more frequently include symptoms of diagnoses lower in the hierarchy. In such situations, the diagnosis that is lower in the hierarchy is not given, even though the patient may meet the criteria for that diagnosis. In other words, certain diagnoses preempt others. After the publication of DSM-III, however, it became apparent that many psychiatric diagnoses could and frequently do coexist.

Strictly applied, DSM-III-R uses hierarchies in two main areas. First, the presence of an organic mental disorder preempts other diagnoses that may have similar presentations. This preemption should apply only when an organic etiology is identified or presumed to explain the onset or development of the clinical presentation. For example, in a depressed patient the diagnosis of an organic mood disorder would preempt the diagnosis of a mood disorder such as major depression; in an anxious patient the diagnosis of an organic anxiety disorder would preempt the diagnosis of panic disorder, and so on.

The second application of hierarchies in DSM-III-R is in requiring that more pervasive disorders preempt less pervasive disorders. This preemption would occur only when criteria for the more pervasive disorder have associated symptoms that define the less pervasive disorder. An example given in DSM-III-R is a patient with both schizophrenia and chronic, mild depression. If this patient meets criteria for both schizophrenia, the more pervasive diagnosis, and dysthymia, the less pervasive diagnosis, the proper DSM-III-R diagnosis would be only schizophrenia. Of course, the patient must meet the defining criteria for the more pervasive disorder, which in this example is schizophrenia. Note that there is no specific relationship between hierarchies and the multiaxial system except that the principal diagnosis is assumed to be the Axis I diagnosis unless designated otherwise (as described in the discussion of the multiaxial system).

Applying these hierarchies has advantages. The primary advantage is to focus attention and treatment on the diagnosis that is clinically more important and more likely to be correct. Otherwise, the clinician might be distracted by tangential, misleading, or incorrect diagnoses. Organic causes are potentially serious and often correctable. More pervasive disorders are not only more clinically significant than less pervasive disorders, but may cause them (e.g., schizophrenia itself may contribute to feelings of depression).

But using these hierarchies has disadvantages as well. One conceptual problem involves the inconsistency of identifying or presuming an organic cause in a diagnostic system that purports to avoid causal inferences. Does the use of the hierarchy imply that other diagnoses, such as major depression, have no organic basis? Further, if an organic cause is sufficiently clear, is there any reason to proceed with further descriptive diagnoses? The user of these hierarchies also risks missing clinically important diagnoses. The organic cause of an organic mental disorder may coexist with similar or other processes responsible for additional disorders. A presumed organic cause, prompting consideration only of organic mental disorders, may be wrong. How certain must the clinician be in this presumption in order to eliminate all but the diagnosis of organic mental disorders? Since a more pervasive diagnosis may coexist with

Table 3-2. The five axes

Axis I	Clinical Syndromes and V Codes
Axis II	Developmental Disorders and Personality Disorders
Axis III	Physical Disorders and Conditions
Axis IV	Severity of Psychosocial Stressors
Axis V	Global Assessment of Functioning

Source. DSM-III-R, pp. 15–16.

a less pervasive disorder, why not consider assessment and treatment of both?

Diagnostic hierarchies are another instance in which the clinician should remain flexible when applying DSM-III-R clinically. The advantages of these hierarchies usually outweigh the disadvantages, but not always. As discussed in Chapter 5, a psychiatric diagnostic case formulation may consider a wide range of differential diagnoses prioritized in terms of both likelihood and clinical importance, even though the strict application of DSM-III-R hierarchies might preclude some of these diagnoses.

The Multiaxial System

DSM-III-R continues to apply the multiaxial system introduced in DSM-III, with only minor modifications. Each axis refers to a different category of information. The multiaxial system helps ensure a comprehensive biopsychosocial assessment, including areas that might otherwise be overlooked. Although the official DSM-III-R assessment requires Axes I, II, and III, a complete DSM-III-R assessment uses all five axes (see Table 3-2).

Axis I is for all those DSM-III-R disorders not included in Axis II. Axis I disorders tend to include the disorders that are more acute and time limited.

Axis II is for two main diagnostic categories: developmental disorders, which primarily apply to children, and personality disorders, which primarily apply to adults. The concept behind Axis II is to incorporate long-standing disorders or conditions that have their onset in childhood or adolescence and persist into adulthood in a stable form without periods of remission or exacerbation. Axis II is also reserved for recording prominent personality traits and defense mechanisms, neither of which are considered disorders and neither of which have official codes.

In one sense, the use of Axis II is artificial; Axis II disorders are as much a part of a person's presentation as Axis I disorders or conditions. However, separating Axis II helps ensure that these disorders are not overlooked in diagnosing the more obvious and florid Axis I disorders, and it has also encouraged research into personality disorders. Axis II is a reminder to consider underlying, persistent, and stable aspects of a patient's presentation, whether or not related to the usually acute and primary problem noted on Axis I. Axis II thereby promotes a more comprehensive assessment and understanding of the patient.

All DSM-III-R mental disorders and conditions are included on either Axis I or Axis II. There may be diagnoses on Axis I alone, Axis II alone, or on both Axis I and Axis II. The principal diagnosis, the primary reason for the assessment, is assumed to be the Axis I diagnosis unless the Axis II disorder is followed by the designation "(principal diagnosis)." There may be multiple diagnoses on Axis I or on Axis II. Multiple diagnoses within an axis should be prioritized according to the order of attention or treatment.

Axis III is for current physical disorders or conditions that are potentially relevant to the understanding or management of the case. They may be relevant to elucidating causes of the presentation, or in identifying any issue related to care.

Axis IV is for recording psychosocial stressors and their severity. The general rule is to rate the severity of stressors that have occurred during the year preceding the assessment, although posttraumatic stress disorder is an exception in which stressors from the more remote past may be rated. Stressors may have contributed to the onset, recurrence, or exacerbation of a disorder and may pertain to either Axis I or Axis II disorders. More than one stressor may be evaluated, but the severity rating usually reflects those that are most severe. Stressors should be listed in order of importance. The stressor itself should be noted and characterized as either "predominantly acute events" (less than 6 months) or "predominantly enduring circumstances" (longer than 6 months). Finally, the severity of the stressor should be rated in comparison to an "average" person's response to the stressor under similar circumstances and should exclusively reflect the stressor itself rather than a patient's particular vulnerabilities. The severity rating is based on the Severity of Psychosocial Stressors Scale (see Table 3-3).

Axis V is for recording overall psychological, social, and occupational functioning. Ratings should be made for two time periods: 1) current functioning, and 2) highest level of functioning during the past year. The Axis V rating is based on the Global Assessment of Functioning Scale (see Table 3-4).

Table 3-3. Severity of Psychosocial Stressors Scale

		Adults	
Code	*Term*	*Examples of stressors*	
		Acute events	*Enduring circumstances*
1	None	No acute events that may be relevant to the disorder	No enduring circumstances that may be relevant to the disorder
2	Mild	Broke up with boyfriend or girlfriend; started or graduated from school; child left home	Family arguments; job dissatisfaction; residence in high-crime neighborhood
3	Moderate	Marriage; marital separation; loss of job; retirement; miscarriage	Marital discord; serious financial problems; trouble with boss; being a single parent
4	Severe	Divorce; birth of first child	Unemployment; poverty
5	Extreme	Death of spouse; serious physical illness diagnosed; victim of rape	Serious chronic illness in self or child; ongoing physical or sexual abuse
6	Catastrophic	Death of child; suicide of spouse; devastating natural disaster	Captivity as hostage; concentration camp experience
0	Inadequate information, or no change in condition		

		Children and adolescents	
Code	*Term*	*Examples of stressors*	
		Acute events	*Enduring circumstances*
1	None	No acute events that may be relevant to the disorder	No enduring circumstances that may be relevant to the disorder
2	Mild	Broke up with boyfriend or girlfriend; change of school	Overcrowded living quarters; family arguments
3	Moderate	Expelled from school; birth of sibling	Chronic disabling illness in parent; chronic parental discord
4	Severe	Divorce of parents; unwanted pregnancy; arrest	Harsh or rejecting parents; chronic life-threatening illness in parent; multiple foster home placements
5	Extreme	Sexual or physical abuse; death of a parent	Recurrent sexual or physical abuse
6	Catastrophic	Death of both parents	Chronic life-threatening illness
0	Inadequate information, or no change in condition		

Source.   DSM-III-R, p. 11.

Table 3-4.   Global Assessment of Functioning Scale

Consider psychological, social, and occupational functioning on a hypothetical continuum of mental health-illness. Do not include impairment in functioning due to physical (or environmental) limitations. See p. 20 for instructions on how to use this scale.

Note: Use intermediate codes when appropriate, e.g., 45, 68, 72.

Code

90 | | | | 81	**Absent or minimal symptoms** (e.g., mild anxiety before an exam), **good functioning in all areas, interested and involved in a wide range of activities, socially effective, generally satisfied with life, no more than everyday problems or concerns** (e.g., an occasional argument with family members).
80 | | | 71	**If symptoms are present, they are transient and expectable reactions to psychosocial stressors** (e.g., difficulty concentrating after family argument); **no more than slight impairment in social, occupational, or school functioning** (e.g., temporarily falling behind in school work).
70 | | | 61	**Some mild symptoms** (e.g., depressed mood and mild insomnia) **OR some difficulty in social, occupational, or school functioning** (e.g., occasional truancy, or theft within the household), **but generally functioning pretty well, has some meaningful interpersonal relationships.**
60 | | 51	**Moderate symptoms** (e.g., flat affect and circumstantial speech, occasional panic attacks) **OR moderate difficulty in social, occupational, or school functioning** (e.g., few friends, conflicts with co-workers).
50 | 41	**Serious symptoms** (e.g., suicidal ideation, severe obsessional rituals, frequent shoplifting) **OR any serious impairment in social, occupational, or school functioning** (e.g., no friends, unable to keep a job).
40 | | | | 31	**Some impairment in reality testing or communication** (e.g., speech is at times illogical, obscure, or irrelevant) **OR major impairment in several areas, such as work or school, family relations, judgment, thinking, or mood** (e.g., depressed man avoids friends, neglects family, and is unable to work; child frequently beats up younger children, is defiant at home, and is failing at school).
30 | | | 21	**Behavior is considerably influenced by delusions or hallucinations OR serious impairment in communication or judgment** (e.g., sometimes incoherent, acts grossly inappropriately, suicidal preoccupation) **OR inability to function in almost all areas** (e.g., stays in bed all day; no job, home, or friends).
20 | | 11	**Some danger of hurting self or others** (e.g., suicide attempts without clear expectation of death, frequently violent, manic excitement) **OR occasionally fails to maintain minimal personal hygiene** (e.g., smears feces) **OR gross impairment in communication** (e.g., largely incoherent or mute).
10 | 1	**Persistent danger of severely hurting self or others** (e.g., recurrent violence) **OR persistent inability to maintain minimal personal hygiene OR serious suicidal act with clear expectation of death.**

Source.   DSM-III-R, p. 12.

The text of DSM-III-R provides a more detailed discussion of each axis and examples of how to record a multiaxial evaluation. Although additional areas, such as a systematic review of a patient's functioning within the family, may deserve clinical attention, the multiaxial system reflects a broad biopsychosocial approach to diagnosis.

DSM-III-R Text and Criteria

After the introductory chapters, the main text of DSM-III-R defines criteria for each diagnosis. Several types of diagnostic criteria may be employed for a given diagnosis: content of symptoms, duration of symptoms, severity of symptoms, course of illness, inclusion criteria, and exclusion criteria. In addition to specific criteria, DSM-III-R describes characteristic features of various disorders. Three controversial diagnoses are included in Appendix A, Proposed Diagnostic Categories Needing Further Study.

Finally, DSM-III-R includes several additional appendixes and indexes that the clinician may find helpful: Decision Trees for Differential Diagnosis; Glossary of Technical Terms; Annotated Comparative Listing of DSM-III and DSM-III-R; Historical Review, ICD-9 Glossary and Classification, and ICD-9-CM Classification; DSM-III-R Field Trial Participants; Alphabetic Listing of DSM-III-R Diagnoses and Codes; Numeric Listing of DSM-III-R Diagnoses and Codes; Index of Selected Symptoms Included in the Diagnostic Criteria; and Index of DSM-III-R Diagnoses and Selected Diagnostic Terms.

An Overview of the DSM-III-R Diagnostic Categories

Mastering DSM-III-R begins with an overview of the major diagnostic categories (see Table 3-5).

At first glance these major categories appear to be a laundry list requiring rote memorization, but at least some principles roughly underlie the arrangement of the DSM-III-R diagnoses. These include developmental chronology, decreasing clinical importance or severity, sometimes increasing specificity, and residual categories reflecting clinical uncertainty. Unfortunately, even with these principles in mind, the disturbances in mental functioning and behavior do not fall into a neatly ordered package.

Disorders typically of childhood onset are listed first, reflecting developmental chronology. The remaining disorders are more typical of adults but may also occur in children.

Organic mental disorders are listed next because of their primary clinical importance. They take precedence in the hierarchy of

Table 3-5.   Major categories of DSM-III-R

Axis I
  1. Disorders usually first evident in infancy, childhood, or adolescence
  2. Organic mental syndromes and disorders
  3. Psychoactive substance use disorders
  4. Schizophrenia
  5. Delusional (paranoid) disorder
  6. Psychotic disorders not elsewhere classified
  7. Mood disorders
  8. Anxiety disorders
  9. Somatoform disorders
 10. Dissociative disorders
 11. Sexual disorders
 12. Sleep disorders
 13. Factitious disorders
 14. Impulse control disorders not elsewhere classified
 15. Adjustment disorder
 16. Psychological factors affecting physical condition
 17. V Codes for conditions not attributable to a mental disorder that are a focus of attention or treatment
 18. Additional codes (applies to both Axis I and Axis II)

Axis II
 19. Developmental disorders
 20. Personality disorders

Other
 21. Proposed diagnostic categories needing further study

DSM-III-R, as discussed earlier. The implied organic etiology suggests that these disorders retain the highest priority for clinical attention. Psychoactive substance disorders follow the broad category of organic mental disorders as a more specific but nevertheless organically based set of disorders.

The diagnostic list next moves to disorders primarily identified by psychotic symptoms. These disorders represent the most potentially severe psychiatric disturbances. Schizophrenia, a chronic, possibly severely dysfunctional and widely treated condition, is listed first among the psychotic disorders. It is followed by delusional (paranoid) disorder, a less common and possibly more circumscribed problem. Psychotic disorders not elsewhere classified is the last and residual category for primarily psychotic disorders, reflecting less diagnostic certainty. Note that these disorders, combined with other mental disorders (e.g., mood disorders with psychotic features and certain personality disorders), represent a wide range of possible diagnoses for patients with psychotic symptoms.

The diagnostic list then moves to diagnoses presenting primarily with mood disturbances, followed by anxiety disturbances. This sequence implies a rough hierarchy: psychotic disorders are more clinically significant than mood disturbances, which are more clinically significant than anxiety disturbances. To some extent, this order may reflect earlier diagnostic thinking, in which psychoses were distinguished as more serious disturbances than neuroses. The neuroses, somewhat transformed, are now partly incorporated into several subcategories of mood disorders, anxiety disorders, and other disorders listed later. These conceptual generalizations regarding "diminished" clinical significance should not be applied to the individual case; any of these diagnoses may be quite clinically significant to the individual patient.

Moving from the disorders primarily associated with mental status functions (organic dysfunction, thought disorder as manifested by psychotic symptoms, mood disturbances, and anxiety disorders), the DSM-III-R categories continue with a variety of psychiatric disorders roughly associated with primarily physical symptoms: somatoform disorders, dissociative disorders, sexual disorders, and sleep disorders. These disorders reflect a spectrum from disorders invoking more prominent psychological explanations to those invoking more prominent biological explanations. Factitious disorders follow as a class derived from disorders at the medical-psychological interface but one step further removed: the feigned symptoms of factitious disorder, whether physical or psychological, by definition reflect neither true physical nor true psychological explanations.

Several categories follow that are either less specific, less clinically significant, or less certain. The category impulse control disorders not elsewhere classified impies some specificity ("impulse control disorders") but also reflects a residual nature ("not elsewhere classified"). Adjustment disorders are common and less severe disorders that sometimes function as residual categories. They naturally belong toward the end of the diagnostic list. Psychological factors affecting physical condition is a more specialized category in which physical rather than psychiatric issues are predominant, although the proper significance of this category in DSM-III-R is unclear.

As the least severe of all, V Codes for conditions not attributable to a mental disorder that are a focus of attention or treatment are nearly at the bottom of the Axis I diagnosis list. In fact, these are not even disorders. They are conditions. The additional codes category provides some final coding options, allowing further flexibility for Axis I diagnoses.

The two Axis II diagnoses are examined next: developmental disorders and personality disorders. The first applies to children, the second to adults. Although they may not be completely analogous, they are generally unified in the concept of describing long-standing, persistent, generally stable disorders with onset during childhood or adolescence. The text of DSM-III-R describes developmental disorders in the discussion of disorders usually first evident in infancy, childhood, or adolescence, where they also logically belong. Additional codes are also applicable to Axis II to maximize flexibility.

Finally, the least scientifically supported categories are listed outside the official diagnoses, in Appendix A, entitled Proposed Diagnostic Categories Needing Further Study.

With this broad perspective in mind, the clinician is prepared to understand the place of each category in the overall DSM-III-R scheme. The clinician can then examine each of the major diagnoses and subcategories in more detail.

The DSM-III-R Diagnoses

The DSM-III-R diagnoses and specific diagnostic criteria are the language and foundation for modern descriptive differential diagnoses in psychiatry. Many mental health professionals and several committees of the American Psychiatric Association scrutinized DSM-III-R to ensure accuracy and precision and to achieve a professional consensus. Every word describing a diagnosis or diagnostic criterion has been carefully reviewed. In order to apply DSM-III-R properly, there is no substitute for learning the diagnoses as described in the text of DSM-III-R itself.

The remainder of this chapter is designed as a manual for learning the DSM-III-R diagnoses and may be used as a training guide or for clinical review. It reviews DSM-III-R diagnoses and diagnostic criteria through the use of an overall summary of criteria for each diagnosis, tables, and selected clinical comments or other observations. Reflecting the need for accuracy and precision, definitions of disorders and various tables are necessarily reproduced or closely adapted from DSM-III-R, although sometimes in abbreviated form. DSM-III-R provides the exact criteria and further detailed clinical discussion for each diagnosis. Throughout the remainder of this chapter, therefore, the reader may wish to refer to DSM-III-R itself for more precise and detailed descriptions of diagnoses and their specific criteria.

Disorders Usually First Evident in Infancy, Childhood, or Adolescence

This DSM-III-R heading incorporates a group of disorders held together by one common thread: they are all usually first evident before adulthood. But this thread is tenuous, as evidenced by the wide range of disorders, symptoms, and age groups included under this category.

The difficulty in combining these disorders under one heading reflects two underlying tensions. Classifying disorders based on developmental stages is clinically valuable, but human development is a process lacking clearly demarcated stages. While some disorders seem more clearly associated with one developmental stage, others may occur in more than one stage or in adulthood. Neither age nor other parameters can adequately define the developmental stages, such as childhood or adolescence, for the purpose of this classification. Second, as a descriptive system, DSM-III-R provides no theoretical basis for pinning the onset of a disorder in this category to a specific developmental stage. "Typical age of onset" is somewhat inadequate as the primary clinical phenomenon for grouping these disorders together.

DSM-III-R attempts to reconcile these tensions and introduce flexibility by classifying these disorders based on two key operational terms: the *usual* time at which the disorders are *first evident.* "Usual" implies possible exceptions in which these disorders may first present in adults rather than children. "First evident" implies that these disorders, even though usually first evident before adulthood, may nevertheless require professional attention later, after the patient reaches adulthood.

Although obviously important in working with children, these diagnoses are also important to practitioners who work with adults. Knowledge of early childhood disorders may help the clinician to understand the adult patient's past psychiatric history and the relationship of past history to current problems. Further, several of these disorders, such as the residual phase of attention-deficit hyperactivity disorder and some cases of conduct disorder, may persist into adulthood in some form. Finally, several of these disorders, such as eating disorders or gender identity disorders, may initially come to the attention of the clinician only after the patient is an adult.

Note that practitioners who work primarily with children may

Table 3-6. Disorders usually first evident in infancy, childhood, or adolescence

1. Developmental disorders (recorded on Axis II)
2. Disruptive behavior disorders
3. Anxiety disorders of childhood or adolescence
4. Eating disorders
5. Gender identity disorders
6. Tic disorders
7. Elimination disorders
8. Speech disorders not elsewhere classified
9. Other disorders of infancy, childhood, or adolescence

need to consider DSM-III-R diagnoses not included under this heading. DSM-III-R disorders *not* listed under this heading (i.e., disorders that are usually first evident in adulthood) may occur in children. The clinician must also understand normal childhood development when applying DSM-III-R diagnoses to children. For example, elements of impulsivity and instability in relationships that are characteristic of the adult borderline personality disorder may be normal in an adolescent. Compared with adults, a psychiatric diagnostic assessment of children may require information derived from a variety of additional sources, such as parents, other family members, peers, schools, and formal testing (e.g., IQ or standardized tests of academic skills).

Critics have argued that there is a lack of evidence for the predictive validity and clinical significance of some of the finer subdivisions of the childhood diagnoses. Strictly applied definitions may fail to identify some problems in children. Further, some of these diagnoses may not adequately take into account age-appropriate developmental variation, suggesting that different criteria should perhaps be used for different age groups. Further research may clarify these issues.

There are nine categories of disorders listed under this heading, each of which incorporates additional, more specific disorders (see Table 3-6).

Developmental disorders (recorded on Axis II). Developmental disorders are characterized by a predominant disturbance in the acquisition of cognitive, language, motor, or social skills. They are recorded on Axis II because they tend to be chronic and persist in stable form into adulthood. There are three main subcategories (mental retardation, pervasive developmental disorders, and specific devel-

Table 3-7. Developmental disorders (recorded on Axis II)

1. Mental retardation
   a. Mild
   b. Moderate
   c. Severe
   d. Profound
   e. Unspecified

2. Pervasive developmental disorders
   a. Autistic disorder
   b. Pervasive developmental disorder (NOS)

3. Specific developmental disorders
   a. Academic skills disorders
      1) Developmental arithmetic disorder
      2) Developmental expressive writing disorder
      3) Developmental reading disorder
   b. Language and speech disorders
      1) Developmental articulation disorder
      2) Developmental expressive language disorder
      3) Developmental receptive language disorder
   c. Motor skills disorder
      1) Developmental coordination disorder
   d. Specific developmental disorder NOS

4. Other developmental disorders
   a. Developmental disorders NOS

opmental disorders) and one residual category (other developmental disorders) (see Table 3-7).

Mental retardation requires significantly subaverage general intellectual functioning, defined by an individually administered IQ test score of 70 or below (with a 5-point margin of error), and significant deficits or impairments in adaptive functioning expected for that age and culture, with an onset before the age of 18. The diagnosis is made regardless of coexisting physical or mental disorders. Severity is indicated as follows:

- mild: IQ level of 50–55 to approximately 70 (representing about 85% of the cases).
- moderate: IQ level of 35–40 to 50–55 (representing about 10% of the cases).
- severe: IQ level of 25–35 to 40 (representing about 3% to 4% of the cases).
- profound: IQ level below 20 or 25 (representing about 1% to 2% of the cases).

- unspecified: Formally untestable, but a strong presumption of mental retardation. The V Code "borderline intellectual functioning" is available for intellectual level presumed to be above 70 (usually from 71 to 84).

Pervasive developmental disorders are characterized by qualitative impairments in the development of reciprocal social interaction, communication skills, and imaginative activity. There is one subtype (autistic disorder) and one residual category (pervasive developmental disorder not otherwise specified).

Known by many clinical terms (infantile autism, Kanner's syndrome, atypical development, symbiotic psychosis, childhood psychosis, childhood schizophrenia), the DSM-III-R definition of *autistic disorder* includes a clinical description for different stages of development. See DSM-III-R for the lists of items that may meet the criteria for impaired reciprocal social interaction, communication skills, and imaginative activity. Psychosis is not included so as to distinguish this disorder from other psychotic disorders of adulthood. The diagnosis should specify if childhood onset (after 36 months of age).

Pervasive developmental disorder not otherwise specified (NOS) is the residual category for pervasive developmental disorders.

Specific developmental disorders (recorded on Axis II) may describe inadequate development in one of three areas: academic skills, language and speech skills, and motor skills. These are diagnoses of exclusion: the clinician must first rule out other causes for the specific developmental delay, including physical or neurological disorders, pervasive developmental disorders, mental retardation, and deficient educational opportunities. Mental retardation may coexist with a specific developmental disorder provided the specific area of inadequate skill is significantly below that expected for a child with that level of IQ (even for an IQ within the mental retardation range).

Academic skills disorders are further divided into three subgroups.

The subgroup *developmental arithmetic disorder* requires marked impairment in the development of arithmetic skills as measured by standardized, individually administered tests with results markedly below the expected level given the person's schooling and intellectual capacity. The impairment must significantly interfere with academic achievement or activities that require such skills.

The subgroup *developmental expressive writing disorder* requires marked impairment in the development of expressive writing skills as measured by standardized, individually administered tests with results that demonstrate writing skills markedly below the expected level given the person's schooling and intellectual capacity. The impairment must significantly interfere with academic achievement or activities requiring such skills.

The subgroup *developmental reading disorder* requires reading achievement as measured by standardized individually administered tests to be markedly below the expected level given the person's schooling and individual capacity. The impairment must significantly interfere with academic achievement or activities requiring reading skills.

Language and speech disorders are further divided into three areas.

The subgroup *developmental articulation disorder* requires consistent failure to use developmentally expected speech sounds.

The subgroup *developmental expressive language disorder* requires marked impairment in the development of expressive language attributable neither to another disorder nor to inadequate schooling. The standardized test score for expressive language must be substantially below that obtained from a standardized measure of nonverbal intellectual capacity. The disturbance must significantly interfere with academic achievement or activities requiring such skills.

The subgroup *developmental receptive language disorder* requires marked impairment in the development of language comprehension not explainable by another disorder nor by inadequate schooling. The disturbance must significantly interfere with academic achievement or activities requiring such skills.

Motor skills disorders are divided into one subcategory and one residual category.

The subcategory *developmental coordination disorder* requires marked impairment in the development of motor coordination. The coordination difficulty must significantly impair academic achievement or activities of daily living.

Specific developmental disorder NOS is a residual category for development disturbances of a specific skills area that do not meet the criteria for the other specific developmental disorders.

Developmental disorders NOS is a residual category to describe a developmental disorder that does not meet criteria for mental retardation or any of the developmental disorders.

Disruptive behavior disorders. There are three major subcategories of disruptive behavior disorders: attention-deficit hyperactivity disorder, conduct disorder, and oppositional defiant disorder (see Table 3-8).

Table 3-8. Disruptive behavior disorders

1. Attention-deficit hyperactivity disorder

2. Conduct disorder
   a. Group type
   b. Solitary aggressive type
   c. Undifferentiated type

3. Oppositional defiant disorder

Attention-deficit hyperactivity disorder is characterized by developmentally inappropriate degrees of inattention (including behaviors indicating hyperactivity). At least 8 of 14 items listed in DSM-III-R must be present. These behavioral disturbances must be present for at least 6 months, must be considerably more frequent than those of most people of the same mental age, and must have an onset before the age of 7. This disorder may be characterized as mild, moderate, or severe based on the number of symptoms present and the level of impairment and functioning at home, at school, and with peers.

Conduct disorder is characterized by a persistent pattern of conduct in which the person violates others' basic rights and violates age-appropriate norms or rules. At least 3 out of 13 items listed in DSM-III-R must be present. These behaviors must last at least 6 months. This disorder may be characterized as mild, moderate, or severe depending on the number of items of disturbed behavior and the degree of harm caused by the conduct.

Conduct disorders are subdivided into three types, each of which may be described as mild, moderate, or severe. The **group type** are conduct problems mostly involving group activities with peers. The **solitary aggressive type** are conduct problems mostly involving aggressive physical behavior, usually toward adults and peers, initiated by the child but not as a group activity. The **undifferentiated type** involve a mixture of features that cannot be classified as group type or solitary aggressive type.

Oppositional defiant disorder requires a pattern of oppositional and defiant behavior without meeting criteria for conduct disorder (which involves more serious violations of others' rights and social norms). The disorder requires at least five of nine items listed in DSM-III-R. These behavioral disturbances must have lasted at least 6 months and must be more common than those seen in other people of the same mental age. This disorder may be characterized as mild,

Table 3-9. Anxiety disorders of childhood or adolescence

1. Separation anxiety disorder
2. Avoidant disorder of childhood or adolescence
3. Overanxious disorder

moderate, or severe based on the number of symptoms and degree of functional impairment.

Anxiety disorders of childhood or adolescence. Anxiety is the predominant feature in anxiety disorders of childhood or adolescence. This category is divided into three disorders, the first two involving anxiety focused on a specific situation (separation anxiety disorder and avoidant disorder of childhood or adolescence) and the third involving anxiety generalized to a variety of situations (overanxious disorder) (see Table 3-9).

Separation anxiety disorder requires excessive anxiety, for at least 2 weeks, concerning separation from those to whom the child is attached. This diagnosis requires at least three of nine items listed in DSM-III-R. Onset must be before age 18. The disturbance must not occur only during the course of a pervasive developmental disorder, schizophrenia, or another psychotic disorder.

Avoidant disorder of childhood or adolescence requires excessive avoidance of contact with unfamiliar people, for at least 6 months, severe enough to interfere with social functioning in peer relationships. In addition, there must be a desire for social involvement with familiar people, and generally warm and edifying relationships with family or familiar figures. The child must be aged at least 2½. The child must not meet the more pervasive and persistent behavioral criteria for avoidant personality disorder.

Overanxious disorder requires excessive or unrealistic anxiety or worry for at least 6 months. The diagnosis requires at least four of seven items listed in DSM-III-R. The patient must not meet criteria for generalized anxiety disorder if over age 18, and the disturbance must not occur only during the course of a pervasive developmental disorder, schizophrenia, or another psychotic disorder.

Eating disorders. This category is characterized by gross disturbances in eating behavior. There are four specific eating disorders and one residual category (see Table 3-10).

Anorexia nervosa requires refusal to maintain a minimal normal body weight for age and height, intense fear of gaining weight or becoming fat (even though underweight), a disturbance in how the patient views his or her body (distorted body image), and amen-

Table 3-10.   Eating disorders

1. Anorexia nervosa
2. Bulimia nervosa
3. Pica
4. Rumination disorder of infancy
5. Eating disorder NOS

orrhea in females (three consecutive and expected menstrual cycles do not occur).

Bulimia nervosa requires recurrent episodes of binge eating, a feeling of lack of control over eating behavior during these binges, and the presence of at least one characteristic and regularly practiced behavior (e.g., self-induced vomiting, use of laxatives or diuretics, strict dieting or fasting, vigorous exercise to prevent weight gain). There must be a minimum average of two binge episodes per week for at least 3 months, and persistent overconcern with body shape and weight.

Pica requires at least 1 month of repeated eating of non-nutritive substances, without meeting criteria for autistic disorder, schizophrenia, or Kleine-Levin's syndrome.

Rumination disorder of infancy requires at least 1 month of repeated regurgitation of food, without nausea or associated gastrointestinal illness, following a period of normal functioning. There must be weight loss or failure to achieve an expected weight gain.

Eating disorder NOS is a residual category for eating disorders that do not meet criteria for the other specified eating disorders.

Gender identity disorders.   This category is characterized by an incongruence between biological sex and gender identity. Gender identity is the psychological sense of whether one belongs to the male or female sex, or the awareness of being male or female. Gender identity should be distinguished from gender role, which is what a person says or does to indicate the degree to which that person is male or female. Gender identity disorders, which are rare, should be distinguished from feeling inadequate in fulfilling expectations of a gender role. These disorders were moved from the adult section in DSM-III to the childhood section in DSM-III-R because symptoms usually begin in childhood. However, the patient may first come to professional attention in adult life. There are four subclasses of gender identity disorders (see Table 3-11).

Gender identity disorder of childhood requires persistent and intense distress in a child about the child's assigned sex. The child

Table 3-11.   Gender identity disorders

1. Gender identity disorder of childhood
2. Transsexualism
3. Gender identity disorder of adolescence or adulthood, nontranssexual type
4. Gender identity disorder NOS

either desires or insists that he or she is of the other sex. The child must repudiate his or her sexual organs or engage in other activity (such as aversion to the typical clothing of his or her sex), as described in DSM-III-R. The child must not yet have reached puberty.

Transsexualism requires persistent discomfort and a sense of inappropriateness about the assigned sex after a person has reached puberty. There must be at least 2 years of a persistent preoccupation with getting rid of one's primary and secondary sex characteristics and of acquiring characteristics of the other sex. The clinician should specify whether there is a history of **asexual, homosexual, heterosexual**, or **unspecified** sexual orientation.

Gender identity disorder of adolescence or adulthood, nontranssexual type requires persistent or recurrent discomfort and a sense of inappropriateness about one's assigned sex, coupled with persistent or recurrent cross-dressing in the role of the other sex, in fantasy or actuality. The behavior must not be for sexual excitement (as in transvestic fetishism) and does not include the characteristic preoccupations of transsexualism. This diagnosis may apply only after puberty. The clinician should specify whether there is **asexual, homosexual, heterosexual** or **unspecified** history of sexual orientation.

Gender identity disorder NOS is a residual category for gender identity disorders that do not meet criteria for another specified gender identity disorder.

Tic disorders. A *tic* is defined in DSM-III-R as an "involuntary, sudden, rapid, recurrent, nonrhythmic, stereotyped, motor movement or vocalization" that "is experienced as irresistible, but can be suppressed for varying lengths of time" (p. 78). Tics may be motor or vocal, and simple or complex. For example, eye blinking may be a simple motor tic, grunting may be a simple vocal tic, facial gestures may be a complex motor tic, and repeating words or phrases out of context may be a complex vocal tic. Examples of possible complex vocal tics are coprolalia (use of words that are socially unacceptable, frequently including obscenities), palilalia (repeating sounds or words), and echolalia (repeating last-heard sounds or words).

Table 3-12. Tic disorders

1. Tourette's disorder
2. Chronic motor or vocal tic disorder
3. Transient tic disorder
4. Tic disorder NOS

Tic disorders should be distinguished from other movement disturbances as defined in DSM-III-R. These include the following:

- choreiform movements: dancinglike, random, irregular, non-repetitive movements
- dystonic movements: slower, twisting movements interspersed with prolonged states of muscular tension
- athetoid movements: slow, irregular writhing movements
- myoclonic movements: brief, shocklike muscle contractions affecting parts of muscles or muscle groups, but not synergistically
- hemiballismic movements: intermittent course, large amplitude, unilateral limb movements
- spasms: stereotypic, slower, and more prolonged movements that involve groups of muscles
- hemifacial spasm: irregular, repetitive, unilateral jerks of facial muscles
- synkinesis: movements of the corner of the mouth when closing the eyes, and its converse
- dyskinesia (e.g., tardive dyskinesia): oral-buccal-lingual masticatory movements of the face and choreoathetoid movements of the limbs

In addition, tics do not include movements or behaviors apparently under voluntary control, such as stereotyped movements and compulsions. Tic disorders are subdivided into four disorders (see Table 3-12).

Tourette's disorder requires that both multiple motor and one or more vocal tics be present, although not necessarily concurrently. The tics may occur many times a day, nearly every day, or intermittently throughout a period of more than 1 year. The nature of the tics (anatomical location, number, frequency, complexity, severity) changes over time. Onset must be before age 21. The disturbance must not occur only during psychoactive substance intoxication or as a result of a central nervous system disorder.

Chronic motor or vocal tic disorder requires either motor or vocal

Table 3-13. Elimination disorders

1. Functional encopresis
2. Functional enuresis

tics, but not both, to be present at some time during the illness. This disorder is otherwise similar to Tourette's disorder.

Transient tic disorder is characterized by single or multiple motor and/or vocal tics that occur many times a day, every day for at least 2 weeks, but for no longer than 12 consecutive months. This diagnosis may not be made if there is a history of Tourette's or chronic motor or vocal tic disorder, each of which requires a duration of at least 1 year. Finally, the disturbance must not occur only during psychoactive substance intoxication or as a result of a central nervous system disorder. The clinician should specify **single episode** or **recurrent**.

Tic disorder NOS is a residual category for tic disorders that do not meet criteria for the other specific tic disorders.

Elimination disorders. There are two subclasses of elimination disorders (see Table 3-13).

Functional encopresis is characterized by repeated passage of feces into inappropriate places, whether involuntary or intentional. This diagnosis requires at least one such event a month for at least 6 months, a chronological and mental age of at least 4 years, and no physical disorder causing the fecal incontinence. The clinician should specify **primary type** (no preceding 1-year period of fecal continence) or **secondary type** (a preceding period of fecal continence of at least 1 year).

Functional enuresis is characterized by repeated voiding of urine during the day or night into bed or clothes, whether involuntary or intentional, at an age when control is expected. This diagnosis requires at least two such events per month for children between the ages of 5 and 6, at least one such event a month for older children, a chronological age of at least 5, a mental age of at least 4, and no physical disorder causing the disturbance. The clinician should specify **primary type** (no preceding 1-year period of urinary continence) or **secondary type** (a preceding period of urinary continence of at least 1 year), and whether **nocturnal only**, **diurnal only**, or **nocturnal and diurnal**.

Speech disorders not elsewhere classified. Two disorders are listed under speech disorders not elsewhere classified (see Table 3-14). *Cluttering* requires a disturbance in speech fluency involving

Table 3-14.   Speech disorders not elsewhere classified

1. Cluttering
2. Stuttering

abnormal rate and rhythm that impairs intelligibility. *Stuttering* requires frequent repetitions or prolongations of sounds or syllables, resulting in markedly impaired speech fluency.

Other disorders of infancy, childhood, or adolescence.   Five additional categories are listed under other disorders of infancy, childhood, or adolescence (see Table 3-15).

Elective mutism requires persistent refusal to talk in one or more major social situations, including at school, despite an ability to comprehend spoken language and to speak.

Identity disorder requires severe subjective distress caused by uncertainty about issues related to identity. Such issues must include at least three of the following: long-term goals, career choice, friendship patterns, sexual orientation and behavior, religious identification, moral value systems, and group loyalties. The symptoms must result in impairment of social or occupational functioning with a duration of at least 3 months. Finally, the disturbance must not occur only during a mood disorder or a psychotic disorder, and must not meet the more pervasive and persistent criteria of borderline personality disorder.

Reactive attachment disorder of infancy or early childhood requires markedly disturbed social relatedness in most contexts (failure to initiate or respond to most social interactions, or being socially indiscriminate), beginning before age 5, and not as a symptom of mental retardation or a pervasive developmental disorder. There must also be grossly pathogenic care, as defined by one of three possible items listed in DSM-III-R, which is presumed to be causally related to the disturbance (a presumption supported if poor care preceded the child's disturbance).

Stereotypy/habit disorder requires intentional and repetitive nonfunctional behaviors (e.g., head banging, biting oneself) that

Table 3-15.   Other disorders of infancy, childhood, or adolescence

1. Elective mutism
2. Identity disorder
3. Reactive attachment disorder of infancy or early childhood
4. Stereotypy/habit disorder
5. Undifferentiated attention-deficit disorder

cause physical injury to the child or markedly interfere with normal activity, and that do not meet criteria for a pervasive developmental disorder or a tic disorder.

Undifferentiated attention-deficit disorder is a residual category of marked, persistent, developmentally inappropriate inattention that is not a symptom of another disorder. The validity of this category remains uncertain.

Organic Mental Syndromes and Disorders

Under this heading, DSM-III-R attempts to make a conceptual distinction between syndromes and disorders.

DSM-III-R states that *organic mental syndromes* refer to signs and symptoms without reference to etiology. Therefore, the organic mental syndromes category purports to follow the general rule that DSM-III-R diagnoses are descriptive. A possible point of confusion, not resolved in DSM-III-R, is that the term "organic" appears to qualify the mental syndrome by implying the presence of a physical cause, even though the physical cause is technically not yet presumed or identified. Once a physical cause is presumed or identified, the organic mental syndrome should be reclassified as an organic mental disorder. DSM-III-R does not articulate the degree of certainty required for changing the diagnosis from a syndrome to a disorder.

It is probably clearer to consider the organic mental syndromes as collections of signs and symptoms implying an organic cause *generally*, but without reference to a *specific* organic cause. Note also that the organic mental syndromes are not numerically coded in DSM-III-R. Unlike organic mental disorders, the organic mental syndromes therefore do not qualify as coded, "official" DSM-III-R diagnoses.

Organic mental disorders refer to signs and symptoms (the organic mental syndrome) with the addition that a physical etiology is known or presumed (and would be recorded on Axis III). Whereas most DSM-III-R criteria are purely descriptive, the organic mental disorders require an identified or presumed physical cause. Reflecting a further possible point of confusion, DSM-III-R states that "organic mental disorders" may apply to some situations in which the physical cause is unknown (see the section on organic mental disorders associated with Axis III physical disorders or conditions, or whose etiology is unknown).

It is probably clearer to consider the organic mental disorders as collections of signs and symptoms that, unlike organic mental syndromes, *do* imply a *specific* organic cause. Further, unlike organic mental syndromes, the organic mental disorders *are* numerically coded and may therefore be used as "official" DSM-III-R diagnoses.

Difficulties in classifying organic mental syndromes and disorders may be important theoretically, but they are usually not clinically significant so long as the clinician considers, identifies, and treats organic factors underlying a clinical presentation.

In working with these terms clinically, an organic mental syndrome may be diagnosed based on a description of the patient's signs and symptoms. An organic mental disorder, however, should be diagnosed when two conditions are met: 1) an organic mental syndrome is present, and 2) a specific organic factor or factors may be judged etiologically related to the mental status abnormalities by history, physical exam, or laboratory tests. In some cases, it may be reasonable to infer an organic etiology from the clinical presentation alone if all other mental disorders are ruled out. For example, one can infer an organic factor causing dementia if other mental disorders that may result in a similar presentation, such as major depression, have been ruled out. A wide range of physical disorders or conditions may cause an organic mental disorder, including primary diseases of the brain and systemic illnesses that affect the brain, such as metabolic disturbances, infection, circulatory disturbances, toxic agents, and psychoactive substances, which may have direct effects, residual effects, or effects after discontinuation.

The importance of organic mental disorders is underscored by one application of hierarchies in DSM-III-R, as discussed earlier: an organic mental disorder preempts other diagnoses that have similar presentations. The value of applying this priority is to focus clinical attention on important, correctable causes and to avoid distractions represented by other diagnoses. But the presumed or identified physical cause may coexist with another mental disorder, or may be wrong. In practice, therefore, the clinician should remain flexible and consider other applicable mental disorders in the differential diagnosis, even as the organic mental disorder is being worked up or treated.

Organic mental syndromes. As previously noted, the use of the term "organic" suggests at least some physical basis for these syndromes. In fact, the DSM-III-R criteria require evidence for organic causes of these syndromes. All organic mental syndromes may be the result of either drugs or physical disease, except for intoxication and withdrawal, which are defined as substance related. Distinctions between different types of organic mental syndromes may have

Table 3-16. Organic mental syndromes

1. Delirium
2. Dementia
3. Amnestic syndrome
4. Organic delusional syndrome
5. Organic hallucinosis
6. Organic mood syndrome
7. Organic anxiety syndrome
8. Organic personality syndrome
9. Intoxication
10. Withdrawal
11. Organic mental syndrome NOS

clinical significance with regard to clinical presentation and ultimate identification of the physical cause. Several of the organic mental syndromes are characterized by one predominant abnormal feature of the mental status, provided delirium is excluded.

Ten clinically distinct syndromes and one residual category are described under the heading of organic mental syndromes (see Table 3-16).

The organic mental syndromes may also be conceptually grouped into six categories based on their salient clinical features (see Table 3-17).

As defined in DSM-III-R, *delirium* is an organic mental syndrome primarily characterized by reduced ability to maintain attention to external stimuli and to shift attention appropriately to new external stimuli, with disorganized thinking as manifested by rambling, ir-

Table 3-17. Clinical groupings of organic mental syndromes

Organic mental syndrome	Salient clinical features
1. Delirium and dementia	Relatively global cognitive impairment
2. Amnestic syndrome and organic hallucinosis	Relatively selective cognitive impairment
3. Organic delusional syndrome, organic mood syndrome, and organic anxiety syndrome	Features resemble other psychiatric disorders: schizophrenic disorder, mood disorder, and anxiety disorder
4. Organic personality syndrome	Personality primarily affected
5. Intoxication and withdrawal	Etiologically related to psychoactive substances
6. Organic mental syndrome	Residual category

Source. Adapted from DSM-III-R, p. 100.

relevant, or incoherent speech. The diagnosis of delirium requires at least two of the following symptoms: reduced level of consciousness; sensory misperception; sleep-wake cycle disturbances with insomnia or daytime sleepiness; increased or decreased psychomotor activities; disorientation to time, place, or person; and memory impairment. The clinical features of delirium tend to develop over a short period of time, usually hours to days. The course of symptoms fluctuates over a 24-hour period. Finally, the diagnosis of delirium requires either of the following regarding an organic cause: 1) evidence of a specific organic factor (or factors) etiologically related to the disturbance based on history, physical examination, or laboratory tests, or 2) in the absence of such evidence, the presumption of an etiological organic factor provided the disturbance cannot be accounted for by another nonorganic mental disorder. DSM-III-R discarded the previous vague and imprecise description of delirium as a "clouding of consciousness"; this phrase should no longer be used.

In practice, the term "delirium" is synonymous with other commonly used terms, such as "encephalopathy," "acute organic brain syndrome," and "acute confusional state." Delirium, primarily a syndrome of global cognitive impairment, covers a broad spectrum of clinical presentations. Delirium may be subtle, especially early on when delirium may present with mild irritability or anxiety. Deficits in wakefulness, perception, sleep-wake cycle, level of activity, orientation, memory, or thought processes all may signal delirium. There may be behavioral changes, delusions, or hallucinations, which are often visual but less commonly may be auditory, tactile, or olfactory. In the elderly or in medical settings where many causes of delirium are prevalent, early or subtle forms of delirium are frequently overlooked. When seeing patients in these settings, therefore, the mental health professional should make a special point of screening for delirium.

After making the diagnosis, two tasks are paramount: 1) managing symptoms of delirium, and 2) identifying and treating the underlying cause of the delirium. Managing symptoms may not be sufficient. Identifying and treating the underlying cause, perhaps with medical or neurologic consultation, may save the patient's life.

It may be difficult to distinguish delirium from other nonorganic mental disorders. Delirium tends to be more random, haphazard, fluctuating, and more likely to involve impaired attention and memory. An apparent organic cause may suggest delirium. Finally, laboratory tests may be helpful. For example, an electroencephalogram

(EEG) with generalized slowing of background activity suggests the possibility of delirium.

Delirium may be difficult to distinguish from other organic mental syndromes, such as dementia. In dementia, the person is more likely to be alert, with memory deficit more prominent. Dementia tends to have a more gradual onset and chronic course, although DSM-III-R takes no official position on the nature of dementia's course. Dementia and delirium may also occur together, but the clinician will have difficulty accurately diagnosing the underlying dementia while symptoms of delirium are prominent.

Dementia is an organic mental syndrome primarily characterized by impairment in short- and long-term memory. The memory disturbance must be coupled with at least one of the following: impaired abstract thinking, impaired judgment, disturbances in higher cortical function such as aphasia (language deficits), apraxia (inability to carry out motor activities despite intact comprehension and function), agnosia (failure to recognize or identify objects despite intact sensory function), "constructional difficulty" such as an inability to copy three-dimensional figures or to assemble blocks, and personality change. These disturbances must significantly interfere with work, usual social activities, or relationships with others. Dementia is not diagnosed if these symptoms occur in the course of delirium. As in delirium, dementia requires either of the following regarding an organic cause: 1) evidence of a specific organic factor (or factors) etiologically related to the disturbance based on history, physical examination, or laboratory tests, or 2) in the absence of such evidence, the presumption of an etiological organic factor provided the disturbance cannot be accounted for by another nonorganic mental disorder. Like delirium, dementia may actually be more of a "disorder" than a "syndrome" in requiring evidence for or the presumption of an organic cause. The clinician should specify the severity of dementia as mild, moderate, or severe depending on the degree of impairment in work or social functioning.

DSM-III-R does not imply a particular clinical course or prognosis for dementia. From this perspective, dementia may progress, remain static, or remit. The reversibility of dementia relates to the underlying cause and the availability of treatments that are not part of the descriptive definition for dementia in DSM-III-R.

Dementia must be distinguished from several other clinical presentations. In normal aging, a person does not demonstrate the memory impairment and other features of dementia sufficient to interfere with social or occupational functioning. In delirium, the patient is more likely to demonstrate deficits in alertness rather than memory, and the clinical course will more likely fluctuate, with a more acute onset and shorter course. As previously noted, dementia and delirium may occur together, during which time the underlying dementia may be difficult to assess. Patients suffering from major depression sometimes demonstrate impairment of memory, thinking, concentration, and other intellectual abilities; cognitive impairment should improve as the depression lifts. A treatment trial may be necessary before the diagnosis is clear. More rarely, other mental disorders may be associated with apparent intellectual deterioration.

Clinically, the mental health professional should be familiar with the common causes of dementia. The technical DSM-III-R definition of dementia may be misleading in excluding certain causes that may present a clinical picture similar to dementia; it may be preferable to consider together the differential diagnoses of the underlying causes of either dementia or a dementialike presentation. The two most common causes of dementia or a dementialike presentation receive special, independent treatment in DSM-III-R. The most common underlying process causing dementia is Alzheimer's disease. Even though the actual cause of Alzheimer's disease is unknown, the dementia of Alzheimer's disease is listed under the organic mental disorders as primary degenerative dementia of the Alzheimer's type. The second most common cause of a dementialike presentation is depression, which DSM-III-R does not include as a dementia syndrome. Depression is listed under mood disorders. As previously reviewed when discussing the term "pseudodementia," this listing may reflect a bias toward minimizing the importance of depression-related cognitive deficits. Among other clinically important causes of dementia are vascular disease (multi-infarct dementia), alcohol, normal pressure hydrocephalus, tumors, metabolic disturbances, infection, neuropathic disease, drugs and toxins, and subdural hematomas. The most recently identified cause of dementia is AIDS.

Amnestic syndrome is an organic mental syndrome that requires impairment in short- and long-term memory, does not occur exclusively during the course of delirium, and does not meet criteria for dementia (reflecting impairment in abstract thinking, judgment, higher cortical function, or changes in personality). There must be evidence from history, physical examination, or laboratory tests of a specific organic factor (or factors) thought to be etiologically related to the presentation.

A person with amnestic syndrome may remember events from the remote past in detail, but may not be able to recall more recent events. "Immediate memory" as tested by digit span recall is not impaired. Disorientation may precede the amnesia. The patient may exhibit confabulation. These patients may be apathetic and emotionally bland.

Organic delusional syndrome is an organic mental syndrome that requires prominent delusions, evidence from the history, physical examination, or laboratory tests of a specific organic factor (or factors) thought to be etiologically related to the disturbance, and that does not occur exclusively during the course of delirium.

Clinically, the nature of the delusions of organic delusional syndrome may vary; they may be highly organized and paranoid, or unstructured and chaotic. The many possible causes of organic delusional syndrome include drugs (e.g., amphetamines, cannabis, or hallucinogens). The syndrome may be an interictal phenomenon in some patients with temporal lobe epilepsy, may appear in certain patients with Huntington's chorea, and may be caused by brain lesions, especially of the right hemisphere. An organic delusional syndrome should be considered when delusions occur in a likely setting for organic causes of delusions, as in a patient who uses drugs, or if a paranoid delusional state occurs in a person with no previous psychiatric history, particularly if the person is over 35 years old. When prominent hallucinations coexist with the delusions, the clinician should consider the dual diagnosis of organic delusional syndrome and organic hallucinosis.

Organic hallucinosis is an organic mental syndrome that requires prominent persistent or recurrent hallucinations, evidence from the history, physical examination, or laboratory tests of a specific organic factor (or factors) thought to be etiologically related to the disturbance, and that does not occur exclusively in the course of delirium.

Clinically, hallucinations in organic hallucinosis may vary; they may be simple and uniform, or highly complex and organized. They tend to be visual or auditory, but may occur in any modality depending partly on the cause. The patient may either understand that the hallucinations are not real, or may have a delusional belief that they are real. Prominent delusional thinking would suggest the additional diagnosis of organic delusional syndrome.

Organic mood syndrome is an organic mental syndrome that requires 1) prominent and persistent depressed, elevated, or expansive mood; 2) evidence from the history, physical examination, or laboratory tests of a specific organic factor (or factors) thought to be etiologically related to the disturbance; and 3) evidence that it does not occur exclusively in the course of delirium. Organic mood syndrome may be specified as manic, depressed, or mixed. Severity may range from mild to severe, possibly including delusions or hallucinations.

This syndrome may be similar to a manic or a major depressive episode, except for the evidence of an organic cause. Common causes are toxins and metabolic abnormalities. Examples of some causes are substances (e.g., reserpine, methyldopa, and some hallucinogens may produce depressive syndromes), endocrine disorders (e.g., hyper- or hypothyroidism and adrenocortical abnormalities may cause manic or depressive syndromes), cancer (e.g., carcinoma of the pancreas may be associated with depression), infection (e.g., viral infection may be associated with depression), and structural diseases of the brain, such as hemispheric strokes.

Organic anxiety syndrome is an organic mental syndrome that requires 1) prominent, recurrent panic attack or generalized anxiety; 2) evidence from the history, physical examination, or laboratory tests of a specific organic factor (or factors) thought to be etiologically related to the disturbance; and 3) evidence that it does not occur exclusively during the course of delirium.

DSM-III-R added this category, which was not included in the preceding manual.

This syndrome may be similar to panic disorder or generalized anxiety disorder, except for the evidence of an organic cause. Anxiety is a common symptom associated with many conditions, but in this syndrome the anxiety must be prominent. Common causes include endocrine disorders (e.g., hyper- or hypothyroidism, pheochromocytoma, fasting hypoglycemia, or hypercortisolism), intoxication from stimulants (e.g., caffeine, cocaine, or amphetamines), or withdrawal from depressant substances (e.g., alcohol or sedatives). Less common causes include brain tumors, seizures, pulmonary embolus, chronic obstructive pulmonary disease, aspirin intolerance, collagen-vascular disease, brucellosis, vitamin B_{12} deficiency, demyelinating disease, and heavy metal intoxication.

Organic personality syndrome is an organic mental syndrome that requires 1) a persistent personality disturbance, either life-long or representing a change or accentuation of a previously characteristic trait; 2) evidence from the history, physical examination, or laboratory tests of a specific organic factor (or factors) thought to be etiologically related to the disturbance; and 3) evidence that it does not occur exclusively during the course of delirium, and that it does not meet criteria for dementia. The personality disturbance must include at least one of the following five features: 1) affective instability, 2) recurrent outbursts of aggression or rage out of proportion to the stressor, 3) markedly impaired social judgment, 4) marked apathy and indifference, and 5) suspiciousness or paranoid ideation. The clinician should specify "explosive type" if outbursts of aggression or rage are a dominant feature.

Patterns of personality disturbances may vary, possibly related to the underlying cause. For example, "frontal lobe syndrome" refers to marked apathy and indifference sometimes associated with frontal lobe damage, whereas temporal lobe epilepsy may be associated with religiosity, written and oral verbosity, and exaggerated aggressiveness. Organic personality syndrome may precede intellectual deterioration, eventually resulting in dementia.

Possible causes of organic personality syndrome include structural brain damage (e.g., neoplasms, head trauma, cerebrovascular disease), temporal lobe epilepsy, neuropathic disease (e.g., multiple sclerosis, Huntington's chorea), endocrine disorders, and psychoactive substances.

Intoxication is an organic mental syndrome that requires 1) the development of a substance-specific syndrome caused by the recent ingestion of a psychoactive substance; 2) maladaptive behavior during the waking state caused by the substance's effect on the central nervous system (e.g., belligerence, impaired judgment, or impaired social or occupational functioning); and 3) evidence that it does not meet criteria for any other specific organic mental syndrome.

DSM-III-R applies the term "intoxication" more narrowly than the physiological application. Recreational or social use of psychoactive substances may cause physiologic change but is not considered intoxication without the addition of maladaptive behavior. For example, social drinking by itself is not intoxication according to DSM-III-R.

The precise presentation of intoxication will vary depending on the substance ingested. Different substances may produce a similar presentation. The clinician should be careful to rule out other medical disorders that can produce symptoms resembling substance-induced intoxication.

This is a residual category. A more specific diagnosis will preempt the designation "intoxication syndrome." For example, a mild intoxication syndrome caused by a known agent would include the name of that agent, e.g., "amphetamine intoxication." If a particular disturbance is predominant, a more specific organic mental disorder may apply, such as "amphetamine delusional disorder" if delusions are predominant during an amphetamine intoxication. Other mental syndromes that may be substance induced, such as delirium, organic hallucinosis, organic delusional syndrome, organic mood syndrome, or organic anxiety syndrome, would preempt the residual diagnosis of intoxication.

Withdrawal is an organic mental syndrome that requires the development of a substance-specific syndrome following cessation or reduction in use of a psychoactive substance that the person previously used regularly, and that does not meet criteria for any other specific organic mental syndrome (such as delirium, organic delusional syndrome, organic hallucinosis, organic mood syndrome, or organic anxiety syndrome).

As in intoxication, the presentation of withdrawal will vary depending on the substance involved. The clinician should rule out other possible medical explanations for the presentation.

The clinician should specify withdrawal for the substance involved. Such a diagnosis may be superimposed on any organic mental syndrome except delirium. For example, mild withdrawal from alcohol would be termed "uncomplicated alcohol withdrawal" even in the presence of most other organic mental syndromes, whereas delirium following alcohol withdrawal is called "alcohol withdrawal delirium." Clinically, it may be difficult to distinguish between an organic mental syndrome caused by a substance, and withdrawal superimposed on an independently caused organic mental syndrome.

Organic mental syndrome NOS is a residual category for organic mental syndromes that do not meet criteria for the other specific organic mental syndromes. It still requires maladaptive change during the waking state and evidence from the history, physical examination, or laboratory tests of a specific organic factor (or factors) thought to be etiologically related to the disturbance.

Organic mental disorders. As defined in DSM-III-R, organic mental disorders refer to the signs and symptoms present in the organic mental syndromes, with the additional requirement of an identified or presumed physical cause, recorded on Axis III. Two exceptions are embodied in this category. First, unlike most DSM-III-R disorders, these disorders are not purely descriptive. Second, having established a requirement for causal inferences in these disorders, DSM-III-R creates a further exception: disorders in this category may be diagnosed when the cause is unknown.

Table 3-18. Organic mental disorders: three subgroups

Organic mental disorder	Conceptual basis
1. Dementias arising in the senium and presenium	Emphasis on age
2. Psychoactive substance-induced organic mental disorders	Emphasis on drugs
3. Organic mental disorders associated with Axis III physical disorders or conditions, or whose etiology is unknown	Emphasis on physical illness

A more detailed review of these disorders may help clarify their proper clinical application. In general terms, these disorders may be thought of as more specific and refined descriptions of organic mental syndromes, in which clinical presentations are more clearly defined and related to specific physical causes.

The organic mental disorders are grouped into three categories according to whether the emphasis of the disorder is on age, drugs, or physical illness (see Table 3-18).

Dementias arising in the senium and presenium. This may be thought of as a more specific diagnosis of the previously described organic mental syndrome of dementia. In these disorders, the underlying physical cause is more clearly established.

The new terms "senium" and "presenium" replace the terms "senile" and "presenile," but their exact purpose in DSM-III-R is unclear. The age of 65 is the traditional, albeit somewhat arbitrary, age chosen to distinguish senile onset from presenile onset disorders. As will be discussed below, in primary degenerative dementia of the Alzheimer's type, DSM-III-R makes a distinction between senile onset and presenile onset, but without clear clinical importance. While multi-infarct dementia usually occurs in the elderly, DSM-III-R makes no particular distinction based on age of onset. There are also two residual categories, one for senile onset and one for presenile onset, but the clinical significance of this distinction is again unclear. In fact, these residual categories taken together cover dementias that may occur at any age, including in young adults, and thereby appear to disregard the grouping of these disorders based on age.

Two specific categories and two residual categories are listed under this heading (see Table 3-19).

Primary degenerative dementia of the Alzheimer type is an organic mental disorder that requires the presence of dementia (see discussion under organic mental syndromes) of insidious onset with

Table 3-19. Dementias arising in the senium and presenium

1. Primary degenerative dementia of the Alzheimer type
   a. Senile onset
   b. Presenile onset
2. Multi-infarct dementia
3. Senile dementia
   (specify etiology on Axis III, if known)
4. Presenile dementia
   (specify etiology on Axis III, if known)

a generally progressive deteriorating course, and the exclusion of all other specific causes of dementia by history, physical examination, and laboratory tests. In deference to tradition, the disorder is further divided into two groups based, somewhat arbitrarily, on age at onset: 1) **senile onset**—onset after age 65, and 2) **presenile onset**—onset at or before age 65.

The disorder may be further coded to indicate the presence of other symptoms as follows: **with delirium, with delusions, with depression**, or **uncomplicated**. Alzheimer's disease should be coded on Axis III.

The development of this diagnosis reflects a growing consensus that the histology and pathology of Alzheimer's disease (i.e., senile plaques, neurofibrillary tangles, granulovacuolar degeneration of neurons, and frequently an atrophied brain with widened cortical sulci and enlarged cerebral ventricles) is highly correlated with the development of dementia. Based on this consensus, the less specific term "primary degenerative dementia," available in DSM-III, is not used in DSM-III-R. Alzheimer's disease itself, however, is considered not a mental disorder, but rather a physical disorder to be recorded on Axis III. The term "primary degenerative dementia of the Alzheimer type" refers only to the clinical presentation of the dementia, not specifically to the underlying Alzheimer's disease.

The presentation of this disorder is consistent with the organic mental syndrome of dementia described previously, and usually involves deficits in intellectual abilities such as memory, judgment, abstract thought, and other higher cortical functions, and changes in personality and behavior. Clinically, this disorder should be distinguished from normal changes in the process of aging. Dementia requires clear evidence of progressive and significant deterioration of intellectual and social or occupational functioning. Finally, this is a diagnosis of exclusion. The diagnosis of primary degenerative dementia of the Alzheimer type requires first ruling out other causes of dementia.

Multi-infarct dementia is an organic mental disorder that requires the presence of dementia (see discussion under organic mental syndromes); a stepwise deteriorating course affecting some but not other functions ("patchy" distribution of deficits) early in the course; focal neurological signs and symptoms; and evidence from history, physical examination, or laboratory tests of significant cerebrovascular disease thought to be etiologically related to the disturbance. The disorder may be further coded to indicate the presence of other symptoms as follows: **with delirium, with delusions, with depression**, or **uncomplicated**. The cerebrovascular disease should be coded on Axis III.

In short, as its name implies, multi-infarct dementia is dementia caused by significant cerebrovascular disease. Clinically, the course and presentation are explained by the underlying disease process: cerebrovascular events may be abrupt, focal, and multiple, thus explaining the abrupt onset, stepwise and fluctuating course, and patchy deficits related to the area damaged in the brain. A single cerebrovascular event usually results in focal deficits but is not sufficient to cause dementia. Multiple strokes at different times, however, would probably be sufficient to cause dementia. This disorder is listed under the heading "dementias arising in the senium and presenium" to indicate its association with the elderly, but there is no particular diagnostic significance to whether the onset is before or after age 65.

Multi-infarct dementia is clinically distinguishable from primary degenerative dementia of the Alzheimer type, which usually presents with a more uniform progressive course and no evidence of cerebrovascular disease. Occasionally, both disorders may be present.

Senile dementia NOS and presenile dementia NOS are residual categories for organic mental disorders that involve the presence of dementia, are associated with an organic factor, and cannot be classified as another specific dementia. Senile dementia NOS would apply if onset is after age 65; presenile dementia NOS would apply if onset is before age 65. The underlying cause, if known, should be specified on Axis III.

As already noted, the clinical significance of the distinction between senile and presenile dementia in these residual categories is unclear. Further, these residual categories, taken together, appear to cover all age groups; they are not necessarily based on the concept of emphasizing age. Nevertheless, these residual categories may be used to describe dementia caused by potentially serious and treatable physical disorders. Possible causes include brain tumor, Huntington's chorea, vitamin B_{12} deficiency, Pick's disease, and Jakob-Creutzfeldt's disease. Technically, especially when age is not clinically significant, such cases may more properly be classified under another heading (discussed below), "organic mental disorders (i.e., dementia) associated with Axis III physical disorders or conditions, or whose etiology is unknown."

   Psychoactive substance-induced organic mental disorders. DSM-III-R makes a distinction between two categories of disorders involving psychoactive substances. *Psychoactive substance-induced organic mental disorders* are various organic mental syndromes caused by the direct effects of psychoactive substances on the nervous system (described in this section). *Psychoactive substance use disorders* are symptoms and maladaptive behavior associated with more or less regular use of psychoactive substances that affect the central nervous system, principally involving dependence or abuse (described in the next major DSM-III-R heading).

   Eleven classes of substances and one residual category are listed under this heading, each associated with a variety of possible specific organic mental disorders (see Table 3-20).

   DSM-III-R provides detailed descriptions for each of the organic mental syndromes caused by these psychoactive substances (pp. 123–163). The diagnosis should incorporate the name of the specific substance, if known. Clinical features suggest that these substances may be considered in three groups: 1) alcohol and sedatives, anxiolytics, or hypnotics; 2) cocaine and amphetamines or similarly acting sympathomimetics; and 3) hallucinogens and phencyclidine (PCP) or similarly acting arylcyclohexylamines. DSM-III-R introduced several additional possible syndromes related to substances listed in this section of DSM-III-R, including cocaine withdrawal, amphetamine withdrawal, PCP mood disorder, inhalant intoxication, posthallucinogen perception disorder (for recurrent "flashbacks" following use of hallucinogens), and others.

   These disorders may be difficult to diagnose. Patients with these disorders seem often to use denial, provide unreliable history, withhold information, and alienate clinicians. Laboratory testing may be helpful, but it must be properly interpreted in the clinical context. For example, a negative urine or blood drug screen does not preclude a substance-induced disorder; there may be false negatives or the substance may have cleared. A positive test does not necessarily prove a substance-induced disorder; there may be false positive re-

Table 3-20. Psychoactive substance-induced organic mental disorders*

Substance	Possible syndromes
Alcohol	Intoxication
	Idiosyncratic intoxication
	Uncomplicated alcohol withdrawal
	Withdrawal delirium
	Hallucinosis
	Amnestic disorder
	Dementia associated with alcoholism
Amphetamine or similarly acting sympathomimetic	Intoxication
	Withdrawal
	Delirium
	Delusional disorder
Caffeine	Intoxication
Cannabis	Intoxication
	Delusional disorder
Cocaine	Intoxication
	Withdrawal
	Delirium
	Delusional disorder
Hallucinogens	Hallucinosis
	Delusional disorder
	Mood disorder
	Posthallucinogen perception disorder
Inhalant	Intoxication
Nicotine	Withdrawal
Opioid	Intoxication
	Withdrawal
PCP or similarly acting arylcyclohexylamine	Intoxication
	Delirium
	Delusional disorder
	Mood disorder
	Organic mental disorder NOS
Sedative, hypnotic, or anxiolytic	Intoxication
	Uncomplicated withdrawal
	Withdrawal delirium
	Amnestic disorder
Other or unspecified psychoactive substance-induced organic mental disorders	Intoxication
	Withdrawal
	Delirium
	Dementia
	Amnestic disorder
	Delusional disorder
	Hallucinosis
	Mood disorder
	Anxiety disorder
	Personality disorder
	Organic mental disorder NOS

*An alternate tabular description may be found in DSM-III-R, p. 124.

Table 3-21.   Organic mental disorders associated with Axis III physical disorders or conditions, or whose etiology is unknown

1. Delirium
2. Dementia
3. Amnestic disorder
4. Organic delusional disorder
5. Organic hallucinosis
6. Organic mood disorder (specify manic, depressed, or mixed)
7. Organic anxiety disorder
8. Organic personality disorder (specify if explosive type)
9. Organic mental disorder NOS

sults, or other more accurate DSM-III-R diagnoses in a patient who also uses substances. Finally, the clinician should consider substance-induced disorders in many situations in which a psychoactive substance may mimic another mental disorder.

Organic mental disorders associated with Axis III physical disorders or conditions, or whose etiology is unknown.   This category is for organic mental disorders (recorded on Axis I) associated with a physical disorder (recorded on Axis III). DSM-III-R provides two examples: delirium associated with pneumonia, and dementia associated with a brain tumor. Each of these organic mental disorders corresponds to an organic mental syndrome described earlier, except that intoxication and withdrawal are excluded because they are defined as substance related. There are eight such disorders and one residual category (see Table 3-21).

Psychoactive Substance Use Disorders

Psychoactive substance use disorders involve substance dependence or substance abuse (more technically described as symptoms and maladaptive behavior associated with more or less regular use of these substances). These disorders require the continued use of the substance despite persistent or recurrent social, occupational, psychological, or physical problems, and the person's knowledge that continued substance use may worsen these functions. The clinician should record the name of the specific substance, if known, rather than the general class of the substance. With multiple substance use, multiple diagnoses of psychoactive substance use disorders may apply. The clinician must also consider the cultural context in diagnosing dependence or abuse. For example, use of alcohol (within limits) and caffeine is culturally sanctioned and may not constitute a disorder.

As previously noted, DSM-III-R makes a distinction between these disorders and psychoactive substance-induced organic mental disorders, which involve specific organic mental syndromes directly caused by these substances. Most patients with a psychoactive substance use disorder will also have a psychoactive substance-induced mental disorder.

DSM-III-R uses a single description of dependence and a single definition of abuse, regardless of the substance involved.

Psychoactive substance dependence. DSM-III-R defines dependence as requiring at least three of nine cognitive, behavioral, and physiological symptoms indicating that the person has impaired control over the use of a psychoactive substance and continues to use the substance despite adverse consequences. These symptoms are detailed in DSM-III-R. Certain symptoms may be less significant or may not apply to certain substances. Some symptoms are required to have persisted for at least 1 month, or to have occurred repeatedly over a long period of time. Severity may be designated as mild, moderate, severe, in partial remission, or in full remission.

The list of possible symptoms includes marked tolerance (a "need for markedly increased amounts of the substance . . . in order to achieve intoxication or desired effect, or markedly diminished effect with continued use of the same amount") and characteristic withdrawal syndromes (described in DSM-III-R under specific psychoactive substance-induced organic mental syndromes). But in DSM-III-R, dependence may or may not involve physiological tolerance and/or withdrawal. Some patients have tolerance and withdrawal but do not have dependence (e.g., medical patients using prescribed narcotics). Other patients have dependence despite not having tolerance or withdrawal (e.g., persons with impaired control of cannabis use without tolerance or withdrawal). There is no listing for caffeine dependence. Caffeine abuse usually does not meet the criteria for dependence, despite possible physiological tolerance and withdrawal; coffee drinkers can usually switch to decaffeinated coffee or coffee substitutes. Finally, withdrawal symptoms may not apply to cannabis, hallucinogens, or PCP.

When several substances are involved, the clinician may consider "polysubstance dependence." This diagnosis requires repeated use of at least three categories of psychoactive substances (excluding nicotine and caffeine) for at least 6 months, with no single substance predominating. Further, dependence criteria must be met for the psychoactive substances as a group, but not met for any specific substance. If dependence criteria are met for several individual substances, there may be multiple diagnoses of dependence for each substance rather than polysubstance dependence.

Psychoactive substance abuse.   In DSM-III-R, this is a residual category. It applies when the criteria for dependence are not met but there remains a pattern of maladaptive substance use requiring at least one of the following: 1) continued substance use despite knowledge of having persistent or recurrent social, occupational, psychological, or physical problems caused or exacerbated by use of the substance, or 2) recurrent use in situations in which use is physically hazardous. Some symptoms must have persisted for at least 1 month or have occurred repeatedly over a long period of time. The person must never have met the criteria for psychoactive substance dependence for this substance.

Clinically, this diagnosis will more likely apply to persons who recently began to use such substances, and to involve substances less likely to cause physiological withdrawal, such as cannabis, cocaine, and hallucinogens.

Classes of psychoactive substances.   DSM-III-R provides a specific discussion of dependence and abuse for each class of substances, which will not be reviewed here. Nine classes of psychoactive substances and residual categories are associated with dependence and abuse; one class of psychoactive substances (nicotine) and one additional category (polysubstance dependence) are associated with dependence but not with abuse (see Table 3-22).

Schizophrenia

Historically, descriptions of schizophrenia have varied, emphasizing either clinical course or presenting symptoms. Kraepelin defined a population of patients with the term "dementia praecox" based on severe functional disturbances and a deteriorating clinical course. Bleuler introduced the term "schizophrenia" (meaning "splitting of the mind") to describe a syndrome characterized by disturbances in certain psychological processes, known as the "four A's" of schizophrenia: autism (turning inward, away from the external world), ambivalence, and disturbances in affect and associations (i.e., loosening of associations). Schneider emphasized possible pathognomonic features called "first-rank" symptoms (including hallucinations and delusions). DSM-III-R attempts to synthesize these approaches, combining the focus on symptoms with the focus on clinical course and increasing the reliability for this diagnosis.

In DSM-III-R, schizophrenia requires characteristic psychotic

Table 3-22. Psychoactive substance use disorders

Dependence or abuse
 1. Alcohol
 2. Amphetamines or similarly acting sympathomimetics
 3. Cannabis
 4. Cocaine
 5. Hallucinogens
 6. Inhalants
 7. Opioids
 8. PCP or similarly acting arylcyclohexylamines
 9. Sedatives, hypnotics, or anxiolytics

Residual categories
 10. Psychoactive substance dependence NOS
 11. Psychoactive substance abuse NOS

Dependence only
 1. Nicotine
 2. Polysubstance dependence

symptoms during the active phase of the disorder for at least 1 week (unless the symptoms are treated). This criterion is met if the patient has 1) two of five possible characteristic symptoms that include delusions, prominent hallucinations, incoherence or marked loosening of associations, catatonic behavior, and flat or grossly inappropriate affect, 2) bizarre delusions, or 3) prominent hallucinations of a particular type (i.e., of a voice unrelated to mood content, or providing a running commentary on the patient's thought or conduct, or voices conversing).[1] The diagnosis requires functioning markedly below the highest level achieved before the onset of the disturbance in such areas as work, social relations, and self-care. There must be continuous signs of the disturbance for at least 6 months, which must include an active phase, with or without prodromal or residual phases. Finally, the diagnosis should not be made if the symptoms are due to a mood disorder or schizoaffective disorder, or if it can be established that an organic factor initiated or maintains the disturbance. Course may be coded as **subchronic** (between 6 months and 2 years), **chronic** (more than 2 years), **subchronic with acute exacerbation, chronic with acute exacerbation, in remission**, or **unspecified**. If the disturbance develops after age 45, the clinician should specify **late onset**.

As suggested in the foregoing criteria, there are three possible phases for schizophrenia.

The *active phase* is a period in the course of schizophrenia of prominent characteristic psychotic symptoms, such as delusions, hallucinations, incoherence or marked loosening of associations, catatonic behavior, flat or grossly inappropriate affect (or "bizarre delusions," or "prominent hallucinations" as previously described). DSM-III-R does not describe the active phase any further. A psychosocial stressor may be associated with the onset of the active phase.

The *prodromal phase* is a clear deterioration in functioning before the active phase, not due to mood disturbance or psychoactive substance use disorder, and involving at least two of nine possible symptoms: 1) marked social isolation or withdrawal; 2) marked impairment in role functioning as a wage earner, student, or homemaker; 3) markedly peculiar behavior; 4) marked impairment in personal hygiene and grooming; 5) blunted or inappropriate affect; 6) digressive, vague, overelaborate, or circumstantial speech, or poverty of speech or speech content; 7) odd beliefs or magical thinking that influences behavior and is inconsistent with cultural norms; 8) unusual perceptual experiences; and 9) marked lack of initiative, interests, or energy.

This list includes negative symptoms as well as less prominent positive symptoms (described in following paragraphs), but these symptoms are generally less clinically significant or less florid than the characteristic psychotic symptoms of the active phase. A prodromal phase frequently precedes the active phase of illness.

The *residual phase* is the persistence of at least two of the nine prodromal-phase symptoms following the active phase, not due to mood disorder or psychoactive substance use disorder. Patients with schizophrenia usually develop a residual phase, during which blunt or flat affect and impaired functioning is common. Most patients do not return to their previous level of functioning.

The most common presentation of schizophrenia appears to include a prodromal phase followed by a pattern of acute exacerbations with residual impairment between episodes. Note that the prodromal and residual phases are mainly used to determine whether the 6-month duration criterion is met; there is no separate code for prodromal or residual phase (except for residual type, described below).

Clinicians sometimes classify symptoms into two types, although this distinction is not explicitly used in DSM-III-R diagnoses. **Positive symptoms** are certain characteristic symptoms of schizophrenia typically present during the active phase, such as delusions, hallucinations, incoherence or loosening of associations, and catatonic behavior. **Negative symptoms** are symptoms other than the characteristic psychotic symptoms noted above, such as social withdrawal and lack of initiative.

These distinctions are not always clear-cut. For example, the symptom of "flat or grossly inappropriate affect" may be considered a positive symptom characteristic of the active phase of schizophrenia, or a negative symptom characteristic of the residual phase, depending on the clinical context and application of definitions for these phases and types of symptoms. Further, there is not necessarily an exact correlation between the concept of positive and negative symptoms and the concept of active and prodromal or residual phases of schizophrenia as described in DSM-III-R.

As described in DSM-III-R, schizophrenia usually involves disturbances in several areas of mental functioning, although no single symptom establishes the diagnosis.

Content of thought may involve delusions that are multiple, fragmented, or bizarre, such as persecutory delusions, delusions of reference, thought broadcasting, thought insertion, thought withdrawal, and delusions of being controlled by external forces. Other less common delusions include somatic, grandiose, religious, and nihilistic delusions.

Form of thought ("formal thought disorder") may involve loosening of associations, poverty of speech content, or (less common) neologisms, perseveration, clanging, and blocking.

Perception may involve auditory hallucinations and (less common) hallucinations of any of the other senses. Nonauditory hallucinations are more typically associated with a physical disorder (with the Axis I diagnosis of an organic mental disorder), although auditory hallucinations may be associated with physical disorders as well. Other less common perceptual disturbances include sensations of bodily change, hypersensitivity to perceptual stimuli, illusions, and synesthesias.

Affect may be flat or inappropriate.

Sense of self may involve concern about the patient's identity and purpose for living.

Volition may involve impairment in initiative, goal-directed activity, and work activities.

Interpersonal functioning and relationship to the external world may involve social withdrawal and emotional detachment.

Psychomotor behavior may involve decreased reactivity to the environment; reduced spontaneous movements and activity; unawareness of the environment (catatonic stupor); rigid postures resistant to efforts to effect movement (catatonic rigidity); purposeless, stereotyped, and excited motor movements unrelated to external stimuli (catatonic excitement); voluntary assumption of inappropriate or bizarre postures (catatonic posturing); or resistance to and active counteracting of instructions or attempts to be moved (catatonic negativism). Some patients exhibit odd mannerisms, grimacing, or waxy flexibility.

Other abnormalities may involve disheveled appearance, abnormal psychomotor activity, other speech abnormalities, behavioral abnormalities, dysphoric mood, and disturbances in perception and thought.

Note that formal cognitive function (or higher integrative function) should be intact in schizophrenia, except for impairment related to the exacerbation of a characteristic symptom. Deficits in these areas may require evaluation for an organic mental syndrome or disorder caused by an underlying physical disorder.

Clinically, the diagnostic criteria for schizophrenia are notable in several additional respects.

Schizophrenia requires both characteristic symptoms and impaired functioning; neither alone is sufficient. Certain psychotic symptoms, such as an encapsulated delusion, may not be enough to meet these criteria. Further, the requirement for diminished functioning typically involves impairment in more than one area.

A minimal duration of illness is required; a shorter duration suggests a different diagnosis (schizophreniform disorder, for example). The required course for symptoms of schizophrenia must be over a continuous 6-month period.

Schizophrenia is not limited to illnesses with a deteriorating course. Recovery is considered possible under the DSM-III-R definition.

Schizophrenia does not apply if there is no period of overt psychotic features, even though there may be some prodromal-like symptoms. DSM-III-R does not use terms such as "latent," "borderline," or "simple" schizophrenia. Certain personality traits or disorders may apply to such cases. Further, a personality disorder or trait may precede the development of schizophrenia. In such cases, personality disorders or traits may be noted on Axis II, followed by the term ("premorbid").

Schizophrenia need not begin before a specific age. Onset is usually during adolescence or early adulthood, so the clinician may need to consider whether early symptoms of schizophrenia underlie the presentation of patients in this age group. But schizophrenia

Table 3-23.   Types of schizophrenia

1. Catatonic
2. Disorganized
3. Paranoid (specify if stable type)
4. Undifferentiated
5. Residual

Note.   In any of the above types, specify if late onset.

may develop later as well. Some research suggests a later age of onset in females. The significance of the late onset group requires further study.

When assessing or treating patients for schizophrenia, it may be useful to consider several additional clinical points. The disorder seems to be equally prevalent in men and women and across different cultures. There is probably a genetic component, so family history may be important. Finally, as noted in DSM-III-R, several factors may predict a better prognosis, such as adequate premorbid social functioning, a precipitating event, abrupt onset, onset in midlife, a clinical picture involving mental confusion, a family history of mood disorder, and the absence of premorbid personality disturbance.

Types.   There are five schizophrenia types, based on the predominant clinical presentation that resulted in the most recent evaluation or admission (see Table 3-23).

Catatonic type is dominated by marked psychomotor disturbance involving catatonic stupor, catatonic negativism, catatonic rigidity, catatonic excitement, or catatonic posturing. Extremes of psychomotor activity may alternate. Associated presentations may include stereotypies, mannerisms, waxy flexibility, and mutism.

Disorganized type is dominated by incoherence, marked loosening of associations, or grossly disorganized behavior, with flat or grossly inappropriate affect, and does not meet criteria for catatonic type.

Paranoid type is dominated by preoccupation with one or more systematized delusions or with frequent auditory hallucinations related to a single theme. The patient does not demonstrate symptoms characteristic of catatonic or disorganized type (i.e., the patient does not present with incoherence, marked loosening of associations, flat or grossly inappropriate affect, catatonic behavior, or grossly disorganized behavior). When paranoid type applies, the clinician may further specify **stable type** to indicate that the criteria for paranoid type have been met during all past and present active phases of the illness. Paranoid type may have a later age of onset and a better prognosis than other schizophrenia types.

Undifferentiated type is dominated by prominent psychotic symptoms, such as delusions, hallucinations, incoherence, or grossly disorganized behavior, and does not meet criteria for paranoid, catatonic, or disorganized type. In a sense, this is a "residual" category for schizophrenia type (used when the active phase is present but the other types do not apply), but should not be confused with the technical meaning of "residual" when discussing phases or residual type (see below).

Residual type applies when there is an absence of prominent psychotic symptoms, such as delusions, hallucinations, incoherence, or grossly disorganized behavior, but there is continuing evidence of the disturbance as indicated by at least two of the nine symptoms listed for the prodromal or residual phase. This type applies when there is a history of an episode of schizophrenia with persistent residual symptoms of the illness but no current prominent psychotic symptoms. The course of this type must be either chronic or subchronic. This type is not really a "residual" category for schizophrenia type, but rather indicates a presentation consistent with the technical definition of the "residual" phase of schizophrenia. Therefore, if the current presentation is in the active phase, one of the other four types must apply. However, if the current presentation is in the residual phase, *only* the residual type applies, regardless of the type of clinical presentations during earlier active phases.[2]

Delusional (Paranoid) Disorder

Delusional (paranoid) disorder requires persistent nonbizarre delusions of at least 1 month duration, not due to another mental disorder. Auditory or visual hallucinations, if present, must not be prominent. Apart from the delusions or ramifications of the delusions, the patient's behavior must not be obviously odd or bizarre. The duration of any coexistent mood disturbance must be brief relative to the duration of the delusional disturbance. The diagnosis requires that the patient never have met criteria for schizophrenia and that it cannot be established that an organic factor initiated and maintained the disturbance. The clinician should specify type (see below).

The term "delusional" is preferred to the term "paranoid" in order to avoid ambiguity.

Table 3-24.   Types of delusional (paranoid) disorder

1. Erotomanic
2. Grandiose
3. Jealous
4. Persecutory
5. Somatic
6. Unspecified

Types.   There are five types and one residual type based on the predominant theme of the delusion (see Table 3-24).

In *erotomanic type* the predominant theme of the delusion(s) is that a person, usually of higher status, is in love with the patient.

In *grandiose type* the predominant theme of the delusion(s) is of inflated worth, power, knowledge, identity, or a special relationship to a deity or famous person.

In *jealous type* the predominant theme of the delusion(s) is that the patient's sexual partner is unfaithful.

In *persecutory type* the predominant theme of the delusion(s) is that the patient or someone close to the patient is being malevolently treated in some way.

In *somatic type* the predominant theme of the delusion(s) is that the patient has some physical defect, disorder, or disease.

Unspecified type is a residual category for delusional disorders that do not meet the definitions of the other types.

Psychotic Disorders Not Elsewhere Classified

This is a residual category for psychotic disorders that cannot be classified elsewhere in DSM-III-R (i.e., they cannot be classified as an organic mental disorder, schizophrenia, delusional disorder, or mood disorder with psychotic features). Four disorders and one residual category are listed under this heading (see Table 3-25).

Brief reactive psychosis.   This psychotic disorder requires the presence of at least one characteristic psychotic symptom (incoherence or marked loosening of associations, delusions, hallucina-

Table 3-25.   Psychotic disorders not elsewhere classified

1. Brief reactive psychosis
2. Schizophreniform disorder (specify without or with good prognostic features)
3. Schizoaffective disorder (specify bipolar type or depressive type)
4. Induced psychotic disorder
5. Psychotic disorder NOS (atypical psychosis)

tions, or catatonic or disorganized behavior)[3] and emotional turmoil (rapid shifts of intense affect or overwhelming perplexity or confusion) which must also 1) be in response to a recent and markedly stressful event or events, 2) have a duration of at least a few hours but no more than 1 month, and 3) feature eventual return to the previous level of functioning. Further, this diagnosis should not be made in the setting of certain more pervasive disorders; the diagnosis requires the absence of prodromal symptoms of schizophrenia and the failure to meet criteria for schizotypal personality disorder before the onset of the disturbance. It must not be due to a mood disorder, and it must not be established that an organic factor initiated and maintained the disturbance. The clinician should add the term "provisional" if still awaiting the expected recovery. If the disturbance continues beyond 1 month, the diagnosis should be changed to another applicable psychotic disorder (e.g., schizophreniform disorder, delusional disorder, mood disorder, or psychotic disorder not otherwise specified).

As indicated above, certain diagnoses preempt the diagnosis of brief reactive psychosis. This is an example of the use of hierarchies in DSM-III-R. Other disorders, such as personality disorders other than schizotypal, may predispose to or coexist with brief reactive psychosis.

Schizophreniform disorder.   This psychotic disorder requires the presence of the characteristic psychotic symptoms of schizophrenia, but unlike schizophrenia, an episode of schizophreniform disorder (including prodromal, active, and residual phases) must have a duration of less than 6 months. This diagnosis should be made only if certain exclusion criteria are met: the clinician must rule out schizoaffective disorder and mood disorder with psychotic features (as is also required for schizophrenia); the patient must not meet criteria for brief reactive psychosis; and it must not be established that the disturbance is initiated and maintained by an organic factor. The clinician should add the term "provisional" if still awaiting the expected recovery. Note that there is no minimal duration for schizophreniform disorder (unlike the DSM-III criteria).

The clinician should also specify **without good prognostic features** or **with good prognostic features**. According to DSM-III-R, at least two of the following are required to establish good prognostic features: 1) onset of prominent psychotic features within 4 weeks of the first noticeable change in usual behavior or functioning; 2) confusion, disorientation, or perplexity at the height of the psychotic episode; 3) good premorbid social and occupational function-

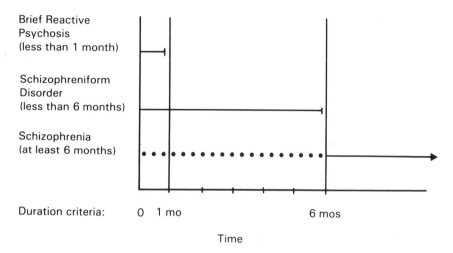

Duration criteria: 0   1 mo   6 mos

Time

Figure 3-1.   Brief reactive psychosis, schizophreniform disorder, schizophrenia: comparison of duration criteria

ing; and 4) absence of blunted or flat affect. However, even these features do not guarantee a good prognosis.

The relationship between schizophreniform disorder and schizophrenia is unclear. According to DSM-III-R definitions, the primary distinction is based on duration: after 6 months, the diagnosis changes from schizophreniform disorder to schizophrenia (see Figure 3-1). Perhaps schizophreniform disorder also involves more emotional turmoil.

Brief reactive psychosis should also be distinguished from schizophreniform disorder. First, duration is a possible distinguishing factor. If the presentation of brief reactive psychosis extends beyond 1 month, the diagnosis must change; such patients may or may not meet criteria for schizophreniform disorder. The clinician should note a potential point of confusion: while a presentation of *more* than 1 month precludes brief reactive psychosis but may permit schizophreniform disorder, a presentation of *less* than 1 month still permits the possible diagnosis of either brief reactive psychosis or schizophreniform disorder (see Figure 3-1).

Second, brief reactive psychosis is more directly related to a stressful event. Finally, DSM-III-R notes that brief reactive psychosis does not usually present with the characteristic psychotic symptoms of the active phase of schizophrenia, although the exact differences are not clearly delineated. In a rare case in which criteria for both are met, the diagnosis of brief reactive psychosis preempts the diagnosis of schizophreniform disorder.

Schizoaffective disorder. This psychotic disorder requires that both psychotic and mood disturbances occur in a particular temporal pattern: at some time during the disturbance there must be *concurrent* psychotic symptoms characteristic of the active phase of schizophrenia *and* a major depressive or manic syndrome. At some other time, there must be psychotic symptoms (delusions or hallucinations for at least 2 weeks) *without* prominent mood symptoms. Thus, there must be some periods with both mood and psychotic symptoms and other periods when only psychotic symptoms are prominent. There are two additional exclusion criteria: 1) schizophrenia must be ruled out, and 2) it must not be established that an organic factor initiated and maintains the disturbance. If the mood disturbance is brief relative to the total duration of the psychotic symptoms, one should consider the diagnosis of schizophrenia. The clinician should specify **bipolar type** (current or previous manic syndrome) or **depressive type** (no current or previous manic syndrome).

In short, this disorder does not meet criteria for either schizophrenia or mood disorder but has significant elements of both. Criteria for this disorder were introduced in DSM-III-R to improve reliability, since the term had been applied in varying ways within the profession. Thus, these criteria are relatively new and require further research. The relationship of schizoaffective disorder to other disorders, such as schizophrenia or mood disorders, remains unclear. Finally, the use of "affective" is somewhat inconsistent with other diagnoses in DSM-III-R; previously designated "affective" disorders, except for "schizoaffective" disorder, were renamed "mood" disorders. The term "schizoaffective" was retained for historical continuity and to reflect current use in the profession.

Induced psychotic disorder. This psychotic disorder requires the presence of a delusion in a second person (not the primary case) in the context of a close relationship with another person or persons (the primary case) who already has an established delusion. The second person's delusion is similar in content to the delusion in the primary case. In short, the same delusions are partially shared by both people. This diagnosis should not be made if the second person suffered from a psychotic disorder or prodromal symptoms of schizophrenia immediately before the onset of the induced delusion.

Typically, the two persons involved in this disorder have lived together for a long time and are isolated from other people. A case involving only two persons is sometimes called a "folie à deux."

Psychotic disorder NOS (atypical psychosis). This is a residual category in which there are psychotic symptoms but the presentation does not meet criteria for any other nonorganic psychotic disorder, or in which there is insufficient information to make a more specific diagnosis among the psychotic disorders. This category should be used only if it cannot be established that an organic factor initiated and maintained the disturbance.

Mood Disorders

DSM-III-R renamed these "mood disorders" (the DSM-III term was "affective disorders") because the disorders in this classification are primarily characterized by disturbances in mood, not "affect."[4] Mood disorders represent a spectrum of possible diagnoses. Three factors usually determine the proper mood disorder diagnosis: 1) the place of the mood disturbance on the mood spectrum (whether depressed, hypomanic, or manic); 2) the temporal course of the mood disturbance (steady or fluctuating, and duration); and 3) the severity of the mood disturbance. Some patients may clearly meet the criteria for a specific disorder, while others may be more difficult to categorize.

Under this heading, DSM-III-R attempts to make a conceptual distinction between syndromes, episodes, and disorders (see Table 3-26).

Mood syndrome refers to mood disturbances and associated symptoms that occur together for a minimal period of time. A mood syndrome may be part of a mood disorder, but it may also be part of a different category of mental disorders. Three primary mood syndromes are 1) major depressive, 2) manic, and 3) hypomanic.

Mood episode refers to a mood syndrome that is not due to a known organic factor and is not part of a nonmood psychotic disorder. There are three mood episodes (one associated with each mood syndrome): 1) major depressive, 2) manic, and 3) hypomanic.

Mood disorder refers to a specific disorder based on the pattern of mood episodes. In addition to residual categories, there are four primary mood disorders: 1) major depression, 2) dysthymia, 3) bipolar disorder, and 4) cyclothymia.

Unlike organic mental syndromes and disorders, mood syndromes and disorders are not distinguished based on whether a particular cause is identified or presumed. Rather, these three terms appear to categorize mood disturbances with increasing diagnostic specificity: "mood syndrome" applies as a generic description of a symptom pattern, although many diagnoses may still apply; "mood episode" implies further diagnostic specificity in requiring that other diagnoses have been ruled out; and "mood disorder" is the most specific, reflecting a well-established pattern of mood episodes. These terms suggest that the differential diagnosis may narrow as diagnostic certainty increases. Note that mood syndromes and mood episodes do not have numerical codes in DSM-III-R, whereas mood disorders do have official diagnostic codes.

Mood syndromes. A *major depressive syndrome* requires at least five of nine possible symptoms that are present during the same 2-week period nearly every day and that represent a change from the patient's previous functioning. At least one of the symptoms must be either depressed mood or significant loss of interest or pleasure. Other symptoms may include significant change in weight or appetite (without dieting); insomnia or hypersomnia; abnormal level of psychomotor activity (agitation or retardation); fatigue or loss of energy; feelings of worthlessness or excessive or inappropriate guilt; difficulty in thinking or concentrating or indecisiveness; and recurrent thoughts of death or suicide (with or without a plan), or a suicide attempt. Symptoms that should not be included are those that are clearly due to a physical condition (this may be difficult to establish, especially in the physically ill), mood-incongruent delusions or hallucinations, incoherence, or marked loosening of associations.

A *manic syndrome* requires a distinct period of abnormally and persistently elevated, expansive, or irritable mood, with the persistence and significant presence of at least three of seven possible symptoms during the period of the mood disturbance (four symptoms are required if the mood is only irritable). The symptoms are 1) inflated self-esteem or grandiosity, 2) decreased need for sleep, 3) unusual talkativeness or pressure to keep talking, 4) flight of ideas or subjective experience that thoughts are racing, 5) distractibility, 6) increase in goal-directed activity or psychomotor agitation, and 7) excessive involvement in pleasurable activities that have a high potential for painful consequences. A manic syndrome also requires that the mood disturbance be severe enough to cause marked impairment in functioning (in work, usual social activities, or relationships with others), or to necessitate hospitalization to prevent harm to self or others.

Clinically, depressed mood may appear to coexist or rapidly alternate with manic mood.

A *hypomanic syndrome* is defined like a manic syndrome except that the elevated, expansive, or irritable mood is not sufficiently severe to cause marked impairment in occupational or social functioning and does not necessitate hospitalization to prevent harm to self or others.

Mood episodes. A *major depressive episode* requires a major depressive syndrome (defined above) with the additional determination that certain other diagnoses do not apply. Specifically, a major depressive episode requires that it cannot be established that an organic factor initiated and maintained the disturbance, that the disturbance is not a normal uncomplicated bereavement in reaction to the death of a loved one, that there have been no delusions or hallucinations during the disturbance for as long as 2 weeks in the absence of prominent mood symptoms, and that the presentation is not superimposed on another nonmood psychotic disorder (such as schizophrenia, schizophreniform disorder, delusional disorder, or psychotic disorders not otherwise specified). In short, a major depressive episode requires at least 2 weeks of depressed mood or loss of interest or pleasure in most activities, and other associated symptoms that represent a change in the patient's functioning (that is, a major depressive syndrome), without evidence for an organic etiology, a normal grief reaction, or a nonmood psychotic disorder.

Clinically, it may be difficult to determine when depressed mood and associated symptoms imply psychopathology. The various symptoms of a major depressive syndrome may also occur with normal sadness, demoralization, grief, or as the direct effect of physical illness.

A major depressive episode may be further specified as to severity, chronicity, and whether it meets criteria for melancholic type.

Severity may be specified as mild, moderate, severe without psychotic features, with psychotic features (specify if mood-congruent psychotic features or mood-incongruent psychotic features), in partial remission, in full remission, or unspecified. In a major depressive episode, mood-congruent psychotic features are delusions or hallucinations consistent with depressive themes, whereas mood-incongruent delusions or hallucinations are not consistent with depressive themes.

The term "chronic" is specified when the current episode has lasted 2 consecutive years without at least a 2-month period free from significant depressive symptoms.

According to DSM-III-R criteria, melancholic type requires at least five of nine possible findings: 1) loss of interest or pleasure in all or almost all activities; 2) lack of reactivity to usually pleasurable stimuli; 3) depression regularly worse in the morning; 4) early morning awakening; 5) psychomotor retardation or agitation; 6) significant anorexia or weight loss; 7) no significant personality disturbance before the first major depressive episode; 8) one or more previous major depressive episodes followed by complete or nearly complete recovery; and 9) previous good response to specific and adequate antidepressant therapy (e.g., tricyclic antidepressants, monoamine oxidase inhibitors, lithium, or electroconvulsive therapy). This list is unusual in DSM-III-R; it includes not only items for symptoms and history but also items based on treatment response. The purpose of this designation is to identify a subtype of major depression more likely based on a biological or genetic cause and more likely to respond to somatic therapy. Unlike the typical DSM-III-R diagnosis, which seeks to remain purely descriptive, this designation implies both an inference regarding cause and a prediction regarding treatment response. While some of these symptoms (e.g., loss of interest in activities, lack of reactivity to usually pleasurable stimuli, anorexia, and early morning awakening) have been associated with medication-responsive depression, more work is needed to determine the extent to which this new definition of melancholia is valid or of increased clinical value. Note that the DSM-III-R definition of melancholic type is quite new and specific, and it may differ from the use of this term in other manuals or other contexts.

A *manic episode* requires a manic syndrome (defined above) with the additional determination that certain other diagnoses do not apply. Specifically, a manic episode requires that there have been no delusions or hallucinations for as long as 2 weeks in the absence of prominent mood symptoms, that the presentation is not superimposed on another nonmood psychotic disorder (such as schizophrenia, schizophreniform disorder, delusional disorder, or psychotic disorders NOS), and that it cannot be established that an organic factor initiated and maintained the disturbance.[5] In short, a manic episode requires a distinct period of abnormally and persistently elevated, expansive, or irritable mood and other associated symptoms that markedly impair functioning or require hospitalization (that is, a manic syndrome), without evidence for an organic etiology or a nonmood psychotic disorder.

A manic episode may be further specified as to severity.[6] Severity may be specified as mild, moderate, severe without psychotic features, with psychotic features (specify whether psychotic features are mood congruent or mood incongruent), in partial remission, in full remission, or unspecified. In a manic episode, mood-congruent psychotic features are delusions or hallucinations consistent with manic themes, whereas mood-incongruent psychotic features are delusions or hallucinations not consistent with manic themes or where there are catatonic symptoms.[7] Severity should be rated for the current manic episode, whether the current bipolar disorder is manic or mixed (discussed below).

A hypomanic episode is defined like a manic episode except that the elevated, expansive, or irritable mood is not sufficiently severe to cause marked impairment in occupational or social functioning and does not necessitate hospitalization to prevent harm to self or others. Compared to a manic episode, symptoms are less severe and may not include delusions. In short, a hypomanic episode is a less severe version of a manic episode.

Mood disorders. There are two major groups of mood disorders (depressive disorders and bipolar disorders), each of which is further subdivided into two disorders and one residual category (see Table 3-26).

There is a logical symmetry to these diagnoses. The two main depressive disorders are major depression itself and the more chronic, less severe dysthymia. Likewise, the two main bipolar disorders are bipolar disorder itself and the more chronic, less severe cyclothymia. The clinician may find it useful to consider a graphic representation when learning the mood disorders (see Figure 3-2).

Depressive disorders. Major depression requires one or more major depressive episodes (described above) without a history of a manic or hypomanic episode. There are two subclassifications based on the number of episodes. **Major depression, single episode**, is a single major depressive episode without a history of a manic or hypomanic episode. **Major depression, recurrent**, is two or more major depressive episodes, separated by at least 2 months of return to more or less usual functioning, without a history of a manic or hypomanic episode. In either case, the clinician may specify severity and, if applicable, seasonal pattern.

As with major depressive episodes (described above), the severity

Table 3-26.   Primary mood syndromes, episodes, and disorders

Mood syndromes
  1. Major depressive
  2. Manic
  3. Hypomanic

Mood episodes
  1. Major depressive
  2. Manic
  3. Hypomanic

Mood disorders
  1. Depressive disorders
     a. Major depression (single episode or recurrent)
     b. Dysthymia (or depressive neurosis)
     c. Depressive disorder NOS
  2. Bipolar disorders
     a. Bipolar (mixed, manic, or depressed)
     b. Cyclothymia
     c. Bipolar disorder NOS

may be specified as mild, moderate, or severe without psychotic features, with psychotic features (specify whether psychotic features are mood congruent or mood incongruent), in partial remission, in full remission, or unspecified.

Seasonal pattern refers to a regular temporal relationship between the onset of a mood disorder episode and a particular 60-day period of the year (i.e., a season). The clinician should not include a seasonally related psychosocial stressor, such as regular winter unemployment. Full remission or a change from depression to mania or hypomania also must occur within a particular 60-day period. For this designation to be made, there must have been at least three episodes of mood disturbance in 3 separate years demonstrating these temporal seasonal relationships, with at least 2 of the years being consecutive. Finally, seasonal episodes must outnumber non-seasonal episodes of the mood disturbance by more than three to one. Seasonal pattern may apply to recurrent major depression, depressive disorder NOS, bipolar disorder, and bipolar disorder NOS. The clinical significance of seasonal pattern is not yet clear.

In adults, dysthymia (or depressive neurosis) requires a history of depressed mood for most days (more days than not) for a duration of at least 2 years.[8] The patient should demonstrate at least two of six possible symptoms while depressed: 1) poor appetite or overeating, 2) insomnia or hypersomnia, 3) low energy or fatigue, 4) low self-esteem, 5) poor concentration or difficulty making decisions,

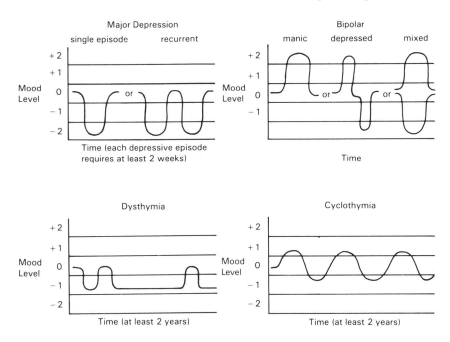

Figure 3-2. Graphic representation of mood disorders. Numerical indications of mood level are meant to convey distinctions in range of mood disturbance severity as compared to normal; graphs are not drawn to scale with regard to time; other clinical patterns are possible. *Source.* Adapted with permission from Webb LJ, DiClemente CC, Johnstone EE, et al. (eds), DSM-III Training Guide. New York, Brunner/Mazel, 1981, pp. 85 and 87.

and 6) feelings of hopelessness. Further, the diagnosis requires that the patient has never been without depressed mood for more than 2 months at a time during the overall 2-year period, and that there is no evidence of a major depressive episode during the first 2 years of the disturbance. If there was an earlier major depressive episode, that episode must have been in full remission before the development of the dysthymia. Finally, there are additional exclusion criteria: there must never have been a manic or hypomanic episode, the presentation must not be superimposed on a chronic psychotic disorder, and it must not be established that an organic factor initiated or maintained the disturbance. In short, dysthymia is similar to major depression except for more chronic course and less severity.

The clinician may specify primary or secondary type, and early or late onset.

Primary type is not related to a preexisting chronic nonmood

Axis I or Axis III disorder. Secondary type is related to a preexisting chronic nonmood Axis I or Axis III disorder. Early onset is onset before age 21. Late onset is onset after age 21.

Dysthymia continues to be a focus for research. The distinction between dysthymia and major depression and the relationship between dysthymia and personality disorders ("characterological" depression or "depressive neurosis" according to other systems) remains unclear. It is possible for a major depression to be superimposed upon dysthymia after the 2-year period; this situation has recently been labelled "double depression" (not an official DSM-III-R diagnosis); both DSM-III-R diagnoses then apply.

Depressive disorder NOS is a residual category for a depressive disorder that does not meet the criteria for the other mood disorders or for adjustment disorder with depressed mood.[9] The clinician should specify **seasonal pattern** if applicable (see above).

Bipolar disorders. Bipolar disorders require one or more manic or hypomanic episodes usually accompanied by one or more major depressive episodes. Bipolar disorders are divided into two disorders (bipolar disorder and cyclothymia) and one residual category. Note that "bipolar disorders" is the name of the heading of these disorders as well as one of the specific disorders listed under this heading.

The term "bipolar" requires some explanation. The "poles" refer to the two possible extremes of mood: depression and mania. By convention and according to current beliefs about psychopathology, the presence of mania alone presumes a disorder that includes disturbances at both poles of mood, and is sufficient to establish a diagnosis of bipolar disorder. This convention reflects the clinical observation that mania is almost invariably associated with some element of depression, or presumably will be associated with depression at some time during the clinical course. In some cases, the depressive element may be subclinical or will not emerge, but the psychopathological process is nevertheless thought to be the same as in cases where depression does emerge. On the other hand, depression alone is not thought to be coupled with mania, so that depression alone is considered "unipolar" (or "unipolar depression"). If mania or hypomania have never occurred in a patient with depression, the term "bipolar" is not used. There is no current application for the concept of "unipolar" mania.

There are three classifications of bipolar disorder based on the clinical features of the current or most recent episode. In bipolar disorder, mixed, the current or most recent episode involves both

manic and major depressive episodes (except for the duration requirement of 2 weeks for depressive symptoms), which are inter-
mixed or rapidly alternate every few days. The prominent depressive
symptoms must last at least a full day.

In bipolar disorder, manic, the current or most recent episode
involves only a manic episode (or partial criteria for a manic episode
if there has been one previously).

In bipolar disorder, depressed, the current or most recent episode involves a major depressive episode (or partial criteria for a
major depressive episode if there has been one previously) and one
or more manic episodes in the past.

In any of these cases, the clinician may specify severity and
seasonal pattern. As with mood episodes (described above), the severity may be specified as mild, moderate, severe without psychotic
features, with psychotic features (specify whether psychotic features
are mood congruent or mood incongruent), in partial remission, in
full remission, or unspecified. Note that the definition of these terms
varies depending on whether one is describing bipolar disorder, mixed
or bipolar disorder, manic (apply definitions of severity as described
under manic episodes) or bipolar disorder, depressed (apply definitions of severity as described under major depressive episode).
Seasonal pattern is as described under depressive disorders.

In adults, cyclothymia requires numerous hypomanic episodes
and numerous periods of depressed mood or loss of interest or pleasure for at least 2 years without meeting criteria for a full major
depressive episode.[10] Further, the diagnosis requires that the patient has never been without hypomanic or depressive symptoms for
more than 2 months at a time during the overall 2-year period, and
that there is no evidence of a major depressive episode or manic
episode during the first 2 years of the disturbance.[11] Finally, there
are additional exclusion criteria: the presentation must not be superimposed on a chronic psychotic disorder, and it must not be
established that an organic factor initiated or maintained the disturbance. In short, cyclothymia is similar to bipolar disorder except
for the more chronic course and milder severity.

Bipolar disorder NOS is a residual category for a disorder with
manic or hypomanic features that does not meet the criteria for the
specific bipolar disorders. The clinician should specify **seasonal pattern** if applicable.

"Bipolar II" (not an official DSM-III-R diagnosis) refers to a mood
disorder in which there is at least one hypomanic episode and one

major depressive episode, but never a full manic episode nor cyclothymia. In DSM-III-R, "bipolar II" would be considered a bipolar disorder not otherwise specified.

Anxiety Disorders (or Anxiety and Phobic Neuroses)

Anxiety disorders are primarily characterized by anxiety symptoms
and/or avoidance behavior. As in mood disorders, several more specific disorders are listed under the heading of anxiety disorders.
Many formerly designated "neuroses" are included under anxiety
disorders, although some former neuroses are included elsewhere
in DSM-III-R.[12] Some patients may clearly meet the criteria for a
specific anxiety disorder, while others may be more difficult to categorize.

DSM-III-R defines anxiety as "apprehension, tension, or uneas-
iness that stems from the anticipation of danger, which may be
internal or external." Although anxiety and fear are distinguishable,
the symptoms are similar and fall into four main groups: motor
tension, autonomic hyperactivity, apprehensive expectation (anxious rumination), and vigilance and scanning. A more specific symptom list is found under generalized anxiety disorder (see below).
Anxiety may be directed toward an object, situation, or activity that
the person seeks to avoid (phobia), or may be unfocused (free-floating
anxiety).

In addition to the anxiety disorders listed here, some disorders
primarily characterized by anxiety are listed elsewhere in DSM-III-
R: separation anxiety disorder (listed under "disorder usually first
evident in infancy, childhood, or adolescence"), organic anxiety syndrome or disorder (under "organic mental syndromes and disorders"), sexual aversion disorder (under "sexual disorders"), and
adjustment disorder with anxious mood. Anxiety symptoms may
also reflect mental disorders that do not usually or primarily present
with anxiety, such as mood disorders, delirium, psychotic disorders,
or personality disorders. An anxiety disorder may coexist with another mental disorder, and dual diagnoses are permitted (which
represents a change from DSM-III). Finally, many physical disorders
and medications may mimic, cause, or contribute to anxiety symptoms, and should be considered in the diagnostic assessment.

There are seven specific anxiety disorders and one residual category (see Table 3-27).

Panic disorder requires discrete, recurring attacks of intense
fear or discomfort ("panic attacks"), which are unexpected (different
from simple phobias) and not the result of being the focus of others'

Table 3-27.   Anxiety disorders (or anxiety and phobic neuroses)

1. Panic disorder
   a. With agoraphobia (specify severity of avoidance and severity of panic attacks)
   b. Without agoraphobia (specify severity of panic attacks)
2. Agoraphobia without history of panic disorder (specify with or without limited symptom attacks)
3. Social phobia (specify if generalized type)
4. Simple phobia
5. Obsessive-compulsive disorder (or obsessive-compulsive neurosis)
6. Posttraumatic stress disorder (specify if delayed onset)
7. Generalized anxiety disorder
8. Anxiety disorder NOS

attention (different from social phobias). Panic attacks require at least 4 of 13 possible symptoms: 1) shortness of breath or feeling smothered, 2) dizziness or feeling unsteady or faint, 3) palpitations or tachycardia, 4) trembling or shaking, 5) diaphoresis, 6) choking, 7) nausea or abdominal distress, 8) depersonalization or derealization, 9) numbness or tingling, 10) flushes or chills, 11) chest pain or chest discomfort, 12) fear of dying, and 13) fear of losing control or of going crazy. Four panic attacks must have occurred within a 4-week period, or one or more panic attacks must be followed by a period of at least 1 month of persistent fear of having another attack. If the attack involves fewer than four symptoms, it is called a "limited symptom attack" rather than a "panic attack." There is another time requirement: during at least some of the panic attacks, at least four of the listed symptoms must develop suddenly and increase in intensity within 10 minutes of the beginning of the first-noticed panic attack symptom. Finally, there is an additional exclusion criterion: it cannot be established that an organic factor initiated and maintained the disturbance (note also that mitral valve prolapse may be associated with panic disorder but does not rule out the diagnosis of panic disorder).

Clinically, panic attacks usually last only minutes but may rarely continue for much longer periods, even hours. The onset of a panic attack usually (but not always) begins with intense anxiety, followed by the other symptoms. Although panic attacks must be initially unexpected, in time they may become associated with certain anxiety-producing situations. Requiring four or more symptoms is arbitrary; usually there are more than six symptoms. Panic disorders commonly appear to include agoraphobia (described below) and frequently coexist with depressive mood disorders.

Panic disorder should be distinguished from other anxiety disorders in which panic attacks may occur, such as simple phobias (in which the occurrence and intensity of the panic attack vary with the approach or withdrawal of the phobic stimulus, whereas the panic attack in panic disorder is less predictable) and social phobia (in which there must be a social phobic situation, described below). Panic disorder may coexist with other mental disorders. Physical disorders and substance intoxication or withdrawal may be associated with panic attacks, and may preclude the diagnosis of panic disorder.

The clinician may specify type and severity. There are two types of panic disorder, based on the presence or absence of agoraphobia: panic disorder with agoraphobia and panic disorder without agoraphobia. **Agoraphobia** is the "fear of being in places or situations from which escape might be difficult or embarrassing or in which help may not be available in the event of a panic attack." This fear results in avoiding travel or requiring a companion when leaving home, or enduring the situation despite anxiety.

Severity is designated as **mild, moderate, severe, in partial remission,** or **in full remission**. For panic disorder with agoraphobia, severity may be indicated for the current severity of agoraphobic avoidance. For either type of panic disorder, severity may be indicated for the current severity of panic attacks. DSM-III-R provides exact criteria for these severity terms.

Agoraphobia without history of panic disorder requires agoraphobia (previously defined) without ever having met criteria for a panic disorder. The clinician should specify **with limited symptom attacks** (involving fewer than four of the characteristic panic attack symptoms) or **without limited symptom attacks.** The relationship between this category and panic disorder is unclear; they may represent different degrees of the same disorder.

Social phobia requires persistent fear of one or more situations (the social phobic situations) in which the patient may be scrutinized by others and fears acting in a way that will be humiliating or embarrassing. This fear must be unrelated to an Axis III or another Axis I disorder, if such a disorder is also present. Exposure to the specific phobic stimulus or stimuli usually provokes an immediate anxiety response during some phase of the social phobia disturbance. The phobic situation must be either avoided or endured with intense anxiety. The avoidant behavior must interfere with occupational or social functioning, or there must be marked distress about having the fear. The person must recognize that this fear is excessive or unreasonable. Finally, if the person is under 18 years of age, the disturbance must not meet the criteria for avoidance disorder of childhood and adolescence.

The clinician should specify **generalized type** if the social phobia includes most social situations. In such cases, avoidant personality disorder may coexist.

Social phobias may be circumscribed (e.g., speaking in social settings, eating food in a restaurant, urinating in a public lavatory) or generalized to most social situations (e.g., fear of saying foolish things or inability to answer questions). Marked "anticipatory anxiety" may occur. Social phobias should be distinguished from avoidance behavior in other contexts, such as normal avoidance behavior in response to common social stress (e.g., formal public speaking), simple phobias (which do not involve the social phobic situation), and panic disorder with agoraphobia (in which avoidance is due to fear or embarrassment concerning having the panic attack itself).

Simple phobias require a persistent fear of a circumscribed stimulus (an object or a situation). Simple phobias do not include fears associated with panic disorder (fear of having a panic attack), agoraphobia without panic disorder, or social phobia (fear of humiliation or embarrassment in certain social situations). Exposure to the specific phobic stimulus or stimuli usually provokes an immediate anxiety response during some phase of the disturbance. The feared object or situation must be either avoided or endured with intense anxiety. The fear or avoidant behavior must significantly interfere with normal routines or usual social functioning, or there must be marked distress about having the fear. The person must recognize that this fear is excessive or unreasonable. Finally, the phobic stimulus must be unrelated to the content of the obsessions of obsessive-compulsive disorder or to the trauma of post-traumatic stress disorder (PTSD).

Examples of simple phobias are fear of specific animals such as snakes, blood injury, closed spaces (claustrophobia), heights (acrophobia), or air travel. Simple phobias may also be called "specific" phobias. Marked anticipatory anxiety may occur. Simple phobias should be distinguished from avoidance behavior in other contexts, such as avoidance in response to delusions in a psychotic disorder (in which the patient does not recognize that the fear is excessive or unreasonable), PTSD (in which the phobic stimuli must be associated with the past trauma, as described below), or obsessions in obsessive-compulsive disorder.

Obsessive-compulsive disorder (or obsessive-compulsive neu-

rosis) requires either obsessions or compulsions that cause marked distress, are time-consuming (taking more than an hour a day), or significantly interfere with the normal routine or occupation or usual social functioning. Obsessive-compulsive disorder may be accompanied by depression or anxiety and may coexist with other mental disorders. Obsessions and compulsions are defined as follows.

Obsessions are recurrent and persistent ideas, thoughts, impulses, or images that are at least initially experienced as intrusive and senseless, and that the person attempts to ignore, suppress, or neutralize. The person must recognize that the obsessions are the result of his or her thoughts, and are not imposed from outside (as occurs with a "thought insertion" delusion). Finally, the content of the obsession must be unrelated to another Axis I disorder that may also be present (e.g., food in an eating disorder, drugs in a psychoactive substance use disorder, guilty or brooding thoughts in a major depression). Examples of obsessions are repetitive thoughts of doing violence, contamination, or doubt about whether one performed a certain act.

Compulsions are repetitive, purposeful, and intentional behaviors that are performed in response to an obsession, according to certain rules, or in a stereotyped fashion. A compulsive behavior must be an unrealistic or excessive attempt to neutralize or prevent discomfort or some dreaded event or situation. In adults, the person must recognize that the behavior is excessive or unreasonable (unless the obsession has evolved into an overvalued idea, in which case compulsion may exist even if the person does not consider the behavior excessive or unreasonable). Examples of compulsions are repetitive behaviors involving hand washing, counting, checking, and touching. Compulsive behaviors may relieve tension, but are usually not pleasurable. Compulsions are distinguished from excessive behaviors in other disorders where they are associated with pleasure (e.g., eating in an eating disorder, sexual behavior in certain sexual disorders, gambling in pathological gambling, and drinking in alcohol dependence or abuse) or are associated with delusions (stereotyped behavior in schizophrenia).

In summary, obsessive-compulsive disorder requires recurrent obsessions or compulsions causing significant distress or dysfunction.

Posttraumatic stress disorder first requires experiencing a traumatic event that is outside the range of normal human experience and that would be markedly stressful to almost anyone. This is followed by at least 1 month's duration of three additional findings:

1) persistent reexperiencing of the traumatic event; 2) persistent avoidance of stimuli associated with the traumatic event or numbing of general responsiveness (not present before the trauma); and 3) persistent symptoms of increased arousal (not present before the trauma).

Each of these three findings may be satisfied by a minimal number of symptoms listed in DSM-III-R. Reexperiencing the event may be indicated by sufficiently severe recollections, dreams, suddenly reliving the event in action or feeling, or psychological distress related to events symbolic of the trauma. Avoidance or numbing requires at least three of seven symptoms: 1) avoidance of thoughts or feelings associated with the trauma, 2) avoidance of activities or situations that arouse recollections of the trauma, 3) psychogenic amnesia about the trauma, 4) markedly diminished interest in significant activities, 5) feeling detached or estranged, 6) restricted range of affect, and 7) a sense of a foreshortened future. Finally, increased arousal requires at least two of six symptoms: 1) difficulty sleeping, 2) irritability or outbursts of anger, 3) difficulty concentrating, 4) hypervigilance, 5) exaggerated startle response, and 6) physiologic reactivity to events symbolic of the trauma.

The clinician should specify **delayed onset** if symptoms began at least 6 months after the trauma.

The traumatic events in PTSD may involve death or serious harm, destruction, or mortal threat to oneself or significant others. Examples of traumatic events include rape, assault, destruction of one's home or community following a natural disaster such as a flood or earthquake, accidental disasters such as a plane or car crash, building collapse, fire, torture, bombings, being held hostage, and military combat. Not included are events within the range of usual experience, such as typical bereavement, chronic illness, business loss, and marital conflict. The specific stressor and severity should be recorded on Axis IV.

Other disorders related to the trauma, such as anxiety disorder, depressive disorder, or organic mental disorder, may coexist with PTSD. PTSD should be distinguished from adjustment disorder, in which the stressor is less severe and within the range of common experience and the characteristic symptoms (reexperiencing, avoidance or numbing, and arousal) are absent. PTSD may occur in children, although symptoms may vary from the adult criteria. For example, in children, one may consider recurrent themes in play, regression of acquired skills, nightmares, or physical symptoms.

Generalized anxiety disorder requires at least 6 months of unrealistic or excessive anxiety and worry (apprehensive expectation) about two or more life circumstances, often experiencing at least 6 of 18 symptoms listed in DSM-III-R (not including symptoms present only during panic attacks). During this period, the person must be bothered more days than not by these worries. The focus of the anxiety and worry must be unrelated to any other Axis I disorder that may be present (such as anxiety or worry about panic attacks in panic disorder, public embarrassment in social phobia, fear of contamination in obsessive-compulsive disorder, or weight change in eating disorder). The anxiety and worry must not occur only during the course of a mood disorder or a psychotic disorder. Finally, there is an additional exclusion criterion: it cannot be established that an organic factor initiated and maintained the disturbance.

The 18 anxiety-related symptoms are grouped into 3 major areas:

- motor tension: trembling, twitching, or feeling shaky; muscle tension, aches, or soreness; restlessness; easy fatigability
- autonomic hyperactivity: dyspnea or smothering sensations; palpitations or tachycardia; sweating or cold, clammy hands; dry mouth; dizziness or lightheadedness; nausea, diarrhea, or other abdominal distress; flushes or chills; frequent urination; trouble swallowing
- vigilance and scanning: feeling keyed up or edgy; exaggerated startle response; difficulty concentrating; difficulty sleeping; irritability

In practice, the clinician may first need to consider physical conditions that may mimic, cause, or contribute to the symptoms associated with a generalized anxiety disorder. There are many such conditions, including respiratory, cardiovascular, endocrine, immunologic, metabolic, neurologic, gastrointestinal, tumor, medication, and other conditions. As indicated above, such physical causes may preclude the diagnosis of generalized anxiety disorder. Next, the clinician may consider the differential psychiatric diagnosis. Anxiety may be present in a variety of mental disorders, including some that do not usually present primarily with anxiety and others that do present primarily with anxiety. Generalized anxiety disorder is not diagnosed in the presence of some of these disorders (see foregoing criteria), but it may coexist with another Axis I disorder if the anxiety is unrelated to that disorder. As previously noted, most mental disorders presenting primarily with anxiety are listed under the anxiety disorders heading, but the clinician may need to consider others listed elsewhere (e.g., separation anxiety disorder, organic anxiety syndrome or disorder, sexual aversion disorder, and adjustment disorder with anxious mood). Finally, generalized anxiety disorder should be distinguished from adjustment disorder with anxious mood, in which the symptoms are less severe, duration is less than 6 months and there is a clear psychosocial stressor (DSM-III-R extended the duration requirement to 6 months in order to exclude transient anxiety reactions).

Anxiety disorder NOS is a residual category reserved for anxiety disorders (involving prominent anxiety or phobic avoidance) that do not meet criteria for another specific anxiety disorder and that cannot be properly classified elsewhere in DSM-III-R (e.g., an adjustment disorder with anxious mood).

Somatoform Disorders

Somatoform disorders are characterized by physical symptoms that suggest physical disorders, but without organic findings or known physiologic mechanisms to explain the symptoms, and with either positive evidence or a strong presumption that the symptoms relate to psychological factors or conflicts. Hence, these disorders are exceptions to the general rule that DSM-III-R is purely descriptive. Somatoform disorders imply a psychological cause based on timing, although DSM-III-R does not go further in delineating the nature of the psychological cause. The role of theory in these and other disorders is discussed in Chapter 4.

In addition to somatoform disorders, a number of other DSM-III-R categories primarily involve symptoms that suggest physical illness (each is described individually later in this chapter). Among these, one important distinction is among somatoform disorders, factitious disorders, and malingering. In somatoform disorders, symptoms are not intentional. In factitious disorders, there is an element of intentional control over symptoms, although there may be primary gain (relief of an internal psychological conflict, considered unconscious). In malingering, symptoms are also intentionally produced, but there is the additional requirement that the symptoms result in secondary gain (external advantages gained from other people or the environment). Another distinction is that in psychological factors affecting physical conditions, physical symptoms are based on an Axis III physical condition or disorder. Finally, adjustment disorder with physical complaints involves a recent stressor and a duration of less than 6 months.

One theme echoing throughout somatoform disorders is the risk of too quickly dismissing symptoms as "nonorganic" and of under-

Table 3-28. Somatoform disorders

1. Body dysmorphic disorder
2. Conversion disorder (or hysterical neurosis, conversion type; specify single episode or recurrent)
3. Hypochondriasis (or hypochondriacal neurosis)
4. Somatization disorder
5. Somatoform pain disorder
6. Undifferentiated somatoform disorder
7. Somatoform disorder

cutting the therapeutic alliance by "disbelieving" patients. On the one hand, certain physical diseases may elude detection on medical evaluation. On the other hand, psychologically based symptoms are just as real to the patient as physiologically based symptoms (and there is often an overlap of psychological and physiological factors). The symptoms are subjective, valid experiences. These disorders do not imply an intentional effort to deceive. These patients frequently seek out physician and medical interventions (with potential iatrogenic complications), while they also tend to minimize or remain unaware of (perhaps unconsciously "denying") the importance of psychological factors. These patients should be recognized as suffering from legitimate disorders; they need professional help.

There are six specific somatoform disorders and one residual category (see Table 3-28).

Body dysmorphic disorder.   This diagnosis requires preoccupation with an imagined defect in physical appearance in an otherwise normal-appearing person. (Grossly excessive concern about a slight physical defect would also qualify.) The belief must not be delusional (as in delusional disorder, somatic type) and must not occur only during the course of anorexia nervosa (preoccupation with body weight) or transsexualism (preoccupation with gender-related physical traits).

This diagnosis should not be made for adolescents who normally worry about minor defects, such as acne, or for adults whose excessive concern about appearance occurs in other disorders but is not the predominant disturbance. This disorder was previously known as "dysmorphophobia," a term that was inaccurate because the disorder does not involve phobic avoidance.

Conversion disorder (or hysterical neurosis, conversion type). This diagnosis requires a loss or change in physical functioning that suggests a physical disorder but in which psychological factors are judged to be etiologically related to the symptom because of a temporal relationship between a psychosocial stressor (apparently related to a psychological conflict or need) and the initiation or exacerbation of the symptom. Thus, conversion disorder implies a psychological cause based on timing. The symptoms must not be intentionally produced (as in factitious disorder or malingering) and must not be a culturally sanctioned response pattern. Appropriate investigations must be unable to provide a physical explanation for the symptoms. Finally, conversion disorder should not be diagnosed if the presenting symptoms are limited to pain (as in somatoform pain disorder, described below, which reflects a different course and treatment) or to sexual functioning (as in certain sexual disorders, in which it is difficult to separate a physiological reaction to anxiety from a conversion symptom). The clinician should specify **single episode** or **recurrent**.

Examples of possible conversion symptoms include paralysis, blindness, anesthesia, inability to stand or walk ("astasia-abasia"), vomiting, "globus hystericus" (sensation of a lump in the throat that inhibits swallowing), and pseudocyesis ("false pregnancy"). Symptoms usually appear suddenly in the setting of significant psychological stress. The symptom may symbolically represent a solution to underlying psychological conflict or need (providing primary gain) and may also help the patient to achieve some obvious and recognizable gain, support, or some other advantage from the environment (providing secondary gain). For example, paralysis may prevent acting on violent impulses and foster dependency (primary gain), and result in avoiding other social responsibilities (secondary gain). This disorder may be associated with histrionic personality traits and the phenomenon of "la belle indifférence" (notable lack of concern or affect regarding the symptoms).

The diagnosis of a conversion disorder requires careful consideration of possible underlying physical causes. Some disease processes (such as multiple sclerosis or systemic lupus erythematosis) produce symptoms that may be mistaken for conversion symptoms. In other cases, medical investigation may simply fail to reveal the physical cause for the symptom (such as an undetected brain tumor in a patient with headaches). Symptoms of a physical disorder may intermix with conversion symptoms, as in epileptic seizures and pseudoseizures, making diagnosis difficult.

Conversion symptoms may be suggested by inconsistencies between symptoms, physical findings on examination, and known human physiology. For example, sensory abnormalities may be inconsistent with the anatomical distribution of the nervous system, inability to walk may be inconsistent with muscle strength on exam, or blindness may be inconsistent with pupillary response or evoked potentials. Also, patient history may reveal models for the conversion symptoms, such as earlier physical disorders or significant others with physical symptoms.

Conversion disorders should also be distinguished from physical disorders in which psychological factors are important (e.g., asthma), other mental disorders in which conversion symptoms may occur (only the more pervasive disorder is usually diagnosed), and hypochondriasis (physical symptoms are usually present, but with no functional loss or distortion).

Historically, cases involving conversion symptoms, at first within the province of neurology, formed the initial basis for Freud's developing theory about the unconscious. These cases appear to be rarer today, suggesting a cultural influence in the development of conversion symptoms. Earlier diagnostic systems refer to these cases as hysterical neurosis, conversion type, a term that is still sometimes used.

Hypochondriasis (or hypochondriacal neurosis). This diagnosis requires at least a 6-month preoccupation with the fear of or belief in having a serious disease based on interpretation of physical signs or sensations as evidence for physical illness. An appropriate physical evaluation must not support diagnosing a physical disorder to account for the physical signs or sensations or for the patient's interpretation of these signs or sensations. However, a coexisting physical disorder may be present. The symptoms must not be merely symptoms of a panic attack. The fear of or belief in the disease must persist despite medical reassurance. Finally, the fear or belief must not be delusional (as in delusional disorder, somatic type).

Hypochondriasis may be associated with long medical histories, seeking many doctors, and repeated episodes of problematic doctor-patient relationships. As in conversion disorder, patient history may reveal physical disorders in the patient or significant others, as well as possible predisposing psychosocial stressors. Frequently seen in medical practices, these patients exhibit much denial of the psychological aspects of their presentation and usually refuse to see mental health professionals.

As in conversion disorder, the differential diagnosis should carefully consider organic causes for symptoms, especially organic processes that may not yet be detectable by usual laboratory studies or examination. However, the clinical picture may be complicated by the possible coexistence of physical disorders. Other mental disorders may present with somatic complaints and should be distinguished from hypochondriasis (e.g., somatic delusions in psychotic disorders, somatic complaints in nonpsychotic disorders). In other disorders, somatic complaints are usually not long-standing preoccupations. It is possible for hypochondriasis to coexist with other mental disorders.

Somatization disorder. This diagnosis requires a history of recurrent and multiple physical complaints or the belief that one is sickly, beginning before age 30 and persisting for several years. The patient must suffer from at least 13 of 35 possible symptoms (see Table 3-29), and two or more of the seven boldfaced items provide a screen suggesting a high likelihood for somatization disorder. Either these symptoms must not have an organic explanation or, when there is an organic explanation, the complaint or resulting social or occupational impairment must be grossly in excess of what would be expected from the physical findings. The symptoms must not have occurred only during a panic attack. Finally, the symptoms must have caused the person to take medicine (other than over-the-counter pain medication), seek a doctor, or alter lifestyle.

This disorder, sometimes called Briquet's syndrome, seems more prevalent among females. Of note, DSM-III-R redefined somatization disorder to eliminate differences in the number of symptoms based on sex. These patients frequently seek professional medical help and may be subjected to multiple and unnecessary surgeries. Life is usually chaotic and dominated by involvement with the professional medical system. Many psychiatric diagnoses may be associated with somatization disorder, including psychoactive substance disorders related to prescription medication, anxiety and depressed mood, psychotic symptoms (more rarely), and personality disorders or traits.

As in other somatoform disorders, the diagnosis of somatization disorder requires careful consideration of possible underlying physical causes, especially those that may be undetected by usual laboratory tests or examination or that may have inexplicit, multiple, or confusing presentations. Somatization disorder should be distinguished from other mental disorders that may present with somatic complaints (e.g., somatic delusions in psychotic disorders, somatic complaints in nonpsychotic disorders). In panic disorder, cardiopulmonary symptoms (which may also occur in somatic disorder) occur only within the context of panic attacks. However, panic disorder and somatization disorder may coexist if the symptoms also occur outside the context of panic attacks. Conversion disorder involves one or more conversion symptoms without full criteria for

Table 3-29.   Symptom list for somatization disorder

Gastrointestinal symptoms
   1. **Vomiting (other than during pregnancy)**
   2. Abdominal pain (other than when menstruating)
   3. Nausea (other than motion sickness)
   4. Bloating (gassy)
   5. Diarrhea
   6. Intolerance of (gets sick from) several different foods

Pain symptoms
   7. **Pain in extremities**
   8. Back pain
   9. Joint pain
  10. Pain during urination
  11. Other pain (excluding headaches)

Cardiopulmonary symptoms
  12. **Shortness of breath when not exerting oneself**
  13. Palpitations
  14. Chest pain
  15. Dizziness

Conversion or pseudoneurologic symptoms
  16. **Amnesia**
  17. **Difficulty swallowing**
  18. Loss of voice
  19. Deafness
  20. Double vision
  21. Blurred vision
  22. Blindness
  23. Fainting or loss of consciousness
  24. Seizure or convulsion
  25. Trouble walking
  26. Paralysis or muscle weakness
  27. Urinary retention or difficulty urinating

Sexual symptoms for the major part of the person's life after opportunities for sexual activity
  28. **Burning sensation in sexual organs or rectum (other than during intercourse)**
  29. Sexual indifference
  30. Pain during intercourse
  31. Impotence

Female reproductive symptoms judged by the person to occur more frequently or severely than in most women
  32. **Painful menstruation**
  33. Irregular menstrual periods
  34. Excessive menstrual bleeding
  35. Vomiting throughout pregnancy

Note.   The seven items in boldface may be used to screen for the disorder. The presence of two or more of these items suggests a high likelihood of the disorder.
Source.   DSM-III-R, pp. 263–264.

somatization disorder. In factitious disorder with physical symptoms, the patient has control over symptoms.

Somatoform pain disorder. This diagnosis requires preoccupation with pain for at least 6 months in the absence of any physical finding to account for the pain and its intensity. Either an appropriate evaluation must fail to uncover an organic explanation or, when there is an organic explanation, the complaint of pain or resulting social or occupational impairment must be grossly in excess of what would be expected from the physical findings.

This disorder may or may not reflect causal psychological factors or secondary gain. As in other somatoform disorders, patients with somatoform pain disorder may seek out many doctors without satisfaction, subject themselves to surgery, overuse medications, exhibit denial regarding the role of psychological factors in their symptoms, and take up the sick role. The pain may or may not have symbolic significance. This disorder may be associated with other mental symptoms and disorders, such as conversion symptoms, depression, histrionic personality traits, and, rarely, la belle indifférence.

As in other somatoform disorders, this disorder should be distinguished from the presentation of pain due to organic disease. Organic pain that seems excessive does not warrant the diagnosis of somatoform pain disorder. Other mental disorders may also present with pain symptoms, but in these cases pain is usually not the dominant symptom. In malingering, the person intentionally produces pain symptoms for secondary gain (such as to obtain narcotics).

Clinicians should apply the diagnosis of somatoform pain disorder cautiously. Pain itself is a subjective experience. Our understanding of pain is incomplete. Nonacceptance of the legitimacy of a patient's pain risks unfair prejudice against the patient, deterioration of the therapeutic alliance, and error. A patient's pain should not be inappropriately dismissed by the pejorative notion that it is merely "psychogenic."

Undifferentiated somatoform disorder. This diagnosis is reserved for patients who do not meet the full criteria for somatization disorder. Thus, undifferentiated somatoform disorder functions as a residual category of somatization disorder, although this residual category is more common than somatization disorder itself. The diagnosis requires one or more physical symptoms (not the 13 required for somatization disorder) for at least 6 months. Either an appropriate evaluation must fail to uncover an organic explanation

Table 3-30.   Dissociative disorders (or hysterical neurosis, dissociative type)

1. Multiple personality disorder
2. Psychogenic fugue
3. Psychogenic amnesia
4. Depersonalization disorder (or depersonalization neurosis)
5. Dissociative disorder NOS

or, when there is an organic explanation, the physical complaints or resulting social or occupational impairment must be grossly in excess of what would be expected from the physical findings. The diagnosis should not be made if the symptoms occur exclusively during the course of another somatization disorder, sexual dysfunction, mood disorder, anxiety disorder, sleep disorder, or a psychotic disorder.

This disorder is distinguishable from adjustment disorder with physical complaints, the duration of which is less than 6 months. Psychological factors affecting physical condition require physical complaints based on an organic process (on Axis III).

Somatoform disorder NOS.   This is a residual category for disorders with somatoform symptoms that do not meet criteria for any other specific somatoform disorders or adjustment disorders with physical complaints.

Dissociative Disorders (or Hysterical Neuroses, Dissociative Type)

Dissociative disorders are primarily characterized by a disturbance or alteration in the normally integrated functions of identity, memory, or consciousness. Earlier diagnostic systems classified these disorders as hysterical neurosis, dissociative type. Note that sleepwalking disorder is similar to a dissociative disorder, but is classified in DSM-III-R as a sleep disorder.

There are four dissociative disorders and one residual category (see Table 3-30).

Multiple personality disorder.   This diagnosis requires the existence of two or more distinct personalities or personality states in one individual. Each personality must have its own relatively enduring pattern of perceiving, relating to, and thinking about the environment. At least two of these personalities or personality states must recurrently take full control over behavior.

There may be a wide range of presentations. Multiple personality may involve mixtures of 2 to perhaps more than 100 fully developed personalities (which extend over a wide range of social and personal contexts) and personality states (which extend over a narrower range of contexts). Different personalities or personality states may share common features, but in classic cases each is unique. Transitions between personalities may be rapid or gradual and may or may not be precipitated by psychosocial stress, meaningful cues, or conflicts among personalities; according to a plan by the personalities; or following suggestion in hypnosis or an amobarbital interview. Personalities may or may not be aware of one another and may show different objective physiological or psychological characteristics (e.g., eyeglass prescriptions, response to medication, IQ). One personality hearing another's voice or talking with another personality must be distinguished from other forms of hallucinations and delusions. These disorders are frequently associated with abuse or severe emotional trauma in childhood, often including sexual abuse. This disorder may not be as rare as previously believed.

Multiple personality disorder should be distinguished from other mental disorders. In particular, psychogenic fugue and psychogenic amnesia are usually limited to a single, brief episode and do not involve repeated shifts of identity. Hallucinations or delusions suggest a psychotic disorder such as schizophrenia or mood disorder with psychotic features. Instability of mood, self-image, and interpersonal behavior suggests borderline personality disorder. Malingering involves intentional deception for secondary gain and may be difficult to rule out. Finally, simply "feeling" like two or more different people is insufficient to warrant this diagnosis.

Psychogenic fugue.   This diagnosis requires sudden, unexpected travel away from home or customary workplace with the assumption of a new identity (partial or complete) and an inability to recall the previous identity. The disturbance must not be due to multiple personality disorder or to an organic mental disorder.

Clinically, the fugue may follow a severe psychosocial stress, is usually brief (hours or days), and involves only limited travel, but rarely it may extend for months and involve complex travel. The assumed identity may be limited or extensive. Significant alcohol use seems to predispose to this disorder.

Psychogenic fugue should be distinguished from other mental disorders. In particular, multiple personality disorder more typically involves repeated shifts of identity, more than a single episode, and a history of identity disturbances since childhood. Psychogenic amnesia usually lacks purposeful travel or the assumption of a new identity (travel in psychogenic amnesia is really "confused wandering"). In temporal lobe epilepsy, episodes are not precipitated by psychosocial stress, mood is more dysphoric, and there is no assumption of a new identity. Malingering involves intentional deception for secondary gain and may be difficult to rule out.

Psychogenic amnesia. This diagnosis requires an episode of sudden inability to recall important personal information that is too extensive to be explained by ordinary forgetfulness. The disturbance must not be due to multiple personality disorder or an organic mental disorder.

Amnesia typically occurs suddenly and follows a severe psychosocial stress. Amnesia may also follow unacceptable impulses, perhaps unconscious, or unacceptable life circumstances. There are four possible types of amnesia.

- localized amnesia (the most common type): failure to recall all events occurring during a circumscribed time period
- selective amnesia: failure to recall some but not all events occurring during a circumscribed time period
- generalized amnesia: failure to recall one's entire life
- continuous amnesia: failure to recall events extending continuously from a previous time period up to and including the present

   Psychogenic amnesia should be distinguished from other disorders. In particular, organic mental disorders are usually not related to stress, tend to demonstrate amnesia for recent events, disappear more slowly (if at all), and are more often accompanied by attention deficits and affective disturbance. In psychoactive substance-induced intoxication, substance intoxication (an organic cause) causes the amnesia. For example, alcohol amnestic disorder usually involves short-term memory impairment, blunted affect, confabulation, and lack of awareness of the memory impairment. In postconcussive amnesia, the memory is more often retrograde (involving the period before the trauma), whereas memory impairment in psychogenic amnesia is usually antegrade (involving the period after the trauma). Epilepsy usually involves a sudden onset of memory impairment, motor abnormalities, and abnormal findings on EEG. Catatonic stupor usually involves catatonic symptoms (i.e., rigidity, posturing, negativism) without memory deficits. Psychogenic fugue is a more accurate diagnosis when the patient travels and assumes another identity. Finally, malingering may be difficult to rule out.

Depersonalization disorder (or depersonalization neurosis). This diagnosis requires the persistent or recurring experience of depersonalization. Depersonalization is indicated either by feeling detached from one's mental processes or body (as if an outside observer), or by feeling like an automaton or as if in a dream. Reality testing must remain intact. The experience must be sufficiently severe and persistent to cause marked distress. Finally, the depersonalization disturbance must be predominant and must not be secondary to another mental disorder such as schizophrenia, panic disorder, agoraphobia without history of panic disorder, or temporal lobe epilepsy.

Single, brief episodes of depersonalization may occur in adults, but they would not warrant this diagnosis unless they are recurrent and cause significant occupational or social dysfunction. Note that depersonalization disorder is listed as a dissociative disorder even though it does not involve a disturbance in memory.

Dissociative disorder NOS. This is a residual category for disorders in which the primary feature is a dissociative symptom but in which the patient does not meet the criteria for one of the other specific dissociative disorders. Examples include Ganser's syndrome (giving "approximate answers" to questions, usually associated with amnesia, disorientation, perceptual disturbances, and conversion symptoms), trance states, and dissociative states following coercive "brainwashing" or terrorist indoctrination.

Sexual Disorders

Sexual disorders are divided into two main groups (paraphilias and sexual dysfunctions) and one main residual category (other sexual disorders).

Paraphilias. Paraphilias are recurrent, intense sexual urges and sexually arousing fantasies in response to objects or situations that are not considered part of normal arousal-activity patterns and that interfere with the capacity for reciprocal, affectionate sexual activity. The paraphilic object or situation need not always be required for sexual arousal. The person must act on these urges or be markedly distressed by them (imagery or fantasy alone is not sufficient for the diagnosis). The disturbance must extend for at least 6 months. Severity is specified as mild (patient was markedly distressed but never acted on the paraphilic urge), moderate (patient acted on the paraphilic urge), or severe (patient repeatedly acted on the paraphilic urge). Thus, severity is based on distress and frequency of acting, not on the nature of the paraphilia itself.

These disorders, previously called "sexual deviations," were re-

Table 3-31. Sexual disorders: paraphilias

1. Exhibitionism
2. Fetishism
3. Frotteurism
4. Pedophilia (specify same sex, opposite sex, same and opposite sex; if limited to incest; exclusive or nonexclusive type)
5. Sexual masochism
6. Sexual sadism
7. Transvestic fetishism
8. Voyeurism
9. Paraphilia NOS

named to emphasize deviation ("para") to that object or situation to which the person is attracted ("philia").

Paraphilias represent a range of disorders. Various paraphilias may involve people (consenting in some disorders, nonconsenting in others) or objects, and may represent either harmless or potentially dangerous behavior. These patients frequently deny the disorder and may come to professional attention only after conflict with their sexual partners or within the context of the legal system (for example, following harm to others or arrest for a sex offense). More than one paraphilia may occur in a patient. Other mental disorders may be associated with a paraphilia (e.g., sexual dysfunctions or personality disorders). Paraphilias are rarely diagnosed in women, except for sexual masochism (which is reportedly much more common in women than men).

Eight specific paraphilias and one residual category are listed in DSM-III-R (see Table 3-31).

Exhibitionism involves exposing one's genitals to an unsuspecting stranger. There may or may not be masturbation. The stranger is usually not in physical danger and there are no further attempts at sexual activity.

Fetishism involves the use of nonliving objects by themselves, not including only articles of female clothing used in cross-dressing (as in transvestic fetishism, described below) or devices designed for the tactile genital stimulation (e.g., vibrators). The object may at other times be used with a sexual partner.

Fetishism may involve masturbation and should be distinguished from nonpathologic sexual experimentation (in which the object is not persistently preferred or required).

Frotteurism involves touching and rubbing against a nonconsenting person. It is the act of touching that is sexually exciting, not the coercive nature of the act.

These behaviors are usually performed in a public place where it is easy to avoid detection and arrest. Frotteurism is distinguished from normal sexual activity because the person touched is not consenting. Patients with other mental disorders, such as mental retardation or schizophrenia, may touch nonconsenting persons primarily due to poor judgment or deficient social skills.

Pedophilia involves sexual activity with a prepubescent child or children (usually age 13 or younger). The patient must be at least 16 years old and at least 5 years older than the prepubescent child or children. These cutoff ages were arbitrarily chosen. A late adolescent involved in a sexual relationship with a 12- or 13-year-old would not qualify for this diagnosis. The clinician may specify **same sex, opposite sex, same and opposite sex;** if **limited to incest;** and **exclusive type** (attracted only to children) or **nonexclusive type** (attracted to adults as well).

This disorder includes a wide spectrum of possible behaviors, including looking, exposure, masturbating, gentle touching and fondling, and forceful sexual contact. Patients usually rationalize their behavior and may be generous and attentive to the children in other respects (sometimes to prevent them from reporting the sexual activity). Patients frequently have a history of childhood sexual abuse themselves.

In other mental disorders, isolated sexual acts with children may primarily reflect impaired judgment, deficient social skills, or problems with impulse control. Exhibitionism may involve exposure to a child but without further sexual activity. In rare cases, sexual sadism may be associated with pedophilia. An isolated sexual act with a child in response to a time-limited stress does not necessarily warrant the diagnosis of pedophilia.

Sexual masochism involves the real act of being humiliated, beaten, bound, or otherwise made to suffer.

Sexual masochism should be distinguished from normal erotic fantasies that may include masochistic ideas but do not involve acting on the urge or marked distress caused by the ideas. Crossdressing may be present, but the humiliation of cross-dressing must cause the arousal (not the cross-dressing itself, as in transvestic fetishism). Self-defeating personality traits involve the need to be humiliated or disappointed, but are not associated with sexual excitement.

Sexual sadism involves real acts in which psychological or physical suffering (including humiliation) of the victim is sexually exciting to the patient.

Patients typically repeat their behavior until they are arrested. Most people who commit rape or sexual assaults do not suffer from this disorder. Sexual sadism should be distinguished from sadistic acts, which do not involve sexual arousal.

Transvestic fetishism involves heterosexual male cross-dressing. The person must not meet criteria for gender identity disorder of adolescence or adulthood, nontranssexual type, or transsexualism. Transvestic behavior may be occasional or extensive, and associated with masturbation or images of other men being attracted to the patient.

If cross-dressing does not directly cause sexual excitement, another diagnosis or condition may apply (e.g., gender identity disorder of adolescence or adulthood, nontranssexual type; transsexualism; homosexuals wishing to attract other males; female impersonators). The person with transvestic fetishism does not feel his male sex is inappropriate. Sexual masochism may involve the desire to be forced to cross-dress, but the primary purpose is sexual arousal from the humiliation, not from the cross-dressing itself.

Voyeurism involves the act of observing an unsuspecting person who is naked, undressing, or engaging in sexual activity.

The secretive, illegal nature of the behavior is usually especially arousing. Voyeurism should be distinguished from normal sexual activity, in which such observations usually do not involve an unsuspecting partner and occur in preparation for further sexual activity with the person observed. Watching pornography is distinguishable because people know they will be observed.

Paraphilia NOS is a residual category for paraphilias that do not meet criteria for the other specific paraphilias.

Sexual dysfunctions. Sexual dysfunctions are disorders in which there is an inhibition in the appetitive or psychophysiological responses that characterize the four phases of the normal sexual response cycle. The dysfunction must be "persistent or recurrent," but DSM-III-R does not define "persistent or recurrent"; this is left to clinical judgment. The clinician may further specify sexual dysfunctions as **psychogenic only, psychogenic and biogenic** (biogenic only would be coded on Axis III and would not warrant the Axis I diagnosis of a sexual dysfunction), **lifelong or acquired,** and **generalized or situational**.

These disorders may be understood as abnormalities in one of the four phases of the sexual response cycle.

- desire (or appetitive): sexual fantasies and desires
- excitement: sexual pleasure and accompanying physiological changes (males experience penile tumescence, erection, and Cowper's gland secretions; females experience pelvic vasocongestion, vaginal lubrication, external genitalia swelling, narrowing of the outer third of the vagina by increased muscle tension and vasocongestion—known as the orgasmic platform, vasocongestion of the labia minora, breast tumescence, and lengthening and widening of the inner two thirds of the vagina)
- orgasm: peaking of sexual pleasure, release of sexual tension, and rhythmic contraction of the perineal muscles and pelvic reproductive organs, and other muscle tension or contractions, including involuntary pelvic thrusting (males also experience the sensation of inevitable ejaculation followed by contraction of the prostate, seminal vesicles, urethra, and resulting emission of semen; females also experience contractions of the wall of the outer third of the vagina)
- resolution: general and muscular relaxation (males are refractory to further erection and orgasm for a variable period of time; females may be able to respond to further stimulations almost immediately)

Sexual dysfunctions are described for the first three phases; there is no specific disorder for the resolution phase.

The clinician should consider whether organic factors (i.e., physical disorders or medication) completely or partially explain the symptoms. Both physical and psychological factors may be involved (the physical disorder would be recorded on Axis III and the sexual dysfunction on Axis I, specified as both psychogenic and biogenic), but sexual dysfunctions should not be diagnosed if exclusively due to organic causes. Physiological tests (lack of nocturnal penile tumescence during rapid eye movement [REM] sleep, abnormal endocrine studies) and history (symptoms that are chronic, unchanging, and independent of the situation) provide evidence for an organic factor. Further, sexual dysfunctions should not be diagnosed if solely due to another Axis I mental disorder. However, sexual dysfunctions may coexist with another mental disorder or condition; both should then be diagnosed. More than one sexual dysfunction may coexist,

Table 3-32.   Sexual dysfunctions

Sexual desire disorders
  1. Hypoactive sexual desire disorder
  2. Sexual aversion disorder

Sexual arousal disorders
  1. Female sexual arousal disorder
  2. Male erectile disorder

Orgasm disorders
  1. Inhibited female orgasm
  2. Inhibited male orgasm
  3. Premature ejaculation

Sexual pain disorders
  1. Dyspareunia
  2. Vaginismus

Sexual dysfunction NOS

in which case they should all be recorded in order of clinical importance. Finally, the diagnosis of sexual dysfunction involving excitement or orgasm should not be made if the sexual stimulation is inadequate.

There are four subheadings (each incorporating additional specific disorders) and a residual category for sexual dysfunctions (see Table 3-32).

Sexual desire disorders involve abnormalities in the desire (appetitive) phase of the sexual response cycle.

Hypoactive sexual desire disorder involves persistent or recurrent deficiency or absence of sexual fantasies and desire for sexual activity (taking into account all relevant factors affecting sexual functioning). The disturbance must not occur exclusively during the course of another Axis I disorder other than another sexual dysfunction.

Sexual aversion disorder involves persistent or recurrent extreme aversion to, and avoidance of, all or almost all genital sexual contact with a sexual partner. The disturbance must not occur exclusively during the course of another Axis I disorder other than a sexual dysfunction.

Sexual arousal disorders involve abnormalities in the excitement phase of the sexual response cycle.

Female sexual arousal disorder involves persistent or recurrent partial or complete failure to attain or maintain the lubrication-swelling response of sexual excitement until completion of the sexual activity, or persistent or recurrent lack of a subjective sense of sexual excitement and pleasure during sexual activity. The disturbance must not occur exclusively during the course of another Axis I disorder other than a sexual dysfunction.

Male erectile disorder involves a persistent or recurrent partial or complete failure to attain or maintain erection until completion of the sexual activity, or a persistent or recurrent lack of a subjective sense of sexual excitement and pleasure during sexual activity. The disturbance must not occur exclusively during the course of another Axis I disorder other than a sexual dysfunction.

Orgasm disorders involve abnormalities in the orgasm phase of the sexual response cycle.

Inhibited female orgasm involves persistent or recurrent delay in, or absence of, orgasm following a normal sexual excitement phase during sexual activity that the clinician judges to be adequate in focus, intensity, and duration. (Note that some females are normally able to experience orgasm during coitus; others normally require manual clitoral stimulation.) The disturbance must not occur exclusively during the course of another Axis I disorder other than a sexual dysfunction.

Inhibited male orgasm involves persistent or recurrent delay in, or absence of, orgasm following a normal sexual excitement phase during sexual activity that the clinician judges to be adequate in focus, intensity, and duration. Usually, the patient can achieve orgasm with masturbation but is unable to achieve orgasm in the vagina. The disturbance must not occur exclusively during the course of another Axis I disorder other than a sexual dysfunction.

Premature ejaculation involves persistent or recurrent ejaculation with minimal sexual stimulation, or ejaculation before, upon, or shortly after penetration and before the person wishes the ejaculation to occur. In making this diagnosis, the clinician must consider factors that affect the duration of the excitement phase (e.g., patient's age, novelty of the sexual partner or situation, frequency of sexual activity).

Sexual pain disorders involve pain rather than an abnormality in a specific phase of the sexual response cycle.

Dyspareunia involves recurrent or persistent genital pain in either a male or a female before, during, or after sexual intercourse. The disturbance must not be caused exclusively by a lack of lubrication or by vaginismus.

Vaginismus involves recurrent or persistent involuntary spasm of the musculature of the outer third of the vagina that interferes with coitus. The disturbance must not be caused exclusively by a physical disorder or by another Axis I disorder.

Sexual dysfunction NOS is a residual category for sexual dysfunctions that do not meet the criteria for the other specific sexual dysfunctions.

Other sexual disorders. *Sexual disorder NOS* is a residual category for sexual disorders that cannot be classified as either a paraphilia or a sexual dysfunction. Patients who may have been diagnosed under "ego-dystonic homosexuality" in DSM-III (a category eliminated in DSM-III-R) may be diagnosed under this category. The diagnostic implications of homosexuality, however, still remain controversial.

Sleep Disorders

Sleep disorders are a new official category (previously an appendix to DSM-III). Clinical experience and research with this category remain somewhat limited.

There are several important clinical considerations when applying these diagnoses. First, the sleep disturbance must exist for more than 1 month. Briefer sleep disturbances are excluded. Second, the sleep disturbance must be the predominant complaint. Sleep disturbance may accompany other mental and physical disorders, but may not qualify as a sleep disorder if not the predominant complaint. Third, the clinician should note that certain disorders with primary sleep disturbances are not listed here. For example, certain physical disorders associated with primary sleep disturbances, such as sleep apnea and narcolepsy, are not separately listed in this scheme (although they may be considered within a subcategory, such as hypersomnias related to a known organic factor, where the physical disorder is recorded on Axis III). Nocturnal enuresis is also not listed here (although consistent with the definition of a parasomnia, this disorder is included under disorders usually first evident in infancy, childhood, and adolescence as functional enuresis). Fourth, sleep recording data are not included in sleep disorder criteria, although such data may be clinically and diagnostically useful. Finally, certain terms take on specific meanings in this category: "daytime" refers to the major period of wakefulness (which may be at night, for example, in people who work night shifts); "primary" (in primary insomnia and primary hypersomnia) refers to the lack of known relationship to a physical or mental condition, not to whether the sleep disorder occurred first or is more important than another disorder.

Table 3-33. Sleep disorders

Dyssomnias
1. Insomnia disorder
   a. Related to another mental disorder (nonorganic)
   b. Related to a known organic factor
   c. Primary insomnia
2. Hypersomnia disorder
   a. Related to another mental disorder (nonorganic)
   b. Related to a known organic factor
   c. Primary hypersomnia
3. Sleep-wake schedule disorder (specify type)
4. Other dyssomnias: dyssomnia NOS

Parasomnias
1. Dream anxiety disorder (nightmare disorder)
2. Sleep terror disorder
3. Sleepwalking disorder
4. Parasomnia NOS

There are two subheadings (each incorporating additional specific disorders) for sleep disorders: dyssomnias and parasomnias (see Table 3-33).

Dyssomnias. Dyssomnias involve disturbances in the amount, quality, and timing of sleep. There are three dyssomnias and one residual category.

Insomnia disorders require difficulty in initiating or maintaining sleep, or nonrestorative sleep (apparently adequate sleep that nevertheless results in feeling unrested). This disturbance must occur at least 3 times a week for at least 1 month and must be sufficiently severe to result in significant daytime fatigue or symptoms (as observed by others) attributable to the sleep disturbance (e.g., irritability or impaired daytime functioning). The disturbance must not occur exclusively during the course of a sleep-wake schedule disorder or a parasomnia.

Although insomnia may accompany many mental and physical disorders, the additional diagnosis of insomnia disorder should be made only if this sleep disturbance is the predominant complaint. Because sleep patterns vary, the clinician should assess what constitutes "normal" sleep for the person being evaluated. Some people normally require little sleep. Sleep patterns may also normally change with age (the elderly typically require less sleep).

There are three further subcategories of insomnia disorders.

Insomnia related to another mental disorder involves another Axis I or Axis II mental disorder but should not be used if the other

Axis I mental disorder involves a known organic factor (e.g., psychoactive substance use disorders).

Insomnia related to a known organic factor involves a known organic factor (e.g., physical disorder, psychoactive substance use disorder, or medications). The physical disorder or medication should be listed on Axis III. Psychoactive substance use disorder should be listed on Axis I.

Primary insomnia involves insomnia that is not apparently maintained by any other mental disorder or known organic factor.

Hypersomnia disorders require either excessive daytime sleepiness (tendency to fall asleep easily and quickly) or sleep attacks (discrete periods of sudden or irresistible sleep) not accounted for by an inadequate amount of sleep or by "sleep drunkenness" (a prolonged transition to the fully awake state on awakening). This disturbance must occur nearly every day for at least 1 month or episodically for longer periods of time. The disturbance must be sufficiently severe to result in impaired occupational or social functioning. The disturbance must not occur exclusively during the course of a sleep-wake schedule disorder.

Although hypersomnia may be associated with physical or other mental disorders, the additional diagnosis of hypersomnia should be made only if this sleep disturbance is the predominant complaint. Hypersomnia may occur daily (e.g., in sleep apnea or narcolepsy) or episodically (e.g., in Kleine-Levin's syndrome). Seizures may mimic sleep attacks but usually include additional characteristic motor movements.

As in insomnia disorders, there are three subcategories of hypersomnia disorders.

Hypersomnia related to another mental disorder (nonorganic) involves another Axis I or Axis II mental disorder.

Hypersomnia related to a known organic factor involves a known organic factor (e.g., physical disorder, psychoactive substance use disorder, or medications). The physical disorder or medication should be listed on Axis III. Psychoactive substance use disorder should be listed on Axis I. Among disorders that may be diagnosed under this heading are sleep apnea, narcolepsy, and sleep-related myoclonus. Narcolepsy may be associated with cataplexy (an episodic loss of muscle tone triggered by strong emotions, sometimes resulting in falls); hypnagogic hallucinations (as one falls asleep) or hypnopompic hallucinations (as one wakes from sleep); and sleep paralysis (inability to move while falling asleep or upon suddenly waking up). Obstructive sleep apnea may be associated with obesity, systemic and pulmonary hypertension, cardiac arrhythmias, and other symptoms (more rarely including impotence and headaches). Hypersomnia periods in Kleine-Levin's syndrome may be associated with increased eating and increased sex drive.

Primary hypersomnia involves hypersomnia that is not apparently maintained by any other mental disorder or known organic factor.

Sleep-wake schedule disorder requires a mismatch between the sleep-wake schedule demanded by the person's environment and the person's normal circadian sleep-wake pattern, resulting in a complaint of either insomnia or hypersomnia (as defined above).

Although sleep-wake schedule disturbances may accompany other mental and physical disorders, the additional diagnosis of sleep-wake schedule disorder should be made only if this sleep disturbance is the predominant complaint. Note also that a depressive syndrome may involve a sleep-wake schedule disturbance (e.g., early morning awakening), but additional symptoms of depression would be present. The diagnosis of sleep-wake schedule disorder applies only if the sleep disturbance would persist after removal of the external factor, such as an environmental demand or medication, and only if the insomnia or hypersomnia is sufficiently frequent and severe to meet the criteria for insomnia disorder or hypersomnia disorder. History may reveal the source of the sleep-wake schedule mismatch, such as rapid travel between time zones, changing work shifts, or an erratic social schedule. Early in the course of this condition, the insomnia or hypersomnia improves if the person is able to follow his or her own sleep-wake schedule for a sufficient period of time.

The clinician may further specify **type** of sleep-wake schedule disorder. In **advanced or delayed type**, the beginning and end of sleep are considerably advanced (patient awakens earlier and goes to sleep earlier) or delayed (patient awakens later and goes to sleep later) compared to what the patient desires. In **disorganized type**, there is no daily period of major sleep because of disorganized and variable sleep and waking times. In **frequently changing type**, sleep-wake schedule disturbance is the result of frequent changes in sleep and waking times.

Dyssomnia NOS is a residual category for insomnias, hypersomnias, or sleep-wake schedule disturbances that cannot be classified as one of the other dyssomnias.

Parasomnias. Parasomnias involve an abnormal event occurring during sleep or at the threshold between sleep and wakefulness. There are three parasomnias and one residual category.

Dream anxiety disorder (nightmare disorder) requires repeated awakenings (usually occurring during the second half of the sleep period) from major sleep periods or naps, with detailed recall of extended and extremely frightening dreams (usually involving threats to survival, security, or self-esteem). The person must rapidly become oriented and alert upon awakening from the dream (unlike the confusion and disorientation seen in sleep terror disorder and some forms of epilepsy). The dream or resulting sleep disturbance must cause significant distress. Finally, this diagnosis requires that it cannot be established that an organic factor initiated or maintains the disturbance.

Clinically, episodes of dream anxiety may best be understood by their association with REM sleep. Because of this association, dream anxiety is more likely to occur later in sleep (when REM sleep is more abundant), without body movements or much autonomic activity (due to loss of muscle tone associated with REM sleep) and with vivid dream recall (dreams are associated with REM sleep). Sleep terror disorder (described below), on the other hand, is not associated with REM sleep and therefore occurs more often in the first third of sleep, accompanied by body movement and autonomic discharge, and usually without vivid dream recall. Dream anxiety disorder should not be diagnosed when nightmares are due to organic factors, such as medications or drugs (as may especially occur with REM rebound following withdrawal from REM-suppressant substances). Nightmares apparently due to organic factors may be classified under the residual category "parasomnia NOS."

Sleep terror disorder requires recurrent episodes of abrupt awakening from sleep, lasting from 1 to 10 minutes. The episodes usually occur during the first third of the major sleep period; begin with a panicky scream; and include intense anxiety (the person may look frightened), signs of autonomic arousal (e.g., tachycardia, rapid breathing, profuse perspiration, dilated pupils, piloerection), and several minutes of confusion, disorientation, and perseverative motor movements, but they do not include detailed dream recall. Efforts to comfort the person are unsuccessful. The diagnosis requires that it cannot be established that an organic factor initiated and maintains the disturbance. Another name for this disorder is "pavor nocturnus."

Clinically, episodes of sleep terror disorder may best be understood by their association with non-REM sleep, which usually involves EEG delta waves and stages 3 and 4 of sleep. Because of this association, sleep terror disorder is more likely to occur during the first third of the major sleep period (when non-REM sleep is more abundant). This contrasts with dream anxiety disorder (described above), which is associated with REM sleep. Sleep terror should also be distinguished from hypnogogic hallucinations (which may be associated with anxiety) and seizures during sleep (a sleep EEG may be needed to diagnose seizures). Sleep terror disorder usually begins in childhood but is not consistently associated with other mental disorders in children. Adult onset, however, may be associated with other disorders, such as an anxiety disorder. Usually, the person does not recall the episode of sleep terror the following morning.

Sleepwalking disorder requires repeated episodes of sleepwalking, a sequence of complex behaviors that includes arising from bed during sleep and walking about (and may include semipurposeful acts). The episode usually occurs during the first third of the major sleep period. During an episode of sleepwalking, the person usually has a blank, staring face, is relatively unresponsive to others, and can be awakened only with great difficulty. Upon awakening from a sleepwalking episode or the next morning, the person does not recall the episode. If awakened from sleepwalking, the person may experience an initial short period of confusion or disorientation, but within minutes there is no impairment of mental activity or behavior. Sleepwalking disorder should be diagnosed only if it cannot be established that an organic factor initiated and maintains the disturbance.

Clinically, sleepwalking is associated with non-REM sleep, which usually involves EEG delta waves and stages 3 and 4 of sleep and therefore shares characteristics previously described for sleep terror disorder. Sleepwalking disorder usually begins in childhood, disappears by adulthood, and is not consistently associated with other mental disorders in children (except perhaps other non-REM sleep disorders such as sleep terror disorder). Adult onset, however, may be associated with other disorders, such as personality disorders. Sleepwalking disorder should be distinguished from several other disorders. In a seizure disorder, the patient is usually unresponsive to the environment, demonstrates characteristic motor movements, does not return to bed, and shows similar behavior while awake; a sleep EEG may be needed to diagnose seizures. Psychogenic fugue is rare in children, typically begins when the person is awake, lasts longer (hours or days), does not involve a disturbance of consciousness, and is associated with other psychopathology. "Sleep drunkenness" is a prolonged transition to the fully awake state that occurs after awakening and is often associated with depression. Episodes of sleepwalking usually last from minutes to about a half hour, and may be hazardous.

Parasomnia NOS is a residual category reserved for sleep disturbances that do not meet criteria for another specific parasomnia.

Factitious Disorders

Factitious disorders require physical or psychological symptoms that are intentionally produced or feigned (i.e., they are factitious or "not real") to enable a person to assume the sick role. Although the diagnosis seems straightforward, it may be difficult to determine if symptoms are produced "intentionally." The clinician must first determine that behavior is voluntary—not always easy in these patients. Further, while such behavior may appear to be under voluntary control, especially if designed to avoid detection, it also reflects involuntary or unconscious motives, especially since these behaviors frequently seem compulsive and result in primary gain (attaining the sick role). For this diagnosis, behaviors are considered "intentional" when they appear deliberate, purposeful, or voluntary to an outside observer, even though they may result from unconscious motivations and serve apparently unintentional goals.

Factitious disorders require excluding "real" organic causes of the symptoms or behavior, but factitious disorders may also coexist with true organically based symptoms. Further, factitious disorders should be distinguished from malingering, although this distinction may be difficult to make. Both involve "intentional" production of symptoms, but they differ in the patient's purpose. In malingering (considered a V Code, described later), the purpose is to achieve secondary gain, an obvious and recognizable gain, support, or some other advantage from the environment (e.g., avoiding a legal responsibility or manipulating a transfer to another facility). In factitious disorders, the purpose is to achieve primary gain, a solution to an underlying psychological conflict or need (i.e., achieving the sick role itself, as when symptoms require continued hospitalization). Factitious disorders imply psychopathology, which may include severe personality disturbances or psychoactive substance use disorders.

There are two forms of factitious disorders and one residual category (see Table 3-34).

Factitious disorder with physical symptoms requires the intentional production or feigning of physical symptoms, but not psychological symptoms. The patient must demonstrate a psychological need to assume the sick role, with an absence of external incentive

Table 3-34.   Factitious disorders

1. Factitious disorder with physical symptoms
2. Factitious disorder with psychological symptoms
3. Factitious disorder NOS

for the behavior (as in malingering) such as economic gain, better care, or physical well-being. This diagnosis should not be made if the symptoms occur exclusively during the course of another Axis I disorder.

Symptoms may be made up, the result of self-injury, or an exaggeration or exacerbation of a physical condition. Münchausen's syndrome is a chronic form of this disorder, characterized by multiple dramatic but vague descriptions of symptoms, multiple hospitalizations and procedures (many surgeries may result in "gridiron abdomen"), extensive medical knowledge, the dominance of medical contacts and hospitals in the person's life, "pseudologia fantastica" (a tendency to tell dramatic but implausible lies about oneself), and social isolation. Once admitted, these patients become demanding and noncompliant, deny fabricating symptoms when confronted, usually sign out of the hospital even if against medical advice, and may travel extensively seeking rehospitalizations.

In particular, this disorder should be distinguished from true physical illness, malingering (symptoms are intentionally produced, but for secondary gain), and somatoform disorders (symptoms are not due to a true physical disorder, but are not intentional).

Factitious disorder with psychological symptoms requires the intentional production or feigning of psychological symptoms, but not physical symptoms. The person must demonstrate a psychological need to assume the sick role, with an absence of external incentive for the behavior (as in malingering) such as economic gain, better care, or physical well-being. This diagnosis should not be made if the symptoms occur exclusively during the course of another Axis I disorder.

In particular, this disorder should be distinguished from a true mental disorder and from malingering (symptoms are intentionally produced, but for secondary gain). Several clinical observations may suggest a factitious disorder rather than a true mental disorder. The patient may seem to "acquire" symptoms based on the examiner's suggestions. Symptoms may not be consistent with the usual known presentation of a mental disorder (even though consistent with the patient's notion of the mental disorder). Symptoms may appear to

Table 3-35.   Impulse control disorders not elsewhere classified

1. Intermittent explosive disorder
2. Kleptomania
3. Pathological gambling
4. Pyromania
5. Trichotillomania
6. Impulse control disorder NOS

worsen when the patient believes he or she is being observed. Some patients demonstrate "vorbeierden," giving approximate answers or talking past the point, but this may also occur in other disorders. Patients may or may not be uncooperative when questioned. Inconsistent history by other informants, projective psychological testing (bypassing defenses), and mental status examination may help identify this disorder (for example, cognitive testing may demonstrate nearly correct answers rather than the gross deficits one would more commonly expect in an organic mental syndrome or disorder).

Factitious disorder NOS is a residual category for factitious disorders that cannot be classified as one of the other specific categories, such as a factitious disorder in which the patient feigns both physical and psychological symptoms.

Impulse Control Disorders Not Elsewhere Classified

This major heading is itself a residual category for impulse control disorders that do not fall within any other DSM-III-R category. Three criteria must be met: 1) failure to resist an impulse, drive, or temptation to perform a harmful act (whether or not consciously resisted or planned); 2) increased tension or arousal before committing the act; and 3) at least at first, pleasure, gratification, or release upon committing the act (regret, self-reproach, or guilt may or may not follow later).

Under this heading there are five disorders and one residual category (see Table 3-35).

Intermittent explosive disorder involves several discreet episodes of loss of control over aggressive impulses, resulting in serious assaultive acts or property destruction. The aggressiveness must be grossly out of proportion to the stressors. Between episodes, there must be no signs of generalized impulsiveness or aggressiveness. Finally, the diagnosis requires that the episode not occur during the course of several other disorders that may also be associated with loss of control (e.g., a psychotic disorder, organic personality syndrome, antisocial or borderline personality disorder, conduct disorder, or intoxication with a psychoactive substance).

The validity of this disorder is unclear; clinicians should consider whether these patients may actually suffer from another mental disorder.

Kleptomania involves recurrent failure to resist impulses to steal objects not needed for personal use or for their monetary value (as would be the case in ordinary stealing). There must be increased tension immediately before the theft, and pleasure or relief when committing the theft. The theft must not be committed in order to express anger or vengeance. Finally, the diagnosis requires that the stealing must not be due to a conduct disorder or antisocial personality disorder (or other disorders that may be associated with stealing, but in which stealing is not the primary problem).

Pathological gambling involves maladaptive gambling behavior and requires at least four of nine possible findings (detailed in DSM-III-R). In brief, the findings provide evidence for a chronic and progressive inability to resist an impulse to gamble, resulting in social and/or occupational dysfunction. This diagnosis must be distinguished from social gambling and gambling behavior associated with a manic or hypomanic episode.

Pyromania involves more than one episode of deliberate and purposeful fire setting. There must be tension or affective arousal before the fire-setting act, and pleasure, satisfaction, or relief when committing the act (or when observing or participating in the results of the act). There must also be fascination, interest, curiosity, or attraction to fire and associated contexts or characteristics (e.g., paraphernalia, uses, consequences, or exposure to fire). Finally, the diagnosis requires that the fire setting must not be done for the purpose of monetary gain, to express a sociopolitical ideology, to conceal criminal activity, to express anger or vengeance, to improve living circumstances, or in response to delusions or hallucinations.

Clinically, fire setting due to pyromania should be distinguished from accidental fire setting, age-appropriate experimentation by children, intentional fire setting for a specific purpose, (e.g., for profit or retaliation), or fire setting that is a consequence of another mental disorder (e.g., response to delusions or hallucinations in a psychotic disorder, or out of confusion in an organic mental syndrome or disorder).

Trichotillomania involves recurrent failure to resist impulses to pull out one's own hair. Noticeable hair loss results. There must be increased tension immediately before pulling out the hair, and gratification or relief when performing the act. The diagnosis requires that the hair pulling be neither associated with a preexisting inflammation of the skin nor in response to a delusion or hallucination.

Trichotillomania should be distinguished from normal hair stroking and alopecia (i.e., hair loss) and should be recorded on Axis III.

Impulse control disorder NOS is a residual category for impulse control disorders that do not meet criteria for other specific impulse control disorders.

Adjustment Disorder

Adjustment disorder requires a maladaptive reaction to an identifiable psychosocial stressor or stressors. There are additional time requirements: the reaction must occur within 3 months of the onset of the stressor, and the reaction must persist no longer than 6 months. The maladaptive reaction must involve impaired occupational or social functioning, or symptoms in excess of what would be considered normal or expected. This diagnosis should be made only if the disturbance is not one instance of a pattern of overreaction to stress or an exacerbation of another DSM-III-R mental disorder (e.g., exacerbation of a personality disorder under stress, although adjustment disorder may also apply if there are new symptoms), or if the disturbance meets criteria for any specific mental disorder or uncomplicated bereavement. The stressor and severity of the stressor should be recorded on Axis IV.

Clinically, adjustment disorder is a kind of intermediate diagnosis that introduces flexibility into DSM-III-R. This diagnosis may apply to certain patients who do not meet full criteria for another mental disorder, provided there is a maladaptive reaction to stress within the defined time parameters. Virtually any stressor may qualify, and the severity of the disturbance may be related to the severity of the stressor. DSM-III-R added the 6-month limit to exclude chronic cases; a longer duration for the disturbance requires a different diagnosis. The diagnosis of adjustment disorder implies that the disturbance will end after the stressor ends, or that the patient will achieve a new level of adaptation if the stressor continues. Adjustment disorders should be distinguished from other mental disorders, which may preempt the diagnosis of adjustment disorder, and from V Codes (described later under V Codes for Conditions Not Attributable to a Mental Disorder that Are a Focus of Attention or

Table 3-36. Types of adjustment disorders

Adjustment disorder with
1. Anxious mood
2. Depressed mood
3. Disturbance of conduct
4. Mixed disturbance of emotions and conduct
5. Mixed emotional features
6. Physical complaints
7. Withdrawal
8. Work (or academic) inhibition

Adjustment disorder NOS

Treatment), in which the patient lacks sufficiently impaired occupational or social functioning or sufficiently severe symptoms.

There are eight types of adjustment disorder and one residual category, based on which symptoms predominate (see Table 3-36).

Types of adjustment disorders. *Adjustment disorder with anxious mood* is predominantly characterized by symptoms of anxious mood.

Adjustment disorder with depressed mood is primarily characterized by depressive symptoms.

Adjustment disorder with disturbance of conduct is predominantly characterized by conduct disturbances, involving the violation of others' rights or of societal norms and rules.

Adjustment disorder with mixed disturbance of emotions and conduct is predominantly characterized by both emotional symptoms and conduct disturbances.

Adjustment disorder with mixed emotional features is predominantly characterized by a combination of emotional symptoms (e.g., depression, anxiety, or other emotions).

Adjustment disorder with physical complaints is predominantly characterized by physical symptoms that would not be diagnosed as physical disorders or conditions on Axis III. DSM-III-R introduced this type to the adjustment disorder category because somatoform disorders require that symptoms persist for at least 6 months. A similar case in which symptoms lasted less than 6 months would not qualify for somatoform disorder, but may quality for this type of adjustment disorder.

Adjustment disorder with withdrawal is predominantly characterized by social withdrawal, without significant depressive or anxiety symptoms.

Adjustment disorder with work (or academic) inhibition is predominantly characterized by impaired work or academic functioning (when previous performance in these areas was adequate).

Adjustment disorder NOS is a residual category for an adjustment disorder that cannot be classified as one of the other specific types.

Psychological Factors Affecting Physical Condition

This diagnosis requires that psychologically meaningful environmental stimuli be temporally related to the initiation or exacerbation of a specific physical condition or disorder. The physical condition or disorder, recorded on Axis III, must involve organic pathology or a known pathophysiologic process. This diagnosis requires that the condition not meet criteria for a somatoform disorder (which requires symptoms without organic findings or known physiologic mechanisms and with an implied psychological cause).

Clinically, psychological factors are thought to contribute toward initiating, exacerbating, or maintaining a true physical condition in these patients. The timing of events supports the inference. This category may apply to any physical condition or disorder, including previously designated "psychosomatic" or "psychophysiological" disorders.

Psychological factors affecting physical condition is the diagnosis itself; no further disorders are listed under this heading.

This category represents one attempt in DSM-III-R to bridge the gap between medicine and psychiatry. Critics may argue that this category does not adequately reflect a comprehensive biopsychosocial approach to patients, the history of psychosomatic medicine, or advances at the interface between medicine and psychiatry. From the biopsychosocial perspective, the implied dichotomy between psychological and physical conditions is misleading. Psychological factors arguably affect almost all physical conditions. According to the biopsychosocial approach, psychological, biological, and social factors constantly interact, although one or another factor may predominate in a particular situation. If there is a category for "psychological" factors affecting "physical" conditions, why not also include a category for each possible interaction of the three factors (i.e., physical factors affecting psychological conditions, social factors affecting psychological conditions, and so on)? Further, the history of psychosomatic medicine and advances in psychoimmunology and neuroendocrinology suggests complex relationships between a patient's psychological state and medical condition that are not reflected in this formal DSM-III-R classification.

Personality Disorders

Personality disorders require that characteristic behaviors or traits be pervasive, begin by early adulthood, and be present in a variety of contexts. Each personality disorder consists of a list of between 7 and 10 items and requires the presence of a specific number of between 4 and 6 items for the diagnosis. Other requirements or exclusion criteria apply to certain specific personality disorders. A personality disorder should not be diagnosed if the presentation is limited to a brief time or to a discrete episode of a mental disorder.

Personality disorders are recorded on Axis II. More than one personality disorder may be diagnosed in a patient if criteria are met for each. An Axis I mental illness may be superimposed on the Axis II personality disorder. If an Axis I psychotic disorder is superimposed on a preexisting premorbid personality disorder, the word "premorbid" may be recorded after the personality disorder on Axis II. Prominent personality traits and defense mechanisms may also be listed on Axis II, but these would not receive a DSM-III-R code number (the clinician may record an "additional code" such as no diagnosis or diagnosis deferred on Axis II, as described later).

The concepts of personality, personality traits, and personality disorder should be distinguished. "Personality" refers to long-standing, deeply ingrained patterns of behavior, including ways of relating to, perceiving, and thinking about the environment (including other people) and self. "Personality traits" are relatively stable patterns of relating to, perceiving, and thinking about the environment (including other people) and oneself, exhibited over a wide range of social and personal situations. Personality traits refer to important aspects of one's personality but alone do not imply psychopathology. Clinicians should recall that personality traits may be recorded on Axis II. "Personality disorder" implies rigid, maladaptive personality traits that result in significant functional impairment or subjective distress.

Personality disorders may apply to children and adolescents, but there are certain limitations, particularly with regard to three personality disorders that correspond to three disorders listed under "disorders usually first evident in infancy, childhood, and adolescence." Antisocial personality disorder corresponds to conduct disorder, but antisocial personality disorder should not be diagnosed in a person under age 18. (Note, however, that conduct disorder may be diagnosed in an adult over age 18 if full criteria for antisocial personality disorder are not met.) Avoidant personality disorder corresponds to avoidant disorder of childhood or adolescence, and borderline personality disorder corresponds to identity disorder; these personality disorders may be diagnosed in a child or adolescent who meets criteria for the personality disorder if the disturbance seems pervasive, persistent, and not limited to a developmental stage. Any of the other personality disorders may apply to children or adolescents, although the characteristic traits will rarely appear sufficiently stable to warrant such diagnoses.

Personality disorders, quite useful clinically, are nevertheless a controversial category in DSM-III-R. A great deal remains to be learned about personality and personality disorders.

From the theoretical perspective, DSM-III-R uses a modified "categorical" classification system for personality disorders, in which specific criteria are provided for specific diagnostic categories. In a classical categorical model, not used in DSM-III-R, each category would be homogeneous and all categories would be mutually exclusive. A classical categorical model is too rigid when the boundaries between disorders are not distinct (as in personality disorders); some patients may not be described under any specific category, whereas others may be described by more than one specific category. DSM-III-R, however, permits two or more personality disorders to coexist. Further, all members of a diagnostic category need not be homogeneous; they need only meet a certain number out of a list of items. DSM-III-R personality disorders also apply a "prototypal" model in which there is an implied "ideal" person, the prototype, who perfectly suits each category. One alternative model, not used in DSM-III-R, is a "dimensional" classification system, in which people would be numerically rated along a spectrum for each of several personality traits or dimensions.

In the categorical approach, DSM-III-R uses a "polythetic" system rather than a "monothetic" system. In a monothetic system, all items on a criteria list are required. Monothetic categories may be overrigid and restrictive, but they provide sharply defined boundaries and homogeneous characteristics for each diagnosis. In a polythetic system, a specified number of items on a criteria list are required. Polythetic categories allow more flexibility, but also introduce more variability. In DSM-III-R, all personality disorders are polythetic.[13]

The current personality disorder diagnoses may be criticized for

Table 3-37. Personality disorders (coded on Axis II)

Cluster A (odd or eccentric)
1. Paranoid
2. Schizoid
3. Schizotypal

Cluster B (dramatic, emotional, or erratic)
4. Antisocial
5. Borderline
6. Histrionic
7. Narcissistic

Cluster C (anxious or fearful)
8. Avoidant
9. Dependent
10. Obsessive compulsive
11. Passive aggressive

Other
12. Personality disorder NOS

apparent inconsistencies and arbitrary distinctions lacking empirical support, and for the fact that no attempt is made to weigh different items. Some argue that there are too few categories or that categories are too narrowly defined, thereby failing to provide diagnoses for certain patients. Others argue that there are too many categories or that categories are too broadly defined, thereby creating overlap and loss of diagnostic specificity. More fundamentally, the problems in this area reflect our lack of understanding of personality and personality disorders.

There are 11 personality disorders and one residual category. The 11 personality disorders are grouped into three clusters: Cluster A includes those disorders in which people appear odd or eccentric; Cluster B includes those disorders in which people appear dramatic, emotional, or erratic; Cluster C includes those disorders in which people appear anxious or fearful (see Table 3-37).

Although each personality disorder will be briefly summarized, the clinician should refer to DSM-III-R itself for the exact criteria and a more thorough discussion. The pattern for each personality disorder must begin in early adulthood and present in a variety of contexts, as indicated by a specified number of items from a list provided for each disorder.

Paranoid personality disorder. This disorder involves a pervasive and unwarranted tendency to interpret the actions of people as deliberately demeaning or threatening. This diagnosis requires at least four of seven items: 1) unjustified expectation of being exploited or harmed, 2) questioning others' loyalty or trustworthiness, 3) reading threatening meanings into benign remarks or events, 4) bearing grudges or being unforgiving, 5) being reluctant to confide in others for fear that information will be used against oneself, 6) being easily slighted and quick to react with anger or to counterattack, and 7) questioning the fidelity of a spouse or sexual partner without justification. This disturbance must not occur exclusively during the course of schizophrenia or a delusional disorder (which involves persistent psychotic symptoms such as hallucinations or delusions).

Schizoid personality disorder. This disorder involves a pervasive pattern of indifference to social relationships and a restricted range of emotional experience and expression. This diagnosis requires at least four of seven items: 1) not desiring or enjoying close relationships, including family; 2) almost always choosing solitary activities; 3) rarely claiming or appearing to experience strong emotions; 4) indicating little desire to have sexual experiences with another person; 5) indifference to the praise and criticism of others; 6) having only one or no close friends or confidants other than first-degree relatives; and 7) constricted affect. This disturbance must not occur exclusively during the course of schizophrenia or a delusional disorder.

Schizoid personality disorder should be distinguished from other similar personality disorders. Schizotypal personality disorder, for example, involves characteristic eccentricities of communication or behavior. Unlike the DSM-III definition, the current definition of schizoid personality disorder no longer requires excluding schizotypal personality disorder. Both diagnoses may apply. Note also that DSM-III-R eliminated the category of schizoid disorder of childhood; schizoid personality disorder may now be used for children. Avoidant personality disorder may also involve social isolation; patients with avoidant personality disorder, however, desire to enter into social relationships but are isolated because they fear rejection or criticism. In paranoid personality disorder, paranoid ideation is the prominent feature.

Schizotypal personality disorder. This disorder involves a pervasive pattern of deficits in interpersonal relatedness and peculiarities of ideation, appearance, and behavior. This diagnosis requires at least five of nine items: 1) ideas of reference, excluding delusions of reference; 2) excessive social anxiety; 3) odd beliefs or magical thinking that influences behavior and is inconsistent with subcultural norms; 4) unusual perceptual experiences; 5) odd or eccentric behavior or appearance; 6) only one or no close friends or confidants other than first-degree relatives; 7) odd speech without loosening of associations or incoherence; 8) inappropriate or constricted affect; and 9) suspiciousness or paranoid ideation. This disturbance must not occur exclusively during the course of schizophrenia or a pervasive developmental disorder.

Compared to other Axis II psychotic disorders, psychotic symptoms in schizotypal personality are less severe and more transient. Avoidant personality disorder does not involve the oddities of behavior, thinking, perception, and speech expected in schizotypal personality disorder. Paranoid personality disorder may include suspiciousness and paranoid ideation, but not the other listed oddities of thought or behavior. The relationship between schizotypal personality disorder and schizophrenia requires further study.

Antisocial personality disorder. This disorder involves a pattern of irresponsible and antisocial behavior. The person must be at least age 18. There must be evidence that a conduct disorder began before age 15, based on a history of at least 3 of 12 items: 1) frequent truancy, 2) running away from home, 3) initiating physical fights, 4) using a weapon in fights, 5) forcing another into sexual activity, 6) physical cruelty to animals, 7) physical cruelty to other people, 8) deliberately destroying property, 9) deliberately setting fires, 10) lying, 11) stealing that does not involve confronting a victim, and 12) stealing that does involve confronting a victim. Further, at least 4 of 10 items must currently be present: 1) inability to sustain consistent work or academic behavior, as shown by significant unemployment, absences, or abandonment of jobs when able to work; 2) failure to conform to social norms and laws; 3) irritability and aggressiveness indicated by repeated physical fights or assaults; 4) repeated failure to honor financial obligations; 5) impulsivity and failure to plan ahead as indicated by travel without goals and/or having no regular address for a month or more; 6) disregard for the truth, as shown by lying, using aliases, or "conning" others for profit or pleasure; 7) recklessness regarding safety such as driving while intoxicated or speeding; 8) irresponsibility as a parent; 9) inability to sustain a monogamous relationship for more than 1 year; and 10) lack of remorse for harming, mistreating, or stealing from others.[14] This disturbance must not occur exclusively during the course of schizophrenia or manic episodes.

Note that the diagnosis of antisocial personality disorder is never made in a person under age 18, primarily because a conduct disorder in a child does not provide evidence for a sufficiently stable pattern of behavior to diagnose a personality disorder (the conduct disorder behavior may remit completely or evolve into another mental disorder). Antisocial personality disorder should also be distinguished from adult antisocial behavior (a V Code, described later, in which antisocial behavior does not meet full criteria for the antisocial personality disorder). Antisocial personality disorder may coexist with other mental disorders, including psychoactive substance abuse, but the additional diagnosis of antisocial personality disorder requires meeting the full criteria as described above (including the history of conduct disorder behavior beginning before age 15 and continuing into adulthood).

Antisocial personality disorder is probably the best-studied and most reliable of all DSM-III-R personality disorders, but may be criticized as being narrowly defined and somewhat tautological: people with antisocial personality disorder are people who exhibit a sufficient number of antisocial behaviors. Although the definition may be reliable (i.e., consistently applied), the clinical significance in so defining this group of people, beyond identifying a population exhibiting socially deviant behavior, is less clear.

Borderline personality disorder. This disorder involves a pervasive pattern of unstable mood, unstable interpersonal relationships, and unstable self-image. This diagnosis requires at least five of eight items: 1) a pattern of unstable and intense interpersonal relationships alternating between extremes of overidealization and devaluation; 2) impulsiveness in at least two self-damaging areas other than suicidal behavior; 3) affective instability with marked but brief shifts of mood to depression, irritability, or anxiety; 4) inappropriate and intense anger or lack of control of anger; 5) recurrent suicidal threats, gestures, or behavior or self-mutilating behavior; 6) marked and persistent identity disturbance in at least two areas; 7) chronic feelings of emptiness or boredom; and 8) frantic efforts, other than suicidal behavior, to avoid real or imagined abandonment.

The label "borderline" is both controversial and subject to overuse. Originally, the term borderline referred to patients on the border between psychosis and neurosis, in order to describe the brief psychotic episodes experienced by supposedly neurotic patients undergoing psychoanalysis. According to some theorists, borderline personality disorder refers to patients with a specific primitive internal psychological structure or personality organization. DSM-III-R, however, provides a purely descriptive definition of borderline personality disorder. Borderline personality disorder overlaps with other personality disorders and may thus also coexist with other personality disorders. Borderline personality disorder may also co-exist with other mental disorders, including Axis I disorders. Note that the diagnosis of borderline personality disorder preempts the diagnosis of identity disorder, which is less pervasive and persistent and limited to a developmental stage. Cyclothymia may involve af-fective instability, but there are no hypomanic episodes in borderline personality disorder.

Histrionic personality disorder. This disorder involves a per-vasive pattern of being excessively emotional and attention seeking. This diagnosis requires at least four of eight items: 1) constantly seeking and demanding reassurance, approval, or praise; 2) inap-propriate sexual seductiveness; 3) overconcern with physical attrac-tiveness; 4) inappropriately exaggerated expression of emotions; 5) discomfort with not being the center of attention; 6) rapidly shifting and shallow expression of emotions; 7) being self-centered and seek-ing immediate satisfaction with no frustration tolerance; and 8) using a style of speech that is excessively impressionistic and lacks details.

Histrionic personality disorder should be distinguished from other disorders that may share some features, such as somatization disorder (in which physical complaints are more dominant), depen-dent personality disorder (in which excessive dependency is more dominant without the excessive emotional features), and narcissis-tic personality disorder (in which envy and a grandiose preoccupa-tion with one's sense of self is more dominant). Histrionic personality disorder has elsewhere been called "hysterical personality."

Narcissistic personality disorder. This disorder involves a per-vasive pattern of grandiosity (in fantasy or behavior), lack of em-pathy, and hypersensitivity to the evaluation of others. This diagnosis requires at least five of nine items: 1) feeling rage, shame, or hu-miliation as a reaction to criticism; 2) exploiting others for personal ends; 3) grandiosity; 4) believing one's problems are unique and only understandable by special people; 5) preoccupation with fantasies of unlimited success, power, brilliance, beauty, or ideal love; 6) a sense of entitlement; 7) a need for constant attention and admira-tion; 8) a lack empathy; and 9) a preoccupation with feelings of envy.

Narcissistic personality disorder should be distinguished from other disorders that may share some features, such as antisocial personality disorder (in which there is more impulsivity and ex-ploitation for material gain rather than for personal entitlement and power), histrionic personality disorder (in which there is more emotional exaggeration and dependency or involvement with others), and borderline personality disorder (in which identity disturbance, impulsivity, and emotional features are more prominent). However, these disorders may coexist.

Avoidant personality disorder. This disorder involves a pervasive pattern of social discomfort, fear of negative evaluation, and timidity. This diagnosis requires at least four of a list of seven items: 1) being easily hurt by criticism or disapproval; 2) having only one or no close friends or confidants other than first-degree relatives; 3) being unwilling to get involved with other people unless certain of being liked; 4) avoiding activities that involve significant contact with others; 5) being reticent in social situations because of fear of saying something inappropriate or foolish or of being unable to answer a question; 6) fear of being embarrassed by blushing, crying, or showing signs of anxiety in front of other people; and 7) exaggerating potential difficulties or physical dangers or risks when doing something ordinary but outside usual routines.

Avoidant personality disorder should be distinguished from other disorders that may share some features, such as schizoid personality disorder (in which social isolation is accompanied by little or no desire for social involvement and an indifference to criticism), social phobias (in which a specific situation rather than personal relationships is usually avoided), and agoraphobia (in which avoidance is due to fear of situations in which help may not be available rather than fear of people). Note that in DSM-III-R, unlike DSM-III, avoidant personality disorder and schizoid personality disorder are no longer mutually exclusive. Note also that the diagnosis of avoidant personality disorder should preempt the diagnosis of avoidant disorder of childhood or adolescence, which is less pervasive and persistent and limited to a developmental stage. The relationship between the Axis II avoidant personality disorder and an Axis I anxiety disorder or other frequently associated Axis I disorders requires further study.

Dependent personality disorder. This disorder involves a pervasive pattern of dependent and submissive behavior. This diagnosis requires at least five of nine items: 1) inability to make everyday decisions without excessive advice or reassurance, 2) allowing others to make one's important decisions, 3) agreeing with others even when believing that they are wrong for fear of rejection, 4) having difficulty initiating projects or doing things on one's own, 5) volunteering to do things that are unpleasant or demeaning to win the approval of other people, 6) feeling uncomfortable or helpless when alone or going to great lengths to avoid being alone, 7) feeling devastated or helpless when close relationships end, 8) being frequently preoccupied with fears of being abandoned, and 9) being easily hurt by criticism or disapproval.

Obsessive-compulsive personality disorder. This disorder involves a pervasive pattern of perfectionism and inflexibility. This diagnosis requires at least five of nine items: 1) inability to complete tasks because of perfectionism; 2) excessive preoccupation with details, rules, lists, order, organization, or schedules so that the main point of an activity is lost; 3) an unreasonable insistence that others do things exactly one's way or an unreasonable reluctance to allow others to do things in the belief they will not do them correctly; 4) excessive devotion to work and productivity to the exclusion of leisure activities and friendships; 5) indecisiveness; 6) overconscientiousness, scrupulousness, and inflexibility about morality, ethics, and values not explained by cultural or religious identification; 7) restricted expression of affection; 8) lack of generosity; and 9) inability to discard worn-out or worthless objects even when they have no sentimental value.

Among other disorders, obsessive-compulsive personality disorder should be distinguished from obsessive-compulsive disorder (described under anxiety disorders), in which there are true obsessions and compulsions. Obsessive-compulsive personality disorder does not require true obsessions and compulsions, although features of this personality disorder are consistent with traditional use of the terms "obsessive" and "compulsive." These diagnostic labels should be applied with precision. Note that both disorders may coexist.

Passive-aggressive personality disorder. This disorder involves a pervasive pattern of passive resistance to demands for adequate social and occupational performance. This diagnosis requires at least five of nine items: 1) procrastination; 2) becoming sulky, irritable, or argumentative when asked to do something one does not want to do; 3) seeming to deliberately work slowly or do a poor job on a task that one does not want to do; 4) unjustifiably protesting that others are making unreasonable demands; 5) avoiding obligations by claiming to have forgotten; 6) believing that one is doing a better job than others think one is doing; 7) resenting useful suggestions; 8) obstructing the efforts of others by failing to do one's share; 9) and unreasonably criticizing or scorning others in positions of authority.

Under certain circumstances, passive-aggressive behavior is appropriate and does not warrant this diagnosis. Further, oppositional defiant disorder preempts the diagnosis of passive-aggressive personality disorder in a person under age 18. Note that DSM-III-R eliminated the previous exclusion criteria for passive-aggressive personality disorder.

Personality disorder NOS. This is a residual category for personality disorders that do not meet criteria for one of the other specific personality disorders. One example is a patient presenting with features of more than one specific personality disorder, significant functional impairment, or subjective distress, but not meeting criteria for any one personality disorder (previously designated "mixed personality disorder" in DSM-III, a category eliminated in DSM-III-R). Another example is a personality disorder not officially included in DSM-III-R, such as self-defeating personality disorder or sadistic personality disorder (described later under Proposed Diagnostic Categories Needing Further Study), which may be written with the "proposed" diagnosis in parentheses as follows: personality disorder NOS (self-defeating personality disorder).

V Codes for Conditions Not Attributable to a Mental Disorder That Are a Focus of Attention or Treatment

The heading of this section in DSM-III-R is self-explanatory: these codes, called V Codes, are available for conditions that are not attributable to a mental disorder and are a focus of attention or treatment. V Codes are adapted from ICD-9-CM. These codes may apply if an evaluation does not identify a mental disorder, if an evaluation is as yet inadequate to identify the presence or absence of a mental disorder, or if a present mental disorder is not the focus of attention or treatment.

DSM-III-R lists 13 V Codes (see Table 3-38).

Academic problem. This code refers to an academic problem that is apparently not due to another mental disorder, including intellectual deficits and specific developmental disorders.

Adult antisocial behavior. This code refers to antisocial behavior apparently not due to another mental disorder, particularly not conduct disorder, antisocial personality disorder, or impulse control disorder.

Borderline intellectual functioning (recorded on Axis II). This code refers to IQ in the range of 71–84, distinguished from mental retardation (IQ of 70 or below).

Childhood or adolescent antisocial behavior. This code refers to antisocial behavior in a child or adolescent apparently not due to

Table 3-38. V Codes for conditions not attributable to a mental disorder that are a focus of attention or treatment

 1. Academic problem
 2. Adult antisocial behavior
 3. Borderline intellectual functioning (recorded on Axis II)
 4. Childhood or adolescent antisocial behavior
 5. Malingering
 6. Marital problem
 7. Noncompliance with medical treatment
 8. Occupational problem
 9. Parent-child problem
10. Other interpersonal problem
11. Other specified family circumstances
12. Phase of life problem or other life circumstance problem
13. Uncomplicated bereavement

another mental disorder, particularly not conduct disorder, antisocial personality disorder, or impulse control disorder.

Malingering. This code refers to intentionally produced false or grossly exaggerated physical or psychological symptoms motivated by external incentives (external advantages gained from other people or the environment, known as secondary gain). Note that malingering may be adaptive. Clinical clues to malingering may include the legal context, discrepancies between claimed stress or disability and objective findings, lack of cooperation, and the presence of antisocial personality disorder. Malingering should be distinguished from other mental disorders, particularly factitious disorder (in which there is primary gain in attaining the sick role, although there is still an element of intentional control) and somatoform disorders such as conversion disorder (in which symptoms are not intentionally produced). Suggestion, hypnosis, or an amobarbital interview may be helpful diagnostically.

Marital problem. This code refers to a marital problem apparently not due to another mental disorder.

Noncompliance with medical treatment. This code refers to noncompliance with medical treatment apparently not due to another mental disorder.

Occupational problem. This code refers to an occupational problem apparently not due to another mental disorder.

Parent-child problem refers to either a parent or a child with a parent-child problem apparently not due to another mental disorder (in the person under evaluation).

Other interpersonal problem. This code refers to an interper-

Table 3-39. Additional codes

1. Unspecified mental disorder (nonpsychotic)
2. No diagnosis or condition on Axis I
3. Diagnosis or condition deferred on Axis I
4. No diagnosis on Axis II (recorded on Axis II)
5. Diagnosis deferred on Axis II (recorded on Axis II)

sonal problem other than a marital or parent-child problem that is apparently not due to another mental disorder (in the person under evaluation).

Other specified family circumstances. This code refers to a family situation other than a marital or parent-child problem that is apparently not due to another mental disorder.

Phase-of-life problem or other life circumstance problem. This code refers to a problem related to a developmental phase or other life situation that is apparently not due to another mental disorder.

Uncomplicated bereavement. This code refers to a normal re-action to the death of a loved person. It may be difficult to distinguish normal bereavement from a depressive syndrome. A lengthy bereave-ment period, by itself, is not necessarily abnormal.

Additional Codes

These codes provide flexibility in the DSM-III-R system, permitting a designation on both Axis I and Axis III when it is not possible to provide a more specific diagnosis. There are five additional codes (see Table 3-39).

Unspecified mental disorder (nonpsychotic). This is a resid-ual code used when there is sufficient information to rule out a psychotic disorder but a more specific diagnosis is not possible. More information may permit a more specific diagnosis later. This code is also used for mental disorders not officially listed in DSM-III-R, such as the proposed "late luteal phase dysphoric disorder" (de-scribed later).

No diagnosis or condition on Axis I. This is the code used when there is no Axis I diagnosis for a condition (including V Codes). The use of this code on Axis I is unrelated to whether there is an Axis II diagnosis or condition.

Diagnosis or condition deferred on Axis I. This is the code used when there is insufficient information to make an Axis I di-agnosis.

No diagnosis on Axis II. This is the code used when there is

Table 3-40. Proposed diagnostic categories needing further study

1. Late luteal phase dysphoric disorder
2. Sadistic personality disorder
3. Self-defeating personality disorder

no Axis II diagnosis or condition. The use of this code on Axis II is unrelated to whether there is an Axis I diagnosis or condition.

Diagnosis deferred on Axis II. This is the code used when there is insufficient information to make an Axis II diagnosis.

Proposed Diagnostic Categories Needing Further Study (Appendix A in DSM-III-R)

These proposed diagnostic categories are not official DSM-III-R diagnoses. They were included in an appendix to stimulate research and in response to pressures from various factions (both scientific and political). Three proposed disorders are listed under this heading (see Table 3-40).

Late luteal phase dysphoric disorder. This proposed disorder, commonly known as "premenstrual syndrome," requires characteristic symptoms in most menstrual cycles during the past year. The symptoms must occur during the late luteal phase (last week of the luteal phase) and end within a few days of the follicular phase. Thus, in menstruating women, symptoms occur the week before and a few days after the onset of menses. In some women (e.g., nonmenstruating women who have had a hysterectomy), the timing of these phases may require hormone measurement. At least 5 of 10 items must be present most of the time during each symptomatic late luteal phase: 1) marked affective lability; 2) anger or irritability; 3) anxiety; 4) depressed mood or hopelessness; 5) decreased interest in usual activities; 6) easy fatigability or marked lack of energy; 7) subjective sense of difficulty in concentrating; 8) change in appetite, overeating, or specific food cravings; 9) hypersomnia or insomnia; and 10) other physical symptoms. At least one of the first four of these symptoms must be included. Further, the disturbance must seriously interfere with occupational or usual social functioning and must not be merely an exacerbation of another mental disorder (although this proposed disorder may coexist with other disorders). Finally, the above criteria must be confirmed by prospective daily self-ratings during at least two symptomatic cycles (a provisional diagnosis may be made while awaiting this confirmation).

This proposed disorder is recorded as unspecified mental disorder (late luteal phase dysphoric disorder).

Late luteal phase dysphoric disorder should be distinguished from dysmenorrhea, in which symptoms begin with menses rather than in the premenstrual phase. Note that pain and physical discomfort alone would be insufficient for this proposed diagnosis, even if properly timed.

Sadistic personality disorder. This proposed personality disorder involves a pervasive pattern of cruel, demeaning, and aggressive behavior, beginning by early adulthood. The proposed diagnosis requires the repeated occurrence of at least four of eight items: 1) using physical cruelty or violence to establish dominance in a relationship, 2) humiliating or demeaning people in the presence of others, 3) treating or disciplining someone under one's control unusually harshly, 4) being amused by or taking pleasure in others' psychological or physical suffering, 5) lying to harm or inflict pain on others, 6) frightening others into doing what one wants through intimidation or even terror, 7) restricting the autonomy of significant others, and 8) being fascinated by violence or weapons. The behaviors must not be directed toward only one person and must not occur only in order to attain sexual arousal (as in sexual sadism).

This proposed disorder is recorded as: personality disorder NOS (sadistic personality disorder).

Self-defeating personality disorder. This proposed personality disorder involves a pervasive pattern of self-defeating behavior, beginning by early adulthood. In this proposed disorder, the patient avoids or undermines pleasurable experiences, is drawn into situations or relationships in which he or she will suffer, and prevents others from helping the patient. This proposed diagnosis requires at least five of eight items: 1) choosing people and situations that lead to disappointments, failure, or mistreatment; 2) rejecting help from others; 3) responding to positive personal events with depression, guilt, or behavior that produces pain; 4) inciting angry or rejecting responses from others and then feeling hurt, defeated, or humiliated; 5) rejecting opportunities for pleasure or being reluctant to acknowledge enjoying oneself; 6) failing to accomplish tasks needed for personal objectives despite one's ability; 7) lacking interest in or rejecting those who treat one well; and 8) engaging in excessive and unsolicited self-sacrifice. These behaviors must not occur exclusively in response to or in anticipation of being physically, sexually, or psychologically abused and must not solely occur only when the person is depressed.

This proposed disorder is recorded as personality disorder NOS (self-defeating personality disorder).

Self-defeating personality disorder should be distinguished from behavior that may superficially appear to be self-defeating but that really reflects an effort to cope with a threat or otherwise difficult situation, such as actual or anticipated physical, psychological, or sexual abuse. It was historically known as "masochistic personality disorder." The new name and descriptive behavioral criteria are designed to avoid historical associations with psychoanalytic views regarding female sexuality or unconscious pleasure from suffering.

Notes

[1]These three items appear redundant and require some explication. While "bizarre delusions" alone or "prominent hallucinations" regarding voices alone satisfy this criterion, so would two out of a list of five possible symptoms that include delusions and prominent hallucinations. DSM-III-R is therefore defining delusions that are *bizarre* and *prominent delusions of a particular type* as having more weight diagnostically. "Bizarre" delusions are defined by a phrase in parentheses as "involving a phenomenon that the person's culture would regard as totally implausible. . . ." Perhaps future revisions will examine the adequacy of this criterion and the definition of "bizarre" delusions. For example, does "totally implausible" mean "impossible"?

[2]This system for residual type results in the loss of specification regarding "types" that applied during *earlier* episodes. However, one does not lose this specification of type when the diagnosis is "schizophrenia, in remission"—under this diagnosis the four types still apply, even though the patient is not in the active phase. This suggests a possible inconsistency in that specification of earlier types is lost when applying "residual type," but retained when applying "schizophrenia, in remission"—even though the patient is not technically in an active phase in either case.

[3]Note the similarity between this list of four symptoms and the list of five symptoms used in the criteria for schizophrenia. Although four symptoms are the same on both lists, brief reactive psychosis requires only one, whereas schizophrenia requires two.

[4]"Mood" and "affect" are described in the discussion of the mental status examination in Chapter 2.

[5]If a mood disturbance is apparently precipitated by antidepressant treatment such as tricyclic antidepressants or ECT, this is not considered an organic cause for this purpose and would not rule out a manic episode.

[6]Unlike a major depressive episode, a manic episode is not rated for chronicity or type in DSM-III-R, probably because such descriptions do not appear to have clinical application.

[7]Note that catatonic symptoms are included as mood-incongruent psychotic features of a manic episode, but DSM-III-R does not specifically apply catatonic symptoms when assessing severity of a major depressive episode.

[8]In children or adolescents, the diagnosis of dysthymia may apply to a presentation of irritable mood (rather than depressed mood), and the duration requirement may be 1 year (rather than 2 years).

[9]The term "atypical depression" is sometimes applied to patients in this category, but this term has not yet been officially accepted or defined.

[10]In children or adolescents, the diagnosis of cyclothymia may apply to a duration of 1 year (rather than 2 years as required for adults).

[11]After 2 years, a manic episode or major depressive episode may be superimposed on cyclothymia, requiring the additional diagnosis of bipolar disorder or bipolar disorder NOS.

[12]For example, dysthymia (depressive neurosis); conversion disorder (hysterical neurosis, conversion type); hypochondriasis (hypochondriacal neurosis); dissociative disorders (hysterical neuroses, dissociative type); and depersonalization disorder (depersonalization neurosis).

[13]This represents a change from DSM-III, in which some personality disorders were monothetic while others were polythetic.

[14]Note that in revising the DSM-III criteria for antisocial personality disorder, DSM-III-R added an item for lack of remorse.

CHAPTER 4

The Application of Psychiatric Theory

The application of psychiatric theory is a third component of the psychiatric diagnostic process. Theories frequently provide the crucial link between pure description of a psychiatric problem and selection of a proper treatment. The application of psychiatric theory, therefore, is an indispensable element in diagnosing and treating a patient. It is beyond the scope of this book to examine psychiatric theory in detail. Instead, in this chapter I will provide a broad and brief overview and describe a framework for applying theory in the diagnostic process. In this chapter, "theory" refers to empirically supported schools of thought that seek to explain the origin, development, or causes for the exacerbation of mental disorders.

When assessing and treating patients, mental health professionals are automatically and perhaps inadvertently applying theoretical constructs: pharmacological interventions reflect biological hypotheses; meaningful interactions with the patient invariably reflect dynamic, behavioral, cognitive, or other psychologically oriented techniques; and discussions with or about a patient's family or work associates reflect an emphasis on the social dimension of a mental disorder. The point of this chapter is to make the application of theory explicit, rather than implicit, so that the clinician is more aware of the application of theory, its possible benefits, and the introduction of possible biases.

Descriptive diagnoses alone, as described in the previous chapter, are insufficient for psychiatric diagnosis. We have already seen that even descriptive diagnoses sometimes evoke etiological implications (e.g., organic mental syndromes and disorders and disorders related to psychoactive substances); causal factors may be an integral aspect of some descriptive diagnoses. More fundamentally, however, etiological theories should be considered for all descriptive diagnoses in order to allow the clinician to reach the primary goal of psychiatric diagnosis: to achieve a meaningful understanding (not simply description) of another human being's mental functioning and behavior, incorporating biological, psychological, and social perspectives.

Consider the following comparison: describing the human mind is like describing a cut diamond. In order to appreciate fully the individuality and imperfections of the diamond, one must examine it from several perspectives. Color, cut, clarity, and weight provide the phenomenological description, just as DSM-III-R provides a phenomenological description of mental disorders. But a deeper appreciation requires an understanding of the diamond's chemical structure, environmentally induced imperfections, natural history, and the gem-cutting process. Similarly, a deeper understanding of an individual human mind and behavior requires a consideration of biological, psychological, and social factors. An understanding of an individual human being, like a diamond, requires an examination of its many facets.

The fact that there are many psychiatric theories reflects both the complexity and our primitive understanding of the human mind and behavior. For example, it is estimated that there are several hundred types of psychotherapy, allegedly reflecting different theories, yet there is no clear understanding of the common factors that make psychotherapy effective. While it is difficult to test many psychiatric theories scientifically, it is empirically established that many psychiatric interventions reflecting different theories, including pharmacotherapy, psychotherapy, social interventions, and combinations of treatment, are efficacious when properly applied in at least certain populations.

In keeping with the biopsychosocial perspective, one can divide psychiatric theory into three main groups based on the areas emphasized: biological, psychological, and social. The true etiology for most mental disorders is unknown, and probably involves an interplay among at least several of the factors suggested by current theories.

Biological Theories

Biological theories suggest that biological factors are causally related to mental disorders. In addition to identifiable medical causes of mental disorders (e.g., causes of organic mental syndromes and disorders, and the effects of psychoactive substances), it may be helpful, although somewhat artificial, to divide the biological theories for mental disorders into the areas of genetics, neurochemistry and molecular neurobiology, and neuroanatomy.

Genetic studies have made important contributions to the understanding of mental disorders. Epidemiological and family risk studies have established familial aspects of certain mental disorders, particularly schizophrenia and bipolar disorder, but of many other disorders as well. Although such studies help predict risks for developing a mental disorder and may elucidate possible genetic influences, they cannot establish that a disorder is solely genetically determined. Environmental factors may influence genetic predispositions. Twin and adoption studies help distinguish between genetic and environmental factors, and they have provided support for genetic influences in many psychiatric disorders. Controlled studies of children at high risk provide data about the influence of a putative factor predisposing to a mental disorder. Finally, much work has focused on the genes themselves; this work involves quantitative studies of monogenic or polygenic transmission, including segregation analysis and linkage analysis, and the analysis of specific chromosome abnormalities. Clinically, genetic factors underscore the importance of obtaining a family psychiatric history, suggest areas for further workup, may influence the choice of somatic treatments, and may suggest important focuses for patient and family education and psychotherapy.

Neurochemistry and molecular neurobiology are additional areas generating important biological theories to explain mental disorders. For example, several theories suggest that mental disorders are causally related to defects in chemical communication between neurons, usually involving one or several neurotransmitter systems. One prominent example is the "dopamine hypothesis" of schizophrenia, which argues that a hyperactive dopamine system, particularly D_2 receptors, is a causal factor for schizophrenia. Indirect evidence supporting this theory includes the correlation between relief of characteristic "positive" schizophrenic symptoms and the blockage of dopamine receptors by neuroleptic medications. More direct evidence comes from postmortem brain studies and studies using positron emission tomography (PET) scans. Another prominent example of a neurochemical theory is the "biogenic amine hypothesis" for depression. One early theory attempted to explain depression as a defect in catecholamine effectiveness, especially norepinephrine. Today there are many complex theories involving the neurochemistry of mood and other disorders, with evidence derived from the neuropharmacological effects of medications and from various brain and metabolic studies. In addition to the classic neurotransmitter, research has increasingly identified other molecules and cellular biological processes that may help explain various mental disorders, often overlapping with genetic studies and studies of neuroanatomy.

Neuroanatomical studies also suggest biological causes of mental disorders. Neuronal systems are being mapped and studied in relation to gross brain structures, augmented by advances in immunocytochemical assays and anterograde and retrograde tracing techniques. Neuroanatomical studies may provide evidence to support neurochemical theories. Gross brain structure may be assessed by such techniques as computerized tomography scans and magnetic resonance imaging; gross brain function may be assessed by PET scans, regional cerebral blood flow studies, and other modern techniques. For example, there is currently evidence that some schizophrenic patients have associated structural brain abnormalities, particularly involving cortical atrophy and the frontal lobes. There may also be associated histopathological findings.

In addition to these areas of current psychiatric research and theory, the clinician should recall that other biological factors may explain a patient's mental disorder. One should consider the influence of the neuroendocrine system and of structural, toxic, and other organic effects related to a wide range of medical disorders and conditions.

The increasing popularity of biological theories to explain mental disorders probably reflects a variety of factors: advances in pharmacotherapy and other somatic treatments, technological advances (i.e., clinical and research tools that permit new biological assays and investigations), an increasing knowledge of neurology and the biology of the brain, and cultural factors that appear to value biological or "medical model" explanations of mental disorders. Clinically, the various biologically based theories provide support for trials of somatic treatments and suggest a biologically oriented approach to educating and counselling patients and family about a psychiatric disorder.

Psychological Theories

Psychological theories suggest psychological factors and processes causally related to mental disorders. Although there are many such theories, several currently prominent approaches will briefly illustrate the application of psychological theories in understanding a patient's psychiatric diagnosis.

Psychoanalytic approaches, originally developed by Freud, suggest many clinically important concepts. For example, "psychic determinism" refers to the notion that there is a psychologically causal explanation, usually multidetermined, for any psychological event. Another concept central to psychoanalytic theory is the dynamic unconscious, containing repressed mental material not normally accessible to the conscious mind. The "dynamic" aspect of the mind refers to the interactions, tension, and struggle between psychic forces. An early structural model of the mind, the topographic model, postulated an unconscious, preconscious, and conscious aspect. Freud's later structural model introduced three additional constructs: the id, containing basic drives such as the sexual drive, wishes, and fantasies; the ego, mediating between the id and the superego and the person's interaction with the environment; and the superego, the person's self-critical conscience derived from introjected parental authority. Psychoanalytic theory further emphasizes the importance of stages of psychosexual development, most prominently the oral, anal, and phallic phases. Psychodynamic theory spawned the concepts of defense mechanisms and primary and secondary gain. Many other theorists have expanded or modified various aspects of psychodynamic theory, introducing a more detailed description of defense mechanisms, increased emphasis on the psychology of the ego and object relations, more detailed attention to other developmental periods, a consideration of psychosocial development, and the study of interpersonal factors involved in personality. In addition to the ideas of Freud and his followers, there are many schools of thought invoking psychologically based theories about mental disorders and personality development; each is associated with certain treatment philosophies and techniques.

From the clinical diagnostic viewpoint, psychodynamic and other psychological concepts may be reflected in the patient's presentation. The concepts of transference, resistance, countertransference, and the therapeutic alliance, described in Chapter 2, are derived from a psychodynamic orientation. Further, psychodynamic theory provides hypotheses to explain a wide range of mental disorders. For example, psychodynamic ideas are widely applied to assess and treat long-standing patterns of maladaptive behavior, such as personality disorders or personality traits described on Axis II of DSM-III-R. The criteria for certain DSM-III-R diagnoses, such as conversion disorder (or hysterical neurosis, conversion type), require temporal evidence that psychological conflict or need is etiologically related to symptoms, implying a psychodynamic causal factor. Other DSM-III-R disorders are derived from previously described "neuroses" and may be understood, at least in some cases, in a psychodynamic context (even though the term "neurosis" is relegated to parentheses in DSM-III-R). These include, for example, dysthymia (or depressive neurosis), anxiety disorders (or anxiety and phobic neuroses), obsessive-compulsive disorder (or obsessive-compulsive neurosis), dissociative disorders (or hysterical neuroses, dissociative type), hypochondriasis (or hypochondriacal neurosis), and depersonalization disorder (or depersonalization neurosis). Further, psychodynamic and other developmental theories may be useful in understanding virtually any DSM-III-R diagnosis or condition. Even when there are prominent biological or other causal factors, dynamic factors may help explain why an exacerbation occurred at a particular time, or why a symptom presented in a particular way. Treatment may then address more adaptive resolutions of potential underlying conflict. Finally, a psychodynamic, developmental, and interpersonal perspective may help in understanding personality, even when there is no particular psychopathology.

Behavioral and learning theory represents another theoretical approach useful in psychiatric diagnosis. Rejecting the importance of the unconscious and internal psychological origins of maladaptive conduct, behavioral theory relies exclusively on the notion that behavior is acquired (i.e., "learned") in the context of the environment. Therefore, maladaptive behavior derives from environmental causes and can be controlled or changed according to the basic laws of learning. Classical conditioning involves linking a conditioned stimulus (such as a sound) with an unconditioned stimulus (such as food), so that the conditioned stimulus alone eventually elicits the unconditioned response (such as salivation). Clinically, classical conditioning seems especially important in certain learned anxieties, such as phobias, and in conditioned responses to medical treatment, such as anticipatory nausea and vomiting in a room associated with chemotherapy. Such responses may be "unlearned," for example by extinction techniques (i.e., repeated exposure to the conditioned stimulus without the unconditioned stimulus).

In operant or instrumental conditioning, the person is the freely choosing "instrument," learning that certain behaviors are associated with positive or negative results. Most learning is by operant conditioning. Behavior, according to this theory, is a direct function of its consequences or reinforcers. Primary reinforcers result in the gratification of basic biological needs (e.g., food or sex); secondary reinforcers are learned in relation to primary reinforcers (i.e., social approval). Conditioning may also occur in order to escape or avoid punishment, where punishment is defined as involving either direct aversive results or the withdrawal of positive results. Other behavioral concepts include extinction, stimulus generalization, the effect of reinforcement schedules, behavior modification, learning through modeling, shaping, flooding, and systematic desensitization. These concepts apply to both understanding the origin of symptoms and developing treatment techniques.

As in the psychodynamic approach, behavioral theory provides a means to understand virtually any DSM-III-R descriptive diagnosis, personality, and nonpathological behavior patterns. Psychotic symptoms, depression, anxiety, personality disorders, maladaptive habits and traits, and many other mental disorders or conditions have been attributed, to varying extents, to failing to learn adaptive behaviors or to learning maladaptive behaviors. Adaptive behaviors may similarly be understood as learned. According to this approach, any behavior based on learning can also be unlearned, so that a behavioral perspective leads to the application of behavioral treatment techniques for mental disorders. To some extent, any psychotherapeutic interaction, even the simplest expression or word of encouragement or admonition, involves the application of behavioral technique.

Cognitive theory is an example of yet another psychological approach for understanding the genesis of mental disorders. Cognitive theory focuses on thought processes and internal interpretations in explaining maladaptive behaviors and experiences. Distortions in these processes may result in helplessness, depression, anxiety, and other dysfunctional mental states. Understood in this way, treatment, including psychotherapy and homework assignments, is geared toward identifying and correcting internal cognitive distortions.

Social Theories

Social theories suggest social factors causally related to mental disorders. From the perspective of the field of sociology, higher rates of certain mental disorders seem to be consistently found among certain socioeconomic classes, most frequently lower socioeconomic classes. This situation suggests either "social causation," in which social factors are causally related to the development of mental disorders, or "social selection," in which mentally disordered people are relegated to lower socioeconomic classes by the downward "social drift" of the mentally ill, or by "social segregation" involving the upward mobility of healthy members of the lower class, leaving the mentally ill behind. In addition, several models have attempted to describe the relationship between social stress or significant life events and the development of mental disorders, particularly in persons vulnerable to developing mental disorders because of other factors.

The clinician may consider a wide range of social factors that may contribute to the development or exacerbation of a mental disorder in a particular patient. These would include social stresses, social supports, financial supports, coping and other social skills, family relationships and family dynamics, cultural mores, and religious beliefs. For example, several studies suggest a poorer outcome for schizophrenic patients whose families exhibit high levels of hostility, criticism, and overinvolvement (called "expressed emotion"). Separation and loss may predispose to mental disorders, particularly depression, whereas firm social support may protect against such disorders. Family dynamics may result in scapegoating or identifying a single family member as "crazy" or as a "victim." These and other social factors may suggest a focus for psychotherapeutic discussions, education, and social interventions, and may provide an additional rationale for marital, family, or group psychotherapy. Sometimes the social system, rather than the individual patient, is the proper primary focus for intervention.

A Framework for Applying Psychiatric Theory

The biopsychosocial model and diagnostic process described in this book provides the framework for applying psychiatric theory to diagnosis. The clinician, while developing the empirical data base and generating a differential descriptive diagnosis, should also consider psychiatric theory in order to understand the patient more fully and to develop more successful treatment strategies. In order to proceed systematically, the clinician may consider each major area of theory (biological, psychological, and social) briefly described above. Thus, the biopsychosocial approach provides an overarching and eclectic way to catalogue and screen for clinically useful theoretical ideas. In keeping with other aspects of the diagnostic process, the clinician should remain flexible and tailor the application of theory to the individual patient.

It is deceiving that psychiatric theories appear mutually exclusive in their pure academic forms. When considered closely, virtually all psychiatric theories take cognizance of biology, psychology, and sociology. Biological theories require incorporating psychological, social, and other environmental influences on brain and behavior. Psychological theories are ultimately based on biology (e.g., biologically generated drives in psychoanalytic theory or learning paradigms in behavioral theory) as well as the interaction of the environment and social relations on psychological development. Social theories must consider the underlying biology and psychology of the actors within the social system.

In the clinical setting, it is probable that several theories involving all three biopsychosocial spheres will apply and complement one another. The clinician must be discriminating: one or several theories may be helpful in understanding a particular patient, whereas others may not. The well-rounded clinician should have at least a basic familiarity with the concepts of each of the major psychiatric theories.

The following examples illustrate the application of several theories when evaluating a patient. The most effective treatments for psychotic disorders frequently require medications, reflecting a biological hypothesis to explain the disorder, but also require psychotherapy and social interventions. Certain depressive disorders are particularly responsive to somatic treatment such as medication or electroconvulsive therapy, but others may be equally or more responsive to one or several types of psychologically based treatments; frequently a combination of interventions is most beneficial. Behavioral theory may be crucial for the understanding and treatment of certain anxiety disorders, but pharmacotherapy and psychotherapy may be required for fully effective treatment. While certain long-standing personality traits or personality disorders are traditionally seen as indications for psychoanalytically oriented psychotherapy, clinicians have increasingly considered behavioral, cognitive, social, and even pharmacological interventions for these disorders.

One final point involves proper acknowledgment when applying psychiatric theories or hypotheses. Theory should not be misrepresented as fact. The theory itself or its application to a particular patient may be mistaken. In order to facilitate diagnostic thinking and professional communication, and in order to avoid errors or a misleading sense of certainty, the clinician should clearly acknowledge the use and application of psychiatric theory. A discussion of psychiatric theory merely identifies the clinician's thinking about the causes of the psychiatric disorder. Such acknowledgments should be systematically included in the more formal psychiatric diagnostic case formulation, discussed in the next chapter.

CHAPTER 5

The Psychiatric Diagnostic Case Formulation

The psychiatric diagnostic case formulation is the fourth component in the diagnostic process. The formulation is partly a formal recapitulation of the other components of the diagnostic process, summarizing the empirical data base, the descriptive diagnosis, and the application of psychiatric theory, and identifying areas for ongoing diagnostic synthesis. But the psychiatric diagnostic case formulation goes one step further. It provides the clinical integration and prioritization of the components of the diagnostic process, thus revealing the clinician's diagnostic thinking in detail and providing the justification for selecting areas for additional assessment, predictions, management, and treatment. The psychiatric diagnostic case formulation should be the natural culmination of the diagnostic process.

More specifically, the psychiatric diagnostic case formulation serves several functions. First, the formulation provides a focused yet comprehensive summary of diagnostic information and thinking relevant to the case. Second, it forces the clinician to integrate available data and theoretical ideas while developing and justifying a meaningful differential descriptive diagnosis. Third, it provides a means of clear professional communication of available information and diagnostic thinking. Fourth, it provides a crucial bridge between diagnostic thinking and treatment interventions; the case formulation provides the priority and rationale for ruling other diagnoses in or out, for testing theoretical hypotheses regarding the patient, and for selecting management and treatment strategies. Fifth, the written diagnostic case formulation documents the entire diagnostic process. Finally, the diagnostic case formulation provides a basis for educational and research activities involving case material, including supervision, assessment of the clinician's abilities, and case presentations in educational or other professional settings, and for generating empirical research data.

The psychiatric diagnostic case formulation should be conceptualized within the framework espoused throughout this book. The formulation should reflect the biopsychosocial model. It should be flexible. While striving to be sufficiently comprehensive, it should also be tailored to meet the goal of achieving meaningful understanding of the individual patient within the practical context of the evaluation.

The following are some examples of how the case formulation may be tailored to the individual patient or situation. The formulation may be long and comprehensive to articulate complicated behavior patterns generating an extensive differential diagnosis. On the other hand, the formulation may be short and succinct when the mental disorder is straightforward and the intended audience requires to-the-point communication, as when providing a psychiatric consultation in a general medical hospital setting. The formulation may also emphasize one area over other areas. For example, organic findings and biological theory may be emphasized for a primarily organic presentation, whereas psychodynamic and other psychological factors may be emphasized in a primarily characterological presentation. The differential descriptive diagnosis may be straightforward, neatly meeting DSM-III-R criteria, or it may be complex, requiring a more flexible interpretation of DSM-III-R and a more detailed discussion of each possible diagnosis.

As a general principle, the case formulation should include express acknowledgment when referring to areas that represent professional consensus, such as DSM-III-R, or areas that are not yet scientifically proven, such as psychiatric theory. For example, descriptive diagnoses based on DSM-III-R should be preceded by a phrase such as "according to DSM-III-R criteria . . . ," and psychiatric hypotheses should include a statement that such comments are based on a particular theory, such as "from the perspective of psychodynamic theory. . . ." The clinician thereby identifies areas in the formulation that may be less objective and that may later be interpreted differently or proven incorrect.

The psychiatric diagnostic case formulation, as conceived here, is broad enough to encompass all aspects of diagnostic thinking, all psychiatric patients, and all theoretical perspectives. The formulation may change with time, either when new clinical information becomes available, or when subjective aspects of the formulation, properly identified as such, are reinterpreted or proven incorrect. In most cases, a written formulation is preferable in order to provide documentation and professional accountability, and to help ensure rigorous diagnostic thinking.

The psychiatric diagnostic case formulation may be divided into four components: 1) a succinct and focused summary of the empirical data base, 2) a prioritized descriptive differential diagnosis using DSM-III-R, 3) the application of psychiatric theory to explain the clinical presentation, and 4) areas for further assessment, predictions, management, and intervention.

A Succinct Summary of the Empirical Data Base

The first component of the psychiatric diagnostic case formulation is a succinct summary of the empirical information about the patient. This information should be organized in order to achieve two goals. First, it should be sufficiently comprehensive to provide background and other information in order to cover all reasonably possible diagnoses. Second, it should be sufficiently focused to minimize extraneous information and to build the case for the prioritized differential diagnosis described in the next section of the formulation. These goals may conflict. The proper balance between comprehensiveness and a narrower focus requires clinical judgment and experience.

In general, the summary should include the most important clinical information from each component of the empirical data base, including history, physical examination with particular emphasis on the mental status examination, laboratory data, and any other relevant information from the diagnostic interview, clinical setting, and symptoms (see Chapter 2). This information would ordinarily include a summary of basic demographic information; the chief complaint and/or primary problem; sources of information; a succinct summary of the salient points from the history of present illness, including recent stressors, precipitating events, and diagnostically important behaviors; a brief summary of diagnostically relevant past medical and psychiatric history, family history, personal history, and social history; and a review of systems. Objective information should next be summarized, including diagnostically pertinent positive or negative findings on mental status examination, other aspects of the physical exam, and important laboratory values.

At the conclusion of this summary, all information relevant to the applicable descriptive differential DSM-III-R diagnoses should be available. Further, enough information should be presented to prioritize the DSM-III-R diagnoses in terms of likelihood and importance, as described below. Thus, the review of the empirical data naturally leads to the prioritized descriptive diagnoses.

Prioritized Descriptive Differential Diagnoses Using DSM-III-R

The case formulation should next proceed with a DSM-III-R descriptive differential diagnosis, including clinical syndromes and V Codes on Axis I; developmental disorders, personality disorders, personality traits, and defense mechanisms on Axis II; physical disorders and conditions on Axis III; and in a complete DSM-III-R diagnosis, severity of psychosocial stressors on Axis IV and global assessment of functioning on Axis V (see Chapter 3). The formulation should describe the features of the clinical presentation that support each of the applicable diagnoses, based on the previously summarized empirical data base and the rigorous application of DSM-III-R criteria. The clinician should specifically state that these are DSM-III-R diagnoses, providing a reference for the criteria defining these diagnoses. This component of the formulation should also prioritize the differential descriptive diagnoses, as described below.

The clinician should first consider the broadest possible range of DSM-III-R descriptive diagnoses that could reasonably apply to the patient. Doing so helps ensure that no clinically important diagnosis is overlooked. A strict application of diagnostic hierarchies may prematurely exclude applicable diagnoses. For example, although an organic mental disorder may preclude other diagnoses according to a technical application of DSM-III-R, in the clinical setting the organic mental disorder may not yet be proven, and other disorders may apply instead of or in combination with the organic disorder. In DSM-III-R, hierarchies are based on theoretically definitive diagnostic knowledge (i.e., depression known to be exclusively due to an organic cause must be diagnosed as an organic mood disorder, not a major depression), whereas the case formulation applies to a clinical situation in which no diagnosis is definitive and information continues to evolve. In straightforward clinical cases, experienced clinicians may be able to screen out a broad differential diagnosis rapidly.

The list of descriptive DSM-III-R diagnoses for Axis I and Axis II should then be prioritized in two respects: according to probable likelihood, and according to clinical importance. These two priority lists may or may not coincide.

The descriptive diagnoses should first be prioritized in order of likelihood. The resulting probability-based list directs clinical attention to those diagnoses that are more likely to be correct. The clinician should note any reasons why one diagnosis is more likely than others.

For example, the clinician may describe a patient as most likely suffering from a major depressive episode, based on the previously described empirical information that meets DSM-III-R criteria for this diagnosis. However, other less likely diagnoses may apply to the patient; the formulation should list these alternatives and present the pertinent positive and negative information that applies to them. The formulation should note when full DSM-III-R criteria are not met for a diagnosis, and which criteria are either not yet met or not yet fully evaluated. For example, further laboratory results, such as thyroid function tests, may be needed before ruling out an organic mood disorder in a depressed patient, even though major depression is the more likely diagnosis.

The descriptive diagnoses should also be prioritized in order of clinical importance. The resulting list directs clinical attention to those diagnoses that require more immediate or significant clinical evaluation and intervention, even if not the most likely correct diagnosis. The clinician should note any reasons why one diagnosis is more pressing than others. In particular, those diagnoses that imply correctable, more serious, or potentially fatal underlying pathology should be identified and treated as high priorities.

For example, even though a major depressive episode may be more likely in a given patient, the clinician may initially need to rule out a potentially correctable and serious cause for an organic mood disorder as a higher clinical priority. In the seriously suicidal depressed patient, however, emergency hospitalization and psychiatric treatment may take on as much or even more urgency than the organic evaluation.

Both Axis I and Axis II should be considered when prioritizing the psychiatric descriptive differential diagnoses, although the formulation should discuss each axis separately. Axis I diagnoses are typically more acute and may tend to be listed first when prioritizing is being done according to both likelihood and clinical importance. However, the clinician should consider Axis II diagnoses as well. Axis II may be difficult to assess in the setting of a more florid Axis I presentation, but it may be important for understanding the patient's long-standing behavior patterns and underlying personality factors. In the absence of a more florid Axis I diagnosis, or after the clinician works with a patient for a time, Axis II diagnoses may become more apparent. Recall that, in addition to personality disorders, Axis II may include a description of personality traits and defense mechanisms. An Axis II diagnosis and Axis II descriptions of personality traits and defense mechanisms provide an opportunity to discuss long-standing patterns of behavior and characterological issues.

In short, this section of the case formulation should initially include the widest reasonably applicable descriptive differential diagnoses using DSM-III-R and should prioritize these differential diagnoses according to both likelihood and clinical urgency. This section leads to a discussion of theoretical explanations for the descriptive diagnoses.

The Application of Psychiatric Theory

The third component of the case formulation is a discussion of theoretical applications (see Chapter 4). Theory helps the practitioner to understand the patient's clinical presentation more fully and provides a rationale for identifying areas for further assessment, predictions, management, and intervention described in the subsequent component of the case formulation.

The discussion of psychiatric theory should reflect a biopsychosocial approach—i.e., the clinician should consider biological (e.g., medical disorders and conditions, genetics, neurochemistry and molecular neurobiology, neuroanatomy), psychological (e.g., behavioral, psychodynamic, cognitive), and social theory. The formulation should review ideas and clinical evidence, drawn from the empirical data base and descriptive differential diagnoses, that support or negate theory applied to the patient under evaluation. The length and depth of this theoretical discussion may vary; it should be designed to develop at least the minimal clinical understanding of the patient required by the clinical situation.

It is in this section that one may describe a so-called psychodynamic case formulation, which might include, for example, a detailed discussion of unconscious conflict and underlying anxiety, functioning of the id, ego, and superego, defense mechanisms, transference, resistance, countertransference, and the therapeutic alliance. In addition, a clinician's individual and more personal interpretation of the case may be considered, and may provide a clue to these dynamic factors. Note, however, that the diagnostic case formulation described in this chapter represents a more generic approach to a case formulation, permitting a psychodynamic discussion as well as a discussion from other theoretical orientations and requiring a rigorous application of DSM-III-R.

Recall that theoretical constructs, while appearing to be mutually exclusive in their pure academic form, usually complement one another and may apply simultaneously. The clinician should tolerate the apparent tensions or outright contradictions between theories, provided such theories can be applied to the patient in a way that is clinically useful. The theoretical emphasis should be tailored to the particular patient, guided by the principle of attempting to achieve meaningful understanding of the patient. Finally, the clinician should specifically state that these are theories, thus acknowledging that this discussion in the formulation involves some conjecture, which may be interpreted differently or eventually proven incorrect.

Areas for Further Assessment, Predictions, Management, and Intervention

The fourth and final component of the psychiatric diagnostic case formulation is a description of areas for further assessment, predictions, management, and intervention. These suggestions should follow logically from the preceding components of the formulation. Thus, the empirical data base provides the foundation for the prioritized descriptive differential diagnosis and the application of psychiatric theory, which in turn highlight areas requiring further evaluation and provide the rationale for management and intervention. Among other functions, this last component is the treatment plan.

Further assessment refers to the need to continue to examine and develop the components of the diagnostic process, as embodied by the concept of the "ongoing diagnostic synthesis" (see Chapter 6). This ongoing synthesis may include filling gaps in the empirical data base and attempting to clarify and narrow the differential diagnosis. For example, the clinician may pursue additional medical or psychiatric history, follow the evolution of the mental status examination over time, or pursue the workup of various diagnoses, such as an organic workup to rule out an organic mental disorder. Further assessment should emphasize diagnoses that are considered most likely as well as those that are most clinically significant, even if less likely. As in all aspects of the diagnostic process, the continuation of the assessment should consider biological, psychological, and social areas.

Predictions may now be made regarding the patient's behavior or response to intervention. Predictions are clinically useful as a means to test descriptive diagnoses, hypotheses, and the degree to which the clinician really understands the patient. For example, the DSM-III-R diagnosis of a personality disorder suggests that a particular pattern of behavior or thought will recur, and the application of a psychiatric theory suggests future behavior patterns or a particular reaction or relationship to the clinician and to the treatment. These predictions help establish a standard for reassessing the patient and testing of the validity of a given descriptive diagnosis or theory.

Finally, the case formulation should conclude with suggested management and intervention strategies. This is the culmination of the case formulation. The clinician homes in on the specific treatment intervention that he or she believes will help the patient. Following the data base, descriptive diagnoses, and theories, the clinician should address biological, psychological, and social aspects of management and intervention. As noted with regard to theory, management and interventions based in these three separate spheres are not mutually exclusive. For example, patients may benefit from combinations of biological strategies such as medication; psychological interventions such as behavioral, psychodynamic, or cognitive psychotherapy; and interventions aimed at the patient's social system. One or another of these options may be emphasized; the choices should reflect an effort to tailor management and interventions to the individual patient. In a sense, management and interventions reflect a prediction about what will help the patient.

As new information becomes available, including results from further workup and responses to management and treatment trials, the clinician should be developing and continually revising the formulation. Thus, the diagnostic process continues to evolve, as discussed in the next chapter.

CHAPTER 6

The Ongoing Diagnostic Synthesis

The fifth and final component in the psychiatric diagnostic process is the ongoing diagnostic synthesis. This component stands for the concept that the diagnostic process continues indefinitely or, in practical terms, until the patient is no longer under the clinician's care. The concept of the ongoing diagnostic synthesis is too often overlooked, resulting in prematurely narrowed differential diagnoses and possibly erroneous or wasteful assessment and treatment.

The concept of an ongoing diagnostic synthesis is stressed as a separate component in order to emphasize the importance of continuing the diagnostic evaluation process, even after treatment is well under way. Continuing the process serves two purposes. First, it ensures a continuing effort to consider new clinical information and ideas. Second, it provides a continuing challenge to the accuracy, reliability, and validity of the clinician's diagnostic thinking.

The ongoing diagnostic synthesis applies to each of the other components of the diagnostic process, as reviewed below.

The clinician should continually pursue meaningful information and reevaluate the clinical significance of the empirical data base, including history, physical examination, particularly the mental status examination, and laboratory studies, all in the context of the patient's symptoms and the clinical setting. Every interaction with the patient or another informant may provide valuable diagnostic information.

The prioritized descriptive differential diagnosis according to DSM-III-R may change with additional information or with an evolution of diagnostic thinking. The differential diagnosis may expand or narrow, and there may be a change in the order of the prioritization according to likelihood or clinical importance.

Note that it is important to consider treatment response or lack thereof in the ongoing evaluation of the psychiatric diagnosis. For example, if the patient does not respond to adequate trials of antidepressant medication, the clinician may need to reevaluate the diagnosis of major depression as well as the underlying presumption that a biological theory explains the patient's presentation; the differential diagnosis may need to be broader, and other theoretical approaches or treatment may prove to be more productive.

Clinicians should be wary of several pitfalls with regard to evaluating the success or failure of treatment. First, supposed treatment failures often reflect inadequate trials (e.g., medication given in an insufficient dose or for too short a duration). In such cases, the treatment may be effective if given correctly. Second, it is common for clinicians to pursue successive and multiple treatment trials rather than consider that the initial diagnosis was incorrect. In some of these cases at least, it may be the diagnosis that is mistaken rather than the treatment. Finally, additional coexisting diagnoses may explain an apparent treatment failure, especially when certain diagnoses—such as those on Axis II—are not initially appreciated.

Theoretical constructs applied to a given patient should also be continually reexamined. These theories are somewhat conjectural and may prove to be unreliable, invalid, or misapplied in a particular patient. Even when a theory is initially useful, the clinical picture may change, requiring new theoretical applications. For example, an initial biological explanation for a major depression may warrant treatment with antidepressant medication, but later in the course of the illness, when the depression is better controlled, the clinician may confront noncompliance in taking medication based on psychological factors, such as resistance, or social constraints, such as family scapegoating or lack of finances. At that point, new interventions may need to be developed based on a deeper psychological or social understanding of the patient, even as the biological intervention continues. In other cases, biological treatments may fail altogether, requiring a rethinking of the diagnosis or theoretical understanding of the patient. Each treatment intervention should be continually reevaluated for efficacy and appropriateness with respect to the overall clinical understanding of the patient's presentation.

The psychiatric diagnostic case formulation should also be continually revised throughout the assessment and treatment of the patient. Clinicians should guard against a sense of complacency simply because they have completed a formulation. When a formulation is written, revisions or addenda may be added at any later point. Note that for medical-legal purposes, chart records and other official documentation should always be recorded in a contemporaneous manner. Errors may be crossed out with a single line, labeled as errors, initialed, and dated, but the record itself should not be erased or otherwise destroyed.

Further assessment, predictions, management, and intervention strategies should continually be reassessed as well. Developing information may suggest new areas for clinical assessment. Predictions designed to validate clinical thinking should be tested later in the clinical course, and new predictions should be generated as the case proceeds. The success or failure of management and treatment will suggest whether such interventions should continue or be altered. Ultimately, the diagnostic process is more than an academic exercise; the clinician should continually strive to identify interventions that will best help the patient.

In conclusion, the diagnostic process begins from the moment the patient is seen and continues until the moment the patient is either "cured" or is no longer in the care of the clinician. All components of the diagnostic process are continually evolving. The empirical data base grows with each piece of information and patient interaction. The prioritized descriptive differential diagnosis using DSM-III-R should evolve as empirical information becomes available. Theoretical constructs are applied and reapplied in order to understand the patient better. The psychiatric diagnostic case formulation, the culmination of the diagnostic process, provides a comprehensive yet focused integration of all components of the diagnostic process, resulting in the treatment plan. Finally, all components of the diagnostic process should be continually pursued throughout the assessment and treatment of the patient.

Further Reading

American Psychiatric Association: Diagnostic and Statistical Manual of Mental Disorders, 3rd Edition, Revised. Washington, DC, American Psychiatric Association, 1987

American Psychiatric Association: Quick Reference to the Diagnostic Criteria From DSM-III-R. Washington, DC, American Psychiatric Association, 1987

Bates B: A Guide to Physical Examination and History Taking, 4th Edition. Philadelphia, PA, JB Lippincott, 1987

Blashfield RK, Draguns JG: Toward a taxonomy of psychopathology: the purpose of psychiatric classification. Br J Psychiatry 129:574–583, 1976

Endicott J, Spitzer RL, Fleiss JL, et al: The Global Assessment Scale: a procedure for measuring overall severity of psychiatric disturbance. Arch Gen Psychiatry 33:766–771, 1976

Engel GL: The need for a new medical model: a challenge for biomedicine. Science 196:129–136, 1977

Engel GL: The clinical application of the biopsychosocial model. Am J Psychiatry 137:535–544, 1980

Fink PJ: Response to the presidential address: is "biopsychosocial" the psychiatric shibboleth? Am J Psychiatry 145:1061–1067, 1988

Folstein MF, Folstein SE, McHugh PR: "Mini-Mental State": a practical method for grading the cognitive state of patients for the clinician. J Psychiatr Res 12:189–198, 1975

Gabbard GO: Psychodynamic Psychiatry in Clinical Practice. Washington, DC, American Psychiatric Press, 1990

Goldman HH (ed): Review of General Psychiatry. Los Altos, CA, Lange Medical Publications, 1984

Goodwin DW, Guze SB: Psychiatric Diagnosis, 3rd Edition. New York, Oxford University Press, 1984

Hackett TP, Cassem NH (eds): Massachusetts General Hospital Handbook of General Hospital Psychiatry, 2nd Edition. Littleton, MA, PSG, 1987

Hales RE, Yudofsky SC (eds): The American Psychiatric Press Textbook of Neuropsychiatry. Washington, DC, American Psychiatric Press, 1987

Hall RCW, Beresford TP (eds): Handbook of Psychiatric Diagnostic Procedures, Vol 1. New York, Spectrum, 1984

Hall RCW, Beresford TP (eds): Handbook of Psychiatric Diagnostic Procedures, Vol 2. New York, Spectrum, 1985

Kaplan HI, Sadock BJ (eds): Comprehensive Textbook of Psychiatry/ IV, 4th Edition. Baltimore, MD, Williams & Wilkins, 1985

Katzman R, Brown T, Fuld P, et al: Validation of a short orientation-memory-concentration test of cognitive impairment. Am J Psychiatry 140:734–739, 1983

Lischman WA: Organic Psychiatry: The Psychological Consequences of a Cerebral Disorder, 2nd Edition. Oxford, Blackwell Scientific, 1987

Luborsky L: Clinicians' judgments of mental health. Arch Gen Psychiatry 7:407–417, 1962

Ludwig AM: Principles of Clinical Psychiatry, 2nd Edition, Revised and Expanded. New York, Free Press, 1986

MacKinnon RA, Michels R: The Psychiatric Interview in Clinical Practice. Philadelphia, PA, WB Saunders, 1971

MacKinnon RA, Yudofsky SC: The Psychiatric Evaluation in Clinical Practice. Philadelphia, PA, JB Lippincott, 1986

Menninger K, Mayman M, Pruyser P: The Vital Balance: The Life Process in Mental Health and Illness. New York, Viking, 1963

Mezzich JE: On developing a psychiatric multiaxial schema for ICD-10. Br J Psychiatry 152 (suppl 1):38–43, 1988

Michels R, Cavenar JO (eds): Psychiatry, Revised. Philadelphia, PA, JB Lippincott, 1988

Morey LC: Personality disorders in DSM-III and DSM-III-R: convergence, coverage, and internal consistency. Am J Psychiatry 145:573–577, 1988

Nicholi AM Jr (ed): The New Harvard Guide to Psychiatry. Cambridge, MA, The Belknap Press of Harvard University Press, 1988

Othmer E, Othmer S: The Clinical Interview Using DSM-III-R. Washington, DC, American Psychiatric Press, 1989

Perry S, Cooper AM, Michels R: The psychodynamic formulation: its purpose, structure, and clinical application. Am J Psychiatry 144:543–550, 1987

Rakoff VM, Stancer HC, Kedward HB (eds): Psychiatric Diagnosis (The CM Hincks Memorial Lectures). New York, Brunner/Mazel, 1977

Rapoport JL, Ismond DR: DSM-III Training Guide for Diagnosis of Childhood Disorders. New York, Brunner/Mazel, 1984

Regier DA, Myers JK, Kramer M, et al: The NIMH Epidemiologic Catchment Area Program. Arch Gen Psychiatry 41:934–941, 1984

Rey JM, Stewart GW, Plapp JM, et al: DSM-III Axis IV revisited. Am J Psychiatry 145:286–292, 1988

Robins E, Guze SB: Establishment of diagnostic validity in psychiatric illness: its application to schizophrenia. Am J Psychiatry 126:983–987, 1970

Shaffer D, Gould MS, Brasic J, et al: A children's global assessment scale (CGAS). Arch Gen Psychiatry 40:1228–1231, 1983

Shea SC: Psychiatric Interviewing: The Art of Understanding. Philadelphia, PA, WB Saunders, 1988

Shrout PE, Spitzer RL, Fleiss JL: Quantification of agreement in psychiatric diagnosis revisited. Arch Gen Psychiatry 44:172–177, 1987

Skodol AE: Problems in Differential Diagnosis: From DSM-III to DSM-III-R in Clinical Practice. Washington, DC, American Psychiatric Press, 1989

Skodol AE, Spitzer RL (eds): An Annotated Bibliography of DSM-III. Washington, DC, American Psychiatric Press, 1987

Soreff SM, McNeil GN (eds): Handbook of Psychiatric Differential Diagnosis. Littleton, MA, PSG, 1987

Spitzer RL, Endicott J, Robins E: Reliability of clinical criteria for psychiatric diagnosis, in Psychiatric Diagnosis: Exploration of Biological Predictors. Edited by Akiskal HS, Webb WL. New York, Spectrum, 1978, pp 61–73

Spitzer RL, Williams JBW, Skodol AE: DSM-III: the major achievements and an overview. Am J Psychiatry 137:151–164, 1980

Spitzer RL, Williams JBW, Skodol AE (eds): International Perspectives on DSM-III. Washington, DC, American Psychiatric Press, 1983

Spitzer RL, Williams JBW, Gibbon M, et al: Structured Clinical Interview for DSM-III-R (SCID). Washington, DC, American Psychiatric Press, 1990

Spitzer RL, Gibbon M, Skodol AE, et al: DSM-III-R Casebook. Washington, DC, American Psychiatric Press, 1988

Strauss JS: A comprehensive approach to psychiatric diagnosis. Am J Psychiatry 132:1193–1197, 1975

Strayhorn JM Jr: Foundations of Clinical Psychiatry. Chicago, IL, Year Book Medical, 1982

Talbott JA, Hales RE, Yudofsky SC (eds): American Psychiatric Press Textbook of Psychiatry. Washington, DC, American Psychiatric Press, 1988

Webb LJ, DiClemente CC, Johnstone EE, et al: DSM-III Training Guide for Use With the American Psychiatric Association's Diagnostic and Statistical Manual of Mental Disorders (Third Edition). New York, Brunner/Mazel, 1981

Widiger TA, Frances A, Spitzer RL, et al: The DSM-III-R personality disorders: an overview. Am J Psychiatry 145:786–795, 1988

Williams JBW: The multiaxial system of DSM-III: where did it come from and where should it go? I: its origins and critiques. Arch Gen Psychiatry 42:175–180, 1985

Williams JBW: The multiaxial system of DSM-III: where did it come from and where should it go? II: empirical studies, innovations, and recommendations. Arch Gen Psychiatry 42:181–186, 1985

Zimmerman M. Why are we rushing to publish DSM-IV? Arch Gen Psychiatry 45:1135–1138, 1988

Index